To my daughter Kristin, for always being there for me,
especially during the tough times.
—Gary Williams

To my wife Lori,
whose attendance at hundreds of college basketball games
over the past 23 years proves how much she loves me.
—David A. Vise

Other Books by David A. Vise

The Bureau and The Mole

Eagle on the Street (with Steve Coll)

Contents

Foreword

By Juan Dixon

When people see Coach on the sidelines during games, they think he looks like a nut they could never get along with. They are wrong. He is one helluva guy with a great sense of humor. Every coach does it his own way, and hollering is his style. What people don't understand is that he is a great teacher and a tremendous motivator.

The most important thing he taught me is how to be a winner. You have to hate to lose. He helped me become stronger mentally. He made me believe in myself even more. He wanted to win so badly, you could see it in his eyes and hear it in his tone of voice. It rubbed off on me, and I wanted to win for the guy.

Coach Williams saw things in me I didn't even know were there. He brought out the best in me, including the absolute determination to succeed. He kept me focused and on the right path. He believed in me and brought out all the hunger and determination that I had. In the process, he made me into the player that I am. He taught me to work on a couple of new things each summer. He said, "Juan, this is how you can score in my offense and help us win." I listened and then tried to go out there and perform.

I can relate to what he went through when he was growing up. During tough times, basketball saved both of us. We are so much alike. We respect one another, and when he looked at me, he could see that I am a guy, like him, who is determined to be successful.

I would call him when basketball games were on TV. I was like, "Coach, did you see that?" It would be something he taught me earlier that day. He really knows the game.

Coach Williams brings intensity to practice each and every day, and he is a great recruiter. From the time he first set foot in my home in Baltimore, he got along with me and my relatives well. There was no BS. He told me what I needed to do to be able to play at Maryland, and he believed in me.

Coach sees something in players that other coaches don't see. He looks for people who have the same work ethic that he does. He took a chance on me when people were doubting his recruiting style. He did the same thing with Lonny Baxter. He proved a lot of people wrong. Our Maryland team was not made up of high school players who had a lot of hype. He recruited underrated players, taught us how to win, and then took us all the way. That is one of the things that makes our national championship so sweet.

I'm glad people finally are realizing that he is a great coach. He deserves all the credit he is getting. Just like a player who works hard, he is continuing to improve as a coach. He is very intense on the sidelines, but there were many days in practice when he was very patient. Each year, he promised to come back as a better coach the next season. And he did.

It was meant for us to be together as coach and player and to bring the national championship back to the state of Maryland. I'm glad I am staying in this area and playing for the Washington Wizards. I will be able to go to the Comcast Center in College Park and root for Maryland, and I plan on being there a lot and staying in close touch with Coach Williams. I respect Coach, and I love him like a father.

Juan Dixon
August 2002

PROLOGUE

Gary Williams feared he had made the biggest mistake of his life. Leaving behind a 22-year marriage to his high school sweetheart and a higher-paying job with better perks as head basketball coach at Ohio State University, he had arrived at the University of Maryland only to encounter one nasty surprise after another. He saw no way out, and Williams's triumphant return in 1989 to coach his alma mater was rapidly becoming a complete and total disaster.

For starters, the atmosphere on campus remained poisoned by the tragic, cocaine-induced death of the greatest athlete in the school's history, Len Bias. His shocking death—less than two days after he was drafted by the Boston Celtics in 1986 and signed a lucrative endorsement deal with Reebok—left students, faculty and administrators questioning whether they wanted to field a big-time college basketball team. Unlike at Ohio State, Williams found virtually no base of support on the College Park campus.

Williams had been informed before he took the job that an NCAA investigation into alleged recruiting violations at Maryland before his arrival would, at most, lead to a slap on the wrist. Instead, Williams found his recruiting hands tied behind his back after the NCAA sanctioned the school with what felt like the college sports equivalent of the death penalty: no playing on television or in the NCAA tournament for two years. The NCAA's action slammed the already battered university and its reeling coach with what seemed to be a knockout blow.

As if that weren't enough, Williams inherited charged racial issues too. The job opening at Maryland had been created by the forced resignation of coach Bob Wade. An outstanding high school basketball coach at Baltimore's Dunbar High School, Wade was revered, and his abrupt dismissal fueled tremendous racial tension in the predominately black neighborhoods of East Baltimore. In the ensuing years, its star athletes would enroll at Georgetown, North Carolina—anywhere but College Park. And in Baltimore, Maryland's treatment of Wade was perceived as discrimination by a lily-white university that set up a black man to fail.

If I would have known what things would be like at Maryland, I would never have left Ohio State. I got there three years after Len Bias died, and there were still a lot of faculty and administrators and students on campus who felt basketball was a bad thing. It discredited the school and brought the most negative attention ever given to the university. They felt there was no way basketball could be an ally for the school. As soon as I got there, I realized I had taken on a situation that might end my coaching career.

Maryland Athletic Director Lew Perkins called and asked if I was interested. It was unusual to get the opportunity to go coach a good basketball program where you had played. That doesn't happen very often. And sometimes you make decisions based on emotion, which you shouldn't do, but you do. This was an emotional decision. I was going through a divorce at the time. Sometimes you have to make decisions based on the situation. I tell players you don't get any do-overs. You go through life and make decisions. And hopefully, you get better for the wrong decisions you make.

The hardest thing I have ever done in my life was in those first three or four years at Maryland. I looked at Ohio State winning games, and I asked, 'What am I, nuts?' I had been head coach at American, Boston College and Ohio State, and then I got hit with adversity at Maryland. I never thought I would have this type of adversity in coaching.

The confluence of cataclysmic events made it impossible for Williams to recruit promising high school players, sending the Maryland program into a nosedive that would soon result in a 2-14 win-loss record and a last-place finish in the Atlantic Coast Conference. In more than two decades of coaching, Williams had never experienced anything like the despair he felt at Maryland.

The struggling Williams knew he couldn't turn things around alone. With help from a small band of loyalists and friends from outside the university, the coach devised the strategy and tactics to rebuild the Maryland program and put the pieces of his broken personal life back together. Slowly but steadily, Gary Williams and his Terps began their climb together. Williams met and talked with his cadre of dedicated friends regularly, though there was never any mention of their existence, or influence, in the press or in public forums. What the public saw instead was a raving madman on the sidelines during basketball games, a crazed coach with a crouched back who looked so tightly wound that it appeared his head might explode at any minute.

Gary Williams's intensity as a coach remains his calling card, and the image that most fans have is of a man who appears to be out of control. His players, however, know that while he may be a screamer and exude an angry demeanor, Williams is very much in control of the team and himself during practices and games. Yet few people, other than his daughter Kristin, really know, or understand, the man in full.

"He doesn't have a lot of things that interest him in life, but the things that do interest him are all-consuming," Kristin said. "I knew from as far back as I can remember how important his career was to him. It was more than a career. It was part of his life, but it wasn't a job he went to from nine to five. It was something he was always thinking about. He has always felt a little hurt that people haven't always understood the method to his madness."

Even after restoring the Maryland basketball program to respectability over a period of years, Williams harbored doubts about attaining the lofty goals he had once set for himself as a coach. He knew he was a sound teacher and a good recruiter who fielded hustling teams that played, as he put it, "94 feet for 40 minutes." But only a few years ago, he expressed uncertainty about whether he would ever take the University of Maryland, which had never made it to the Final Four, to the pinnacle of college basketball.

"When I first started coaching, the one goal, the only goal, was the Final Four and the national championship. Now I know it is possible that it might never happen. For a lot of coaches, good coaches, it never does."

1

A QUESTION OF RESOLVE

When the final buzzer sounded, ending one of the most heart-wrenching defeats in Final Four history, University of Maryland fans could do little more than shake their heads in disbelief and dismay. The Maryland-Duke semifinal matchup in Minneapolis on March 31, 2001 had established a new NCAA record, but it was not one the Terrapins had sought when they suited up to play the Blue Devils. In the school's first trip ever to the Final Four, Maryland had jumped out quickly to a 22-point lead, only to succumb to an odd panoply of forces that resulted in Duke emerging victorious. The NCAA record book would note the turn of events as the biggest comeback in Final Four history, leaving emotionally drained Terps supporters dejected. While Duke breathed a collective sigh of relief, the outcome left many of the Maryland faithful flabbergasted.

It didn't take some fans long to find a target for their fury. They placed the blame for the defeat squarely on Maryland Head Coach Gary Williams. Surely, they reasoned, Williams must have done something wrong if the Terps could not hold onto such a large margin. Had he somehow been outmaneuvered? Had his high-strung style left his players too uptight once Duke began mounting its comeback? Had Williams failed to make the right adjustments on the offensive or defensive end? Why couldn't the Terps play well with such a big lead?

Baltimore City Council president Sheila Dixon, an aunt of Maryland star guard and team leader Juan Dixon, was among the fans who lashed out at Williams a few days later at the Baltimore Orioles' opening game at Camden Yards. "I wanted to pour a glass of soda on him for losing," Sheila Dixon recalled. Without identifying herself to her nephew's favorite coach at the baseball game, she shouted, "You know, you really lost that for them." But at the same game, Williams received a standing ovation from the crowd. He had, after all, taken Maryland to its first Final Four.

A fighter by nature, Gary Williams sensed the stakes were high in the aftermath of the school's Final Four defeat by Duke. After more than two decades as a head coach, including a dozen at the helm of the Terrapins program, he knew the fans were with you when you won and second-guessing you when you lost. Williams also knew that expectations remained sky high. He didn't mind that part at all. He knew he was at the helm of a talented veteran squad and that the higher the expectations, the greater the potential to achieve. Yet the coach also knew that in the aftermath of the disappointing Duke defeat, his players were at a crossroads, and there were two divergent paths his Terrapins could take: they could lose confidence in themselves and go into a downward spiral, or they could absorb the lessons from their trip to the Final Four and come back twice as hard next season.

We were upset we lost the game to Duke. The way we lost the game bothered me more than anything else. During the game, I just kept trying to make them understand that Duke was making a run, but we were not playing well.

We could have changed that by playing better basketball. The problem is that when you are playing somebody as good as Duke, there is no leeway. You have to play well all the time.

After the loss to Duke in Minneapolis, I told our players I was really proud of them. I stayed very positive, and we stayed very positive. I said they were the greatest team ever in the history of the University of Maryland.

Our players were not satisfied with just getting to the Final Four, even though that had not been done before in the history of the school. The fact that we had quite a few players returning helped. They wanted the ultimate shot. We thought we were good enough to have won it but didn't play well enough to win it.

Our seniors had strong ideas about where they thought they were on the map of college basketball. We didn't feel we had to take a back seat to any program. I knew Maryland could be as good anybody else. Once I saw our effort at the Final Four in Minneapolis, I thought we had a chance to win it all the next year. I also knew we were going to give it our best shot.

Despite the Final Four defeat, few who knew him doubted Gary Williams's ability to come back, especially when he had his back to the wall. That seemed to be one of his greatest strengths. He knew how to capitalize on defeats by making his team mentally tougher and more focused. That is the way he had always dealt with setbacks: a tireless work ethic, a blazing intensity and a deep-seated hatred of losing. All of this enabled him to live in the moment and immerse himself in the heat of battle, to the point where it seemed the fiery coach on the sidelines, sweating through his suits and shouting at his bench when his players fell short of expectations, had an insatiable, hyperkinetic competitive drive. He had to win, and he had to go into every ballgame believing his team would win. There was no other way. And when he lost, which he knew would happen sometimes, he had to make sure that it was not for lack of effort and that he had done everything possible to win.

"I coach every game," Williams said, "as if it was the most important game I have ever coached."

His extraordinary focus, both during games and throughout the basketball season, has left an indelible impression on his players, rival coaches, the nation's top basketball analysts and others. And his emotion-laden style of coaching—the hunched back, the red face, the catcher's crouch and histrionics on the sidelines—made it seem at times as though he were on the court as the Terps' sixth man. It also led many to misread him and falsely conclude that his emotions got the better of him during games or that he was nothing more than a cold-blooded drill sergeant.

Not so, according to Red Auerbach, who held forth one recent morning on Gary Williams. With a stogie in his mouth at 9:00 a.m., the legendary Auerbach—who in his 80s still scouts for the Boston Celtics and sports his trademark green cap and green cane—appreciates what he sees in the Maryland coach. "What I like about Gary is he is in control," said Auerbach, one of the greatest coaches and general managers in NBA history. "All that intensity he portrays does not take away from the fact that he is in control of his ball club, and he knows what is going on. He is not affected by the surrounding pressures. He is a good teacher, and the ballplayers under him have improved a lot. He substitutes well, he runs his ball club well and he is pretty well liked by his peers. People who know him like him.

"He is a nice guy, but he is a hard worker," Auerbach, a longtime Washington, D.C. resident, continued. "There is no substitute for work. In the game of basketball, there are no shortcuts. You have got to spend the time with each player. He also doesn't appear to be intimidated by the reputation of other coaches. He is focused on his own program and on his own team and he figures that if he gets the best out of what he has got, he will let the chips fall where they may."

Bonnie Bernstein, a Maryland graduate and commentator for CBS Sports who has known Williams for years, said he is in the perfect job that plays to his ability to teach and dedication to developing players. She also said it is easy to misread him. "My early impression of Gary was sweating through five shirts a game and just ranting and raving and screaming," Bernstein said. But as she has gotten to know him better, she has picked up on other traits. "There is something you see when you look in Gary's eyes when he is coaching, and you know there is nowhere else he would rather be than on the court with his kids trying to coach them to victory," she said. "Gary was forced to be a fighter at an early age, and once you develop that mentality, it never goes away."

Despite his outward display of emotion during games, Gary Williams is actually a coach, and a man, who keeps much close to the vest. He has never forgotten his South Jersey roots and remains a regular guy who enjoys a beer with the boys, a victory cigar, and watching and talking sports. But with material success, he also has learned to eat filet mignon, appreciate fine wines, and golf at exclusive clubs. Without becoming unhitched from his past or unable to connect to his players, he has grown with success. Still, Williams has been silent about much that he has endured, and his sideline scowl reflects, in part, a rugged individualism. That angry expression also belies a sentimental side. Time and again in recent years, tears have welled up in his eyes around family and friends, who ascribe it to Williams getting older, achieving career milestones, growing closer to his daughter, and becoming a grandfather. But those closest to him also say there is an elusive quality about the man they cannot explain.

"There is a part of Gary no one knows," said Maryland assistant basketball coach Dave Dickerson. "There is a part to him where it is his moment and no one else's. That is the most intriguing thing about him."

Terry Arenson, one of Williams's closest buddies, said he understands his friend better after attending his father's recent funeral. "Gary is a lot like his dad. His dad liked to walk railroad tracks. He walked the Appalachian Trail. He went out by himself. It was amazing at his father's funeral listening to people talk about him as his own man. Some of his dad's friends spoke at the funeral about feelings his father had later in life for their children and neighbors' children, and it was like he was making up for time lost when Gary and his brothers were growing up. Gary is a lot like his dad now with Kristin and his grandson David. He is getting that same kind of second chance."

Through conversations with Williams, other coaches, and countless fans, shoeshine man Joe Green in Baltimore has developed a sharp eye for evaluating character and talent. He is not easily fooled by appearances or unduly persuaded by what some of those who climb into his bank of chairs for a polish have to say about Maryland basketball and its leader. "Gary Williams coaches you through the stress of surviving," he said. "A key is practice. I guarantee you a man who stands up most of the time as a coach during games stands up during practice too. It is Gary Williams's coaching that has been able to make physically unattractive players into a major force in the ACC."

I think guys can learn to generate more competitive fire, but I think for all the great ones, the most important thing is winning. There is nothing else that matters. Part of being a great winner is that you have to hate to lose. It has to tear you up. When you start accepting losses, it is time to stop playing or coaching. I can't accept a loss. I have to think there is always a way I can win as a coach. As a player, there are games you get beat, and you can't accept it. That has got to be the attitude.

To build a team with a winning attitude, I have to recruit the right kinds of players. Once I develop a gut feeling on a recruit, once I like a guy, it's "Let's go." When I get a positive feeling about a player, I don't care what other people say or write or even how he plays after that. I can find fault with anybody I watch for too long. If I watch a player long enough, I am going to see things I don't like and focus on the things he can't do. And what can happen then is that I don't like him as much by the time I sign him as when I first saw him play.

I move forward when I see what I am looking for in a player. It is not just basketball ability, although that has to be there. It is determination. It is not being satisfied and always wanting to get better. I'm looking for that hunger and thirst. The longer I coach, the more I realize about who wins, and who is good and not good. What is inside a player is something that is hard to judge when I am recruiting. But I really try to look at a guy to see how badly he wants to win and how badly he wants to play. That changes my opinion of a potential recruit. I will take a guy who is 80 percent of another guy in terms of basketball ability but who will outwork the more talented player.

I *never label a kid as too skinny or too small. In recruiting Juan Dixon, I was fortunate to have coached Michael Adams at Boston College who was thought to be not good enough to play in the Big East. I had a little guy at Ohio State in Jay Burson. When you coach guys like that, you get the message that small guys can be big players.*

Everybody thinks there is some big secret on how to improve in sports as a player and a coach. If you want to be a great shooter, you have to spend more time practicing than the other guys and separate yourself from them. If you know how to do something, you have to put in the extra time to perfect it. In coaching, the secret is getting players into the frame of mind to put that extra time in.

Before a Maryland game, I can be nervous all day. But as a coach, I have to get over that feeling. That is one thing I've always been able to do. When I walk into the Maryland locker room two hours before the game, in my mind, we are going to win the game, even if I had doubts before. If I don't believe that, the players won't either.

2

THE BIRTH OF A COACH

Ever since his youth in Collingswood, New Jersey, Gary Williams's life has revolved around basketball. As an All-State point guard for Collingswood High School, and later as a scholarship player for the University of Maryland Terrapins in the mid-1960s, Williams made up for his lack of physical prowess with determination, hustle and hard work. Coaches liked having Williams on the floor; he understood the game and followed their directions with precision. In pick-up games in South Jersey, he was one of the first players chosen; others who wanted to shoot the ball liked having Williams—who was content to dish off good passes—on their side.

A lifelong student of the game, Williams also exuded a never-say-die attitude. He gave his all in practice and competed hard each and every time out, expecting no less from his teammates in practice, during games and on the playground. "Gary is the one guy I always knew would play as hard as I would. His interest was always in winning," said Stan Pawlak, who played high school basketball with Williams and remembers him as a dogged defensive player and fluid passer. "If you got open and Gary was playing guard, the ball was at your fingertips the minute you wanted it to be there."

For the ultra-competitive Williams, basketball presented a challenge he tackled with religious fervor. "His knees were always bleeding," said Ed Pyne, who played with Williams during high school. "He was a lunatic competitor." Basketball was Williams's passion, release and escape, and it provided him with a comfort zone. A self-described gym rat, Williams would need the protection and promise the game offered him, particularly as his life at home grew more painful in his early teen years.

One morning, Gary's father told him in the car on the way to school that he was moving out of the house. Then he dropped him off for the day, just like that. "I was surprised he was leaving," Williams said. The initial separation and subsequent divorce had a profound effect on Williams. It made him more self-reliant—a prominent character trait that has stayed with him over the years—but the divorce also left him feeling like an outsider in Collingswood. "It was one of those things you felt kind of funny about," Williams said. "You think people are talking about you."

While he had not grown up in a close family, in the South Jersey community where Williams lived, divorce was not part of the program. Daily life revolved around family, church and school. Gary remembers being 13 and the only one in his class whose parents were split. "I always felt basketball got me through that period of my life," Williams said. Though he rarely talked about the break-up at the time, his friends noticed. "He kept all that inside of him. It ate him alive. We kind of knew, but you didn't talk about that kind of thing," Pawlak said. To make matters worse, Gary's mother moved to California with another man, leaving Gary and his two brothers—one older and one younger—to live with his dad. His father's growing devotion to strict and traditional Episcopalian religious practices distanced Gary further from him.

Sports were a way to get on equal footing. Once you hit the court, it didn't matter who you were or what your family was like. You either were a player or you were not. One of the greatest things about basketball is that you can play all day and it doesn't cost you anything. I remember dragging home as a kid when it was getting dark after playing for hours and hours. If you are a competitor who works hard to reach goals as a player, it helps you handle tough situations in life, too. Basketball is something you can use to get through difficult times.

Gary received no encouragement for his athletic pursuits at home and became something of a latchkey kid. Neither his older nor his younger brother played sports. "I remember hitting a baseball when I was three or four. I always had good coordination, and I liked to compete. My father thought it was a waste of time." His father, who worked a monotonous job as a check sorter at the Federal Reserve Bank in Philadelphia at night, encouraged him to spend less time playing ball and more time hitting the books. It was to no avail. For Gary, basketball was what mattered most. He enjoyed hoops on the playground and loved journeying whenever possible into Philadelphia to watch college basketball games at the Palestra, where he dreamed of someday playing. At the same time, Williams looked outside his family for camaraderie and support, and he found it among his teammates and coaches. John Smith, his high school basketball coach, served as a mentor, not only encouraging Williams on the court but also inviting him to his home on a regular basis. "John Smith was a father figure more than a high school coach. I used to eat at his house," Williams recalled. "He was a great motivator as a coach. He could really get you to play. He is one reason I got into coaching."

Williams also found refuge in another local domain: the home of his high school sweetheart Diane, whose family lovingly took him in as one of their own. Even before he met Diane, he had met her mother, who worked in the school cafeteria at Collingswood.

Williams, who focused mostly on basketball and never dated much, recalls initially being attracted to Diane's good looks. In the post-World War II era—Williams was born in 1945, the year the war ended—theirs was a traditional courtship. They went to high school games together, shared dates with friends they had in common and never ventured far from their South Jersey community. "Nobody had any money," Williams said. Gary, one year ahead of his girlfriend, went off to Maryland to play basketball, while Diane, described as a "sweetheart, unselfish and very supportive" by Pyne, finished high school and then pursued a nursing degree in Camden.

Before deciding on Maryland, Williams had hoped to join his friend Stan Pawlak at the University of Pennsylvania so he could play in the Palestra and compete in the Big Five—the famed intra-city rivalry in Philadelphia involving Penn, Villanova, La Salle, St. Joe's and Temple. But lacking the grades to get accepted at Penn, Williams visited Clemson, Providence, Pittsburgh and the University of Maryland, where he took one look at Cole Field House and fell in love. Like the Palestra, it had the ambiance of an oversized high school gym. But "the Palestra seated 9,000. Cole seated 15,000 for college games." Williams enrolled to play for Coach Bud Millikan on a Terps basketball scholarship in 1963. While he was not a standout on the court, he turned out to be a smart playmaker. When Williams came to College Park as a freshman, Dean Smith was in his third year as coach of the North Carolina Tar Heels. "He was a tough competitor," Smith said. "Gary was the key guy there. He got the ball in to Jay McMillen. He was what a point guard should be, I think."

In 1966, toward the end of his junior year, Williams attended the historic NCAA championship game at Cole Field House and saw Texas Western's all-black starting five knock off Adolph Rupp and his all-white Kentucky Wildcats. "I snuck in the back door to watch," Williams said. "People said there was no way a good white team would lose to a good black team. Texas Western proved to a lot of people that night that the color of the man who was playing didn't matter. What mattered was how you played."

Williams scored sporadically during his college career, though he did set a Terps record for once hitting eight straight shots. The team's record fell each year from his sophomore year, when the team finished second in the ACC, to his senior year, when Maryland went 11-14.

"When we were losing, he was really irritated. He would not get over it easily," recalled Joe Harrington, who played alongside Williams at Maryland. "It gnawed at him. It really bothered him to lose."

I played for a first-rate coach in Bud Millikan, but after that, nothing was first-rate in the Maryland basketball program. He had Frank Fellows as his one assistant coach, who also had to teach three courses and be the recruiter. We were up against Duke, which had a head coach and a number of full-time assistants, including Chuck Daly. And the way basketball players were treated at Maryland wasn't a good situation either. This was a football school then. We always felt they got much better treatment. I left Maryland after playing for four years feeling kind of bitter. I didn't feel like we got what we should have gotten out of college basketball. And I didn't think the school cared.

Bud coached great individual defensive technique, starting with how to stop the guy with the ball on the perimeter. The defensive stance wasn't much different from what other coaches taught except that any fake a player made before he dribbled, you reacted the same way, with a six-inch slide back and a push off your front foot to cover any situation. Most good offensive players watch your front foot. They try to get you to shift your weight, and then they go the other way. Bud's technique was that whatever fake a player made, you went straight back, and we drilled on that until oblivion. You did a straight slide in case he did dribble so you could cover him. There was no three-point shot. So you kept the defense in tight and kept the ball out of the lane.

You couldn't play for Bud Millikan unless you were willing to play hard on the defensive end of the court. In practice, we would prac-

tice two and a half hours of defense and spend about ten minutes on offense. We got so tired of it that we got to the point where almost every player would rather shoot than play defense. In pick-up games, nobody wanted to play defense.

Under Bud you had to take charges and dive on the ball. I had played that way in high school. But I still had to learn all of his techniques. For instance, if your man didn't have the ball, he knew where you should be on the court, and he demanded that you play a certain distance away from your man. If you didn't play defense his way, you didn't play.

We could play with anybody on our schedule, but we didn't win too many games because we were a very conservative offensive team. We would walk the ball up the floor and run patterns. That made it tough to win. You let lesser teams beat you.

While I played at Maryland, Dean Smith was coaching at North Carolina, Frank McGuire was at South Carolina and Press Maravich was at N.C. State. I saw how their teams played on both ends of the floor. I liked the pressure defense I saw at other ACC schools. I started looking at things in terms of how I might coach and how I would like teams to play. After my junior year in college, I began to feel like I wanted to be a basketball coach.

Williams's first coaching experience came during a fifth year of school he spent at Maryland to complete his undergraduate degree in marketing. He served as an assistant to Tom Davis for Maryland's freshman team and sometimes scrimmaged against the players in practice. Davis would turn out to have an enormous influence on Gary's career and philosophy. Unlike Millikan, Davis employed an aggressive pressing, fast-breaking style of play. He also took a liking to his protégé. "He was way beyond his years in terms of his basketball IQ," Davis said of Williams. "I've talked basketball with a lot of guys, and Gary would rank up there in the top one to two percent in terms of understanding the game."

It was a big year for Williams in other ways, too. While working as an assistant coach in February of 1968, Williams married

Diane McMillan in her family's Methodist church in Collingswood. The two had gotten engaged the previous summer. "I thought I would be married for the rest of my life and never thought anything else," he said.

Soon thereafter, Williams took a job coaching the junior varsity at Woodrow Wilson High School in Camden. The position became available around the time that things were heating up in Vietnam and 50,000 men per month were getting drafted. Williams received an automatic deferment by taking the job coaching the junior varsity, since the school was in the inner city, where teachers were sorely needed. About a year later, his friend Stan Pawlak, who was then teaching elementary school and playing basketball on weekends, found out the head coaching job was opening up at Woodrow Wilson. Pawlak made some inquiries, and, with the help of his dad, he soon found himself as assistant to Gary Williams, the new head basketball coach of Woodrow Wilson High School.

What happened next was nothing short of remarkable. In his first year as head coach of Woodrow Wilson, the varsity team went 27-0 and won the New Jersey state championship. Williams inherited four veterans and a 6'9" player who moved to the area from Chicago. Nevertheless, Pawlak was struck by the 24-year-old Williams's ability to motivate the squad to play to its greatest potential. "He wills his teams to win. It was magical," Pawlak said. After being down by 16 points in the state semifinals, Williams switched defenses at halftime, moving from a full-court press to a half-court zone press. "Our kids came alive, and their kids didn't react to it. Gary made the right calls," Pawlak said. "We ran off the first 21 points of the second half."

In the state championship game played in the Atlantic City Convention Hall, Woodrow Wilson was given little chance against defending powerhouse East Orange High School, which came into the duel undefeated. But Woodrow Wilson came out pressing, executed well and walked away with an 86-72 victory. Meanwhile,

Williams's wife, Diane, seven months pregnant, looked on proudly from the stands. "It was the ultimate to win the state championship," Williams said. "We never trailed. We pressed and they were shocked."

The victory by the upstarts from South Jersey was marred by a riot that broke out on the court immediately after the game. Angry fans from East Orange didn't think the scrappy squad from Camden had a chance. Their growing frustration resulted in a full-scale brawl. One of Williams's players was hit with a cane, taking some of the luster away from the surprise win. But that didn't stop Williams and his pal Ed Pyne from celebrating the victory in style with their wives and a couple of bottles of Cold Duck later that night. And shortly afterwards, his team was honored with a parade and a mayor's reception in Camden. Within two months, Diane and Gary's daughter Kristin was born. Despite the turmoil of the era, 1970 turned out to be a banner year for Gary Williams, with a 27-0 season and a healthy baby daughter.

Just as Williams's high-school coaching career was taking off, another determined basketball man came to Maryland and left an indelible imprint on the Terps' program, the region and the landscape of college basketball. Charles "Lefty" Driesell came to College Park in 1969 after compiling a sterling 176-65 record over nine seasons at Davidson College. He stood six foot five and sturdy, his build a reminder of the old playing days at Duke in the 1950s. With his bald head, sly southern grin, and irrepressible salesmanship, he played the part of a pied piper. When he strode onto the basketball court in Cole Field House for games, the Maryland band played "Hail to the Chief," and borrowing Nixon-era iconography of the day, he flashed the "V-sign" for victory at the crowd.

Seemingly overnight, a team that had been averaging 3,000 spectators per game was now selling out Cole Field House for many games. And "The Lefthander" made sure the fans had something to see. Playing with virtually the same lineup that had sputtered and wheezed to an 8-18 record prior to his arrival, Driesell steered the Terps to a 13-13 mark in his first season. After a last-second upset of the Blue Devils, Maryland students charged the floor and carried their new coach off on their shoulders.

Driesell took a mediocre Maryland program and put it on the national stage, vowing to turn the Terrapins into "the UCLA of the East" during his first press conference. By daring to compare his program to that of UCLA coach John Wooden, the gold standard in college basketball, Driesell offended many purists. Unbowed, the new Maryland coach displayed more of his brash style by placing a full-page ad in *The Washington Post* telling four of the D.C. area's top high school players, in the spirit of a lawman's notice in the Old West, that they were "Wanted" by the Terps. One of the four, Jim O'Brien, went to Maryland, became a three-year starter and played a key role in the program's resurgence.

Driesell was a tireless recruiter who immediately set out to bring the best talent in the country to College Park. He joked that he put his assistant coach Joe Harrington in a car, told him to drive west "and see everybody 6'9" or taller from here to California." In his first full year on the job, Driesell recruited two phenomenal players, shot-blocking center Len Elmore from Manhattan's Power Memorial High School, and Tom McMillen, the consensus No. 1 high school prospect in the nation. McMillen, who also was considering Virginia, chose the Tar Heels, despite his father's personal dislike for Coach Dean Smith. But when his father fell ill, McMillen had second thoughts about going to school far from home. "That reopened the whole thing, and Lefty came on charging," McMillen said. Driesell's persistence paid off, and Maryland eventually won the year's top recruiting prize.

Quick with a colorful quote or a friendly word, Lefty related well to just about everybody. A devoted husband and father who spoke of Christian values, he was a master recruiter. "Ah kin coach," he said in his Tidewater twang. Beneath that veneer lay a whip-smart basketball mind and a fierce drive to win. "The Lefthander was a recruiter, he was the entertainment, he was the entrepreneur and he was the shoe salesman," said Roy Williams, then assistant coach at North Carolina. "He had unbelievable energy and thought recruiting from the first moment of each day until the last moment of each day. He did bring life into the Maryland program."

In the early 1970s, Gary Williams nearly missed an opportunity that would change his basketball trajectory forever. The youthful high school coach received a phone call from Tom Davis, who had gotten the head coaching job at Lafayette University. Davis asked Williams to join him at Lafayette as his assistant college basketball coach just as Williams had done with the freshman team at Maryland. However, there was a condition: Williams had to coach the soccer team, too. Lafayette had never had an assistant basketball coach, and the money in the budget was there to pay for a soccer coach.

Consumed by basketball and ignorant of soccer, Williams flatly turned Davis down. "I can't do it," he said. A week later, Davis called back, urging Williams to reconsider the decision and promising him he would regret it years later if he missed his chance to break into the college coaching ranks and remained a high school coach for life. Coaching, like other professions, depended heavily on who you knew, and Gary didn't know any other college coaches who might offer him that kind of opportunity. Still, he detested the idea of coaching soccer, a game he knew nothing about, and strongly preferred to remain focused on basketball. Besides, he was making \$8,000 a year as a teacher, his wife was making about \$6,000 as a nurse, and for \$14,000, they could afford to go out for dinner once a week and enjoy themselves. The offer from Lafayette to coach was for a cool $6,900. But Tom Davis refused to take "no" for an answer.

"Ever think about being a college coach?" Davis asked in a follow-up phone call after a week had passed.

"Yeah, but not day to day," Williams replied. "I've probably seen two soccer games in my whole life."

"This might be your one chance to ever be a college coach," Davis said. "You have to give yourself the chance."

Williams did. In hindsight, his decision to leave Woodrow Wilson High School for a job coaching basketball and soccer in the college ranks seems obvious. But at the time, Williams still harbored doubts. "I was going to be a high school basketball coach my whole life," Williams said. "I agreed to take that job in a second phone call from Tom Davis. My first day of soccer practice at Lafayette was the most scared I had ever been. I knew every player knew more than I did. They gave me books to read about soccer, but I didn't know anything. We just did a lot of basketball drills that first year."

The soccer team had a successful run in Williams's first year at Lafayette, but it was on the basketball court where he and Davis made their mark. "I never thought of him as an assistant coach," Davis said. "He was much more than an assistant coach. We worked things out together." After an ugly loss to Temple in which the Leopards could not crack the Owls' 3-2 zone, Williams and Davis spent an entire off-season creating an offense heavy on bounce passing to counter that defense. "We learned a lot about zone defense just trying to break it down," Davis said. "It was amazing how much time we put in to figure out this one aspect of the game. But that's how you learn as a coach." With Davis at the helm and Williams in the assistant's chair, Lafayette became a giant-killer along the East Coast. Big-time basketball programs that had signed the Leopards to come play against their team often rescinded their invitation, afraid that they would lose to the tiny school from Easton, PA.

The taciturn Davis and firebrand Williams were gaining a reputation of playing "good cop-bad cop" with referees, but in reality, they were just being themselves. And Williams was "fun to be around," Davis said. "Kids saw that right away. He was an outstanding coach at Lafayette because he could speak their language." And while life as a young assistant—recruiting, scouting and coaching games—often made for long stretches away from his wife and daughter, Williams was doing what he wanted to do and having some wild adventures along the way. "I remember sitting with Gary in a bar in Morgantown after beating West Virginia," Davis said, "when behind us this woman pulls out a gun and starts shooting at her boyfriend.

"I think we decided then it was time to turn in."

3
MOVING ON UP

Gary Williams's philosophy as a basketball coach has been influenced heavily by what he learned about defense as a player for Coach Bud Millikan at Maryland, what he learned about offense and other parts of the game as an assistant to Coach Tom Davis at Lafayette and Boston College, his own observation of other coaches, and an innate sense of the game that he developed as a player. He was described in a 1966 Maryland basketball brochure as a "fierce competitor with a heart as big as his chest," and as a coach, his record is unambiguous: he has improved the basketball programs at all of the universities where he has served over the past two dozen years. In each case, the teams he directed have posted winning records. And his extraordinary intensity and passion for winning have influenced those who suited up to play for him or watched him, in practice and in games, sweating, shouting and scowling.

At every stop along the way, Williams grew as a coach without abandoning the fundamental precepts of the game he had learned from others. As head coach at American University in 1979, Boston College in 1983 and Ohio State in 1986, he sought to meld what he had gleaned with his own hard-charging brand of offense and defense, leaving rival coaches uneasy since it meant that his teams would be tough to beat no matter what players he had on his squad. As the only head coach to serve at the helm of teams in the Big East, the Big Ten and the ACC, Williams developed a unique perspective that, when combined with his passionate work ethic, made every minute of practices and games count.

"I just like to be aggressive. I think that's the key thing," Williams said. "It's hard to separate the offense and defense. If we're aggressive defensively, it seems like we play better offensively."

The old theory was if you pressed a lot, you couldn't play good drop-back defense or run a lot on offense. I thought you could do it. That was my big breakthrough. I thought you could be a pressing team, a fast-breaking team and still play good drop-back defense. I really became a student of the game. I watched as much basketball as I could as I got older. I just knew there was a way to play good defense and run on offense. I knew from Coach Millikan that you had to have good drop-back defense to win. The thing that is toughest to learn as a fast-breaking team is that you still have to be disciplined in your shot selection. You have to take good shots no matter what style of offense you play.

I learned zone defense from Tom Davis since I never learned it from Bud Millikan. On the playground, I had picked up plenty of the 2-3 zone defense. But Tom really knew zone and the proper way to play it. Here I was, after playing for a man who gave me a terrific man-to-man background, and then I got the principles of zone defense as an assistant to Tom for seven years at Lafayette and then Boston College. It was tremendous, and as I look back I see that it provided the foundation for what I am as a defensive coach. If there was a school for basketball, I couldn't have taken courses better than what I learned from being with Bud Millikan and Tom Davis.

Simply put, if you play really good defense, you will always be in the game, even if you are not shooting well. The way we play defense is always going to be an important part of the way I coach. I like the full-court press, combined with a half-court defense where you can gamble a little bit. The full court press is the ultimate weapon. It is not just making the other team take a tougher shot. You can steal the ball before the other team even gets to shoot.

Offensively, you always have to start with the idea of getting the ball inside. With solid inside players, you have to get them the ball. At Maryland, when you have a Lonny Baxter or a Joe Smith or a Keith Booth, you have to get them the ball. We were able to do that.

I've always liked to fast-break and run. If we didn't have a good shot, the next look was to get the ball inside. If we didn't have it, we wouldn't take a quick jump shot. When we play well, we are tough enough not to take the quick jump shot but to try to get it inside. Even if you don't get it inside, you force the defense to collapse a little bit so that when you do shoot from outside, you are more wide open.

Those who remember Gary Williams taking over in 1979 as head basketball coach of American University, a school that didn't even have its own gym to play in, recall his competitiveness, drive and rapid results. Fearful after years as an assistant coach that he might never get a head coaching position, Williams was thrilled to have the $18,000-a-year job. He didn't go after the best players in the area, only the ones he thought he had a reasonable shot at landing. But those who came on board, straight out of high school or as transfer students, shared certain traits with their coach, particularly a strong work ethic and quickness. In just two years, Williams led American to its best season ever, winning the East Coast Conference championship with a 24-6 record that still stands as the best record in school history. Williams won coaching honors while leading the team to multiple postseason appearances. He posted a four-year record at AU of 72-42; the school has not returned to postseason play since his departure in 1983 to take over as head coach at Boston College.

Players say that after practicing under Williams and enduring his outbursts when they failed to give 100 percent, games seemed easy. They also grew to trust his sense that if they played tough, unrelenting defense, virtually anything was possible on a given night. "We worked very hard," Williams said. "We surprised some people, including maybe ourselves. And we were confident. Each win built confidence. By the end, we really believed we could find a way to beat almost anybody. Our guys found out they could play our style—pressing defensively for the entire game—and win."

Williams was as aggressive on the sidelines as he wanted his players to be on the court. He became so animated during one game that he did a full pirouette, accidentally leaving behind a trail of his players' meal money that fell from his pocket onto the court. Though he shouted during games, he rarely received technical fouls from the officials because his ire was aimed at his players on the bench and his assistant coaches. Williams grabbed hold of teaching moments while blowing off steam, a habit that would stick with him throughout his career. "We call him 'Wacko.' He's earned it," said Syracuse University basketball coach Jim Boeheim. "On the court, he's crazed, to put it mildly. Off the court, he's different. He's a low-key guy."

Washington Post sports editor George Solomon has a vivid recollection of sitting down with a calm and composed Gary Williams over lunch and listening to him spell out his desire to ramp up the program at American and help his team and his players reach new heights. "It meant something to him," Solomon recalled. "Every game means something to him." John Feinstein, who covered Williams's collegiate head coaching debut as a reporter for *The Washington Post*, remembers him as smart, driven, hard-working and armed with a plan. Lacking a full-sized gym—American played its home games at Ft. Myer, some 10 miles away in suburban Virginia—did nothing to dampen his long-term ambitions. Said Feinstein, "When I first knew Gary at American, the Final Four was where he wanted to get to."

For a young head coach filled with enthusiasm, American proved to be a launching pad to a better job at a bigger program.

For Williams, the 1982 move to Boston College meant returning to familiar terrain, where he had served as assistant basketball coach under his mentor, Tom Davis. When Davis left Boston College for Stanford University that year, Williams got the job as BC's head coach after turning down a similar offer from Seton Hall. The career move marked a seismic shift into a major conference, the Big East, where he would be coaching against some of the best in the business, including Lou Carnesecca at St. John's, John Thompson at Georgetown, Rollie Massimino at Villanova and Boeheim at Syracuse. And he would be striving to get the job done at B.C., a school better known over the years for hockey and football, and which sported a rising young quarterback in the college game, Doug Flutie.

Williams took the helm of a team at Boston College that was 21-9 under Davis the previous season and had made it to the Elite Eight in the NCAA tournament. Hired on April 6, one week before the signing date for basketball recruits, the coach knew he had to get to work immediately. "The first thing I've got to do is meet the team and then get on the road recruiting," he said.

Over the next four seasons, Williams continued his predecessor's winning ways at Boston College, proving he could coach in what was then the nation's hottest conference and showing that he could win ballgames with small, aggressive players who shared his thirst for winning. The Eagles made it to postseason tournaments every year, scored major upsets and played with passion. The squads Williams coached were generally described as an odd assortment of overachievers who hustled while their energetic coach worked the sidelines and helped them win some tough ballgames against first-tier teams.

The biggest star at Boston College turned out to be the diminutive Michael Adams, who as a 5'11", 160-pound guard was Williams's first in a series of small, spirited guards who could score from anywhere on the floor. Adams was followed at B.C. by 5'10" Dana Barros, who averaged nearly 40 points a game in high school.

And years later, Maryland's Juan Dixon, the best all-around player Williams ever coached, would boast a similar physique to accompany his outsized success.

In his first season at B.C., Williams clung to the pressing defense that his mentor Tom Davis had employed. But adding his own twist, he unleashed a fast-break offense and Boston College led the nation in scoring with an average of 84.3 points per game. Working out of a small office near the school's modest gym, which held a maximum of 4,400, Williams commanded respect from players, who realized that his tirades, which often included booting basketballs into the stands during practice to get their attention, were fierce but short-lived. But above all, his players liked to win, and Boston College did just that. During his best season, the Eagles moved into the top 20, tied for first in the Big East, won a school record 25 games and made it to the round of 16 in the NCAA tournament.

CBS sports reporter Lesley Visser, then a beat reporter for *The Boston Globe* covering B.C., has vivid memories of Williams screaming and stomping on the sidelines, pirouetting during games and wearing a shirt that became a "river of sweat." The first time she laid eyes on him, she wondered if he was crazy and was reassured by a sportswriter for *The Boston Herald* who told her, "No, that's just Gary Williams." Later, Visser described Williams's sideline style as "crouched on the floor, folded like a pocket knife." He brought passion and fun to practices. Mike Jarvis, then coach of Cambridge Latin High School in Boston, used to bring his players to watch the Eagles practice. "Gary always wants his kids to enjoy it and never to forget the journey," Jarvis said. "If you see Gary during a game only, you don't know that. He is teaching these kids all the time. He wanted them to have great memories of it and to make memories."

There were big wins during Williams's tenure at B.C., and one of his sweetest victories came in the 1985 NCAA Tournament, when the Eagles knocked off Duke 74-73 in the second round. The squad, which cut Duke's lead to five before the break, picked up its play after a tongue-lashing from the fiery Williams at halftime. "I was so upset at halftime. I really didn't know if we're supposed to be here," he said. "And I really think the kids woke up in the morning, before the game, and wondered if they were supposed to be here." But the third-seeded Blue Devils went down to the scrappy squad from Boston that played 11 men and hung on under the leadership of point guard Michael Adams. "We don't always look good, sometimes we're even sloppy, but I never question our efforts," Williams said. "That's just the way we play. If the ball's on the floor, it's our game." Switching zone defenses—B.C. went from a 1-2-2 zone to a trapping 1-3-1—disrupted Duke's rhythm. "We were trying to score, but they were holding us defensively," Duke Coach Mike Krzyzewski said after the game.

Things didn't always turn out that way. The following season, the Eagles went on a 10-1 run at the beginning of the second half to build a 12-point second-half lead against the Georgetown Hoyas before 14,218 cheering fans in the Boston Garden. But as the game wore on, the nationally ranked Hoyas came back to win 73-66 after B.C. failed to hit a basket for more than six minutes. "It's frustrating to play the 12th-ranked team in the country and be good enough to beat them most of the way," Williams said. A few weeks later in a rematch, the Hoyas prevailed again in a game where Williams was hit with a rare technical foul after arguing a traveling call that erased an Eagles dunk.

With his strong showing at Boston College and a growing reputation as a focused coach whose players and teams consistently overachieved, Williams continued to attract the attention of other university basketball programs. About a year after turning down an offer to become head coach at Wake Forest and deciding not to pursue a similar post at Arkansas, Williams made it clear he would entertain other offers. Ultimately, he took the next step up the ladder in his coaching career by accepting the head coaching job at

Ohio State in 1986. A school better known for its Buckeye football program, Ohio State had the advantage of playing in Columbus, Ohio, a town that did not have to compete for attention with pro sports teams.

Williams relished the move. "It hasn't been difficult at all. I've had to repeat myself a lot. We talk fast [in the East]. I miss lobster. Columbus is bigger than Boston. Most people don't realize that."

4

THE CRUELEST THING EVER

I was in the coach's office at Ohio State when I heard the news. I had taken the job as head coach at Ohio State less than three weeks earlier. Somebody called me from Maryland, and my initial reaction was, 'You have got to be kidding me.' I can remember walking into Ohio State assistant coach Randy Ayers's office and saying, 'You are not going to believe this one. Bias died.'

Given his unrealized potential and the widespread expectation that he would be an immediate sensation in the NBA, the death of Len Bias marked a seminal moment in sports history. He had a credo: "Live, love and laugh every day as it might be your last, because someday, you'll be right." But everyone knew that June 19, 1986 was not the 22-year-old's time to go, not with his strength of body and force of personality. In its cover story recounting the traumatic event, *Sports Illustrated* called Bias's premature death "The Cruelest Thing Ever." The headline itself was drawn from comments made by Celtics star Larry Bird, who had looked forward to playing with Bias so much that he had promised to show up at rookie training camp if Bias joined the team. Some had called Bias the most graceful and powerful basketball player they had ever seen, a standout they predicted would surpass the great Michael Jordan. "He worked a basketball court in the same style as Muhammad Ali did a ring, with a bold defiance that combined with his overwhelming athletic gifts to create an aura rarely seen," according to *The Washington Post.*

He was built like Superman. He was the one guy who you thought, 'Nothing could bring him down.' For basketball players everywhere, it was a shock when he died. When you look at Bias and the type of player he was, and the physical specimen he was, that added to the shock. There was no way anything could stop him at 22.

Players like Bias, the great ones, they have a power forward's body, 6'8" or 6'9", and the coordination and quickness of a six-foot player. To his credit, Bias worked on his shot. By time he was a junior, he was a legitimate threat from the outside. You had to play him. That allowed him to use his skills to beat people off the dribble. He was a warrior. He became one of those relentless, Jordan-type players who refused to lose. Maryland had played Ohio State that previous season before I got there, and even though they beat Maryland, our players at Ohio State were still talking about Bias.

There is a buzz with the great ones when they come onto the court. I can feel it in an arena when people sense something special is going on out there. Bias was something special. A coach can't put that into a player, where he just walks on the court and thinks he will always find a way to win. That is what Bias had. He was different from anybody else.

A first-team All-American, Bias was ACC Player of the Year his junior and senior seasons and led Maryland to victory in the ACC Tournament in North Carolina. "In my time as a coach, there have been great, great players in our conference, but there have been two who were above the rest in my mind, and one was Michael Jordan and the other was Len Bias," said Duke Coach Mike Krzyzewski. When he shot his jumper, Bias soared straight up like a missile and then hung an extra second at the top of his leap, before releasing his shot high above his head, leaving hapless defenders to drift back to earth. Former Maryland Athletic Director Jack Heise put it succinctly, saying, "Len Bias was poetry in motion."

From the halls of Congress to the streets of Washington and Boston, the death of Len Bias was a topic of endless discussion that sent shock waves through the nation. Only days after his death, 11,000 people jammed Cole Field House to mourn his passing rather than to watch him play. The size of the crowd was an indication of the extraordinary outpouring that followed his demise.

A dark cloud hung over the University of Maryland after the disturbing death, a personal tragedy for the Bias family that generated more negative publicity for the school than anything before. After the university retired Bias's number 34, author John Feinstein said, "It was like hanging a ghost up there in the rafters."

Even as the story unfolded, it was clear this would become a pivotal time in the university's history. The dream, quite literally, had turned into a disaster overnight. For a day, Maryland coach Lefty Driesell had been so pleased that his greatest player was chosen second in the NBA draft by the Boston Celtics. For Bias, a hefty contract with the Celtics and a related endorsement deal with Reebok would make him a millionaire and lift his family out of poverty instantly. Bias celebrated his extraordinary good fortune with friends in his College Park dorm room in June of 1986 by eating crabs. But the partying went on too long, and by morning, Bias died from a heart attack brought on by cocaine, less than 48 hours after being drafted. His stunning death profoundly influenced everything from consciousness about the dangers of drugs to the NCAA's policy on drug testing to the fate of The Lefthander, a coach with the second-best winning percentage in the nation. Within months of Bias's death, Lefty's basketball program, amid intense scrutiny, began to crumble.

"Lefty was a friend of mine and Bias, Lefty said, had it all," said Celtics president Red Auerbach. "He was a competitor, he was tough, he was strong, he was quick, he could shoot, he was a great player. He would have been an All-Star in the NBA. Lenny Bias was examined by us, examined by the Knicks and examined by Golden State a week or so before the draft. He was clean as a whistle. So there you go." Auerbach had been ecstatic that his mighty Boston Celtics drafted Maryland's all-time scoring leader and greatest athlete as its top pick in the 1986 NBA draft. Auerbach had never seen another player like him. "We lost a great player for 10 years—not for one year, for 10 years. He was the ideal pro. He had everything. And he was a good kid. I knew him. He was coachable. He was a helluva kid."

Nothing, Auerbach said, had shaken the city of Boston as much since the 1963 assassination of President John F. Kennedy.

N*obody thought cocaine was that dangerous back then. Then Bias died. The most positive thing that came out of that was that drug testing became part of athletic programs. The drug testing immediately changed on most campuses across the country. Parents used to have these liberal views that said, 'We don't want our children drug tested.' They used to ask, 'Do you have drug testing in your program?' After Bias, the question changed, and you were told by the parents that you had to have drug testing programs. That changed within a week's time. And when kids saw Bias go down, they knew it could happen to them.*

Maryland got a bad rap. And being so close to Washington, it instantly became a national story. The Len Bias story was read up close and personal by everybody in the country. Somehow, because Bias died, it meant Maryland was different from any other school. That was bullshit. I started to get upset. They were using this to say the whole university was bad, that the school was bad and the basketball program was bad. The fact that Bias died was one thing and a major issue, but that didn't make the Maryland team worse than any other team where a guy did cocaine or compromised the university's academic standards. I was upset that the school didn't step up and say, 'Wait a minute. We feel bad about this, but we are a great university with a great basketball program.' That never happened.

In the months following Bias's death, the feisty Driesell came under fire for running a basketball program that attracted some of the nation's top high school athletes but lacked sufficient discipline. A criminal investigation ensued, revealing, to the surprise and dismay of many, that this was not the first time Bias had used cocaine. Chancellor John Slaughter cited the immediate need for a "redirection" involving more focus on academics by basketball players. An internal study of the Len Bias tragedy reinforced Slaughter's view that the academic performance of Maryland's athletes had been unduly influenced by its coaches.

James Bias said Maryland had been "negligent" toward his son and openly accused the school of exploiting athletes. "When they're recruiting these players, they promise them anything, and later the kids find out it's all athletics and Basket Weaving 101." Within months, Driesell was ousted from the Maryland program that had been his life's work. "As a college coach, you are supposed to be responsible beyond a parent and keep your players from doing anything wrong 24 hours a day," Williams said. "But they do the same things other college students do. The toughest part of being a college coach is that responsibility."

Williams had believed that Driesell would be coaching the Terps as long as he wanted to coach. And while he was not contacted by Slaughter about the job, he would have declined, since he had just started the Ohio State job three weeks earlier. And so, as much of America was consumed in the national debate over drugs in college sports, Williams focused on putting the Buckeyes on the path to success.

His players knew he meant business from the start. "I remember the first week Gary Williams came in," said Buckeye Tony White.

"We were used to Coach Eldon Miller, who was mellow and soft-spoken. Gary kicks a ball into a balcony during practice and kicks another one that breaks glass. It signaled the change in Ohio State basketball...for the better." Williams was happy, too, to be coaching at a school that did not face the recruiting challenges he encountered at Boston College, where the team finished 13-15 in his fourth and final season. What Williams did enjoy at B.C., and subsequently at Ohio State, was his total immersion in basketball and the athletes themselves during the season. "I really do like the association with the players. That's the part of coaching I really like. From October 15, when practices start, to the end of the season, you live with your players more than your family."

Within months, Ohio State would play one of the biggest games of Williams's coaching career, when the Buckeyes squared off against top-ranked University of Iowa during his first season in Columbus. Iowa's national ranking would have made the game significant enough, but the dynamics were enhanced further because Gary Williams was taking on his mentor and teacher, Iowa coach Tom Davis.

Before the Buckeyes played Iowa during Williams's first season at Ohio State in 1986, a columnist for *The Columbus Dispatch* paid homage to Davis, who schooled Williams in the art of high-pressure basketball and assisted him in getting each of his first three jobs in college coaching. He characterized Davis as "the best college basketball coach in the country" and said that his presence, along with that of Williams, in the Big Ten would alter the style of play in the conference.

When the big game finally came in Iowa's Carver-Hawkeye arena, Williams had the underdog's advantage and the possibility that his opponent might face a letdown and overlook the Buckeyes. Ohio State had been picked in preseason polls to finish in the bottom half of the Big Ten. Meanwhile, Tom Davis and the Hawkeyes were off to an 18-0 start, setting a new school record for consecutive victories, and had just come off of big wins over three nationally ranked schools, Indiana, Purdue and Illinois.

Williams and his team came prepared to pull off an upset. He employed both sagging man-to-man and zone defenses in a bid to force Iowa—last in the conference in three-point shooting—to put the ball up from the perimeter. He slowed the game down with a half-court offense, using the 45-second shot clock to reduce Iowa's advantage in transition. And he made certain that his team's only major offensive star, senior Dennis Hopson, got the ball in a position to shoot as often as possible.

Even though the smaller Ohio State squad had been outplayed on the boards, the score was knotted at 41 by halftime. Heading into the locker room, the Buckeyes had no doubt that they could pull off the upset. Williams told them that the first several minutes of the second half were critical, and that it was the last 20 minutes of the game that really counted. Less than four minutes into the second half, Ohio State took a 49-48 lead and never trailed again. Iowa made a late run that closed the gap to three points with just over two minutes to play. But the Ohio State squad refused to buckle, hitting a pair of free throws down the stretch before holding on to win, 80-76.

"This is probably my biggest victory because it is against the No. 1 team in the country and a coach I respect more than any other coach in the country," Williams said.

"They just played clearly superior to us in every way," Davis said. "I thought going into this game that people didn't give Ohio State enough respect for being as good as they are."

Ohio State controlled the tempo of the game from the opening tip, in part because Williams, rather than following the model of full-court pressure he had learned from Davis, relied instead upon the drop-back defense drilled into him by his Maryland coach, Bud Millikan. "You have to gamble sometimes against a team like that," Williams said. "You won't shut down everything. We didn't press that much, for example, because we feared their quickness and didn't want to give up transition baskets." On the offensive end, Williams's team executed: Buckeyes star Hopson scored 36 points, nearly half of his team's total.

From that January victory, Ohio State continued to surprise its rivals and made it into the NCAA Tournament in Williams's first year in Columbus. In the first round of the tournament, the Buckeyes advanced by upsetting Kentucky 91-77 before facing Williams's familiar foe: John Thompson and his powerhouse Georgetown squad. The Hoyas had beaten Williams's Boston College teams seven out of eight times they met. "I left Boston College because I didn't want to play Georgetown anymore," Williams joked before the game, adding that he had kept a watchful eye on the Hoyas when he coached at American University to see what he could learn. "I'd go see Georgetown play 10 to 12 times a season to steal some things from them. When you coach, you admire other programs and how those teams play. Georgetown is one of them." But all that Williams learned could not prevent the Hoyas from beating the Buckeyes. Still, the season was a very successful one overall and a promising augur of things to come. After the game, Thompson lavished praise on Williams, saying he was happy to see him move on to the Big Ten. "I was glad [Gary] was gone," Thompson said. "Gary is competitive. You expect pressure and a high level of intensity. That is the way he is, and that is the way his teams play."

As coach of Ohio State, Williams continued to thrive, recruiting outstanding players by reestablishing the school's presence in a state known for producing top-notch high school basketball talent. Into the late 1980s, he poured himself into the job, focusing during the season on practice, preparation, game coaching and scouting, while getting a jump on recruiting during the summers and securing some of the state's finest talent. Along the way, his already high level of enthusiasm for college basketball mounted.

"I wish, just once, every fan could get a chance to go to a Final Four," he said. "The players are so pumped up. Everybody's pumped up. Saturday's the best day, the semifinals, just to feel the building. I know I'm partial. But I talk to the TV people. They say it's up there with the Super Bowl and the World Series in what they like to do. There's just something about college basketball." Williams noted that he marveled listening to Larry Bird and Kevin McHale of the Boston Celtics, with all the great pro games they had played, reflect on their college days. "They still talk about their team in college," he said. "It's still got a grip on them. It's something that never leaves them."

Williams devoted himself to the game he loved, which clearly was his top priority and passion. In a sign of what was to come in his personal life, a story in *The Columbus Dispatch* at the end of the 1988 season hinted at the travails experienced by his wife, Diane, a regular attendee at Ohio State basketball games who had moved five times with her husband as he attained bigger and better coaching jobs. "I still can't get over how intense he gets for every game," she said. "He gets so emotional about every one. You sort of wonder how long his arteries can take it. But, really, he's a different person at home. What you see on the court, he couldn't be that way all the time. He just couldn't."

Still, Gary's focus on college basketball, on getting the most out of every team he coached at every game, exacted a toll on family life.

"He's been a coach ever since we've been married. So it's really the only life I've known," Diane said. "It certainly has a lot of ups and downs. The highs are very high, and the lows are rock bottom. I'm sure a lot of businessmen's wives face the same thing." The article went on to describe Diane's unspoken plight. "Although Diane Williams did not say so," the story said, "we know that it is only with a great deal of patience and understanding that one tolerates a basketball coach. Coaches spend all of their time either playing a game or thinking about playing one. What is good about her husband, Diane Williams said, is that he does not spend much time replaying a game after it has been played. Nor, except when a player has sorely disappointed him, does he tend to bring his problems home. But he has the memory of, well, a hoops nut. (After coaching for decades, he can still name every player on all of his teams.) When John Smith, Gary Williams's basketball coach at Collingswood High School, visited the Williamses, Diane was stunned to discover that a husband who couldn't always remember to bring home a loaf of bread could do a mental play-by-play of a game he played 25 years ago.

Diane knew her husband's dream was the Final Four, which he attended that season in Kansas City without her. "I keep telling him I'm going to wait until we're playing in it," she said. "Someday, we will."

5

FOR ALMA MATER

After three strong Ohio State seasons, a pair of top-rated recruiting classes, and a potential Final Four squad on the horizon, there was little reason for Gary Williams to consider leaving his head coaching job when the season ended in 1989. He had a solid team returning and had recruited Ohio's "Mr. Basketball," Jimmy Jackson, to become a Buckeye. As head coach, Williams had a lucrative job in a city where he had a presence. In addition, his team played in a competitive conference where two rival teams, Indiana and Michigan, won the national championship during his tenure. And Jack Nicklaus had given him a guest membership to his golf club, Muirfield Village, where he could pursue his passion for the links in the off-season.

In May of 1989, the University of Maryland forced the resignation of its basketball coach, Bob Wade, amid allegations of recruiting violations. Williams, who had worked for eight years as an assistant before becoming a head coach at the college level, was not completely surprised that things had not worked out under Wade. It would have been an extremely difficult job for anybody, but Williams believed the odds of Wade succeeding were diminished significantly by his lack of prior college coaching experience. "Even though he had been a very successful high school basketball coach, I felt there were going to be some problems after Bob Wade was hired. I don't know of anybody out there who could have done it without that kind of training."

Propelled by a combination of personal factors and emotions, Gary Williams seriously considered leaving the burgeoning program he had built in Columbus for the head coaching job at his alma mater. Williams had achieved success at three universities, and further job-hopping would not have been likely if a position had beckoned from virtually any other campus. Maryland, however, was special. It was the place where he had played college basketball and been a co-captain himself. The longer he coached and the more emotion he put into the job and the game he loved, the more he came to realize that his feelings ran deep for College Park. People could move from city to city, change jobs, alter their personal lives and make new friends. Yet, Williams realized, athletes and others were profoundly influenced by the one thing they could not change: the university they had played for, or attended, as impressionable undergraduates.

Despite the shortcomings in the basketball program when he played at Maryland, or perhaps because of them, Williams felt a tug at his heartstrings that was unmistakable when the job opened up. The idea of returning to Cole Field House as head coach, a prospect he once thought impossible in the Driesell era, stirred his emotions. "Maryland is unique. It is not just another school," Williams said. "In all my years at American U., Boston College and Ohio State, I never thought I had to return to my alma mater to reach fulfillment as a coach. When you're involved in your job, it's too intense. You put too much into where you are to dwell on it. But after playing at a great basketball school, you do have that certain feeling about it."

It was that intangible feeling, as much as anything else, that distinguished him from other strong candidates for the post when

Williams discussed the job with athletic director Lew Perkins and a selection panel that included former Maryland basketball star Len Elmore. "Gary was the best choice," Elmore said. "At a time when you have an alumnus whose heart bleeds [for Maryland], you know that even when times get tough, he will have the qualities of tenacity and perseverance and wouldn't allow obstacles to get in the way."

In addition, Williams could put some messy personal business behind him by leaving Columbus. Years of focusing more on basketball than family, and the ensuing unhappiness in his marriage, prompted the 44-year-old Williams to separate from Diane and move out of the house in June of 1988. "They went to high school together and got married young. And he was having your typical midlife crisis," said their daughter, Kristin. "I never thought he would actually leave, but I wasn't as shocked as some people might have been. You could kind of see him getting busier and more distant."

Kristin felt angry and hurt. The upheaval was particularly difficult for her, given its timing. "It was two weeks before my high school graduation. It was really strange," Kristin said. "Then to go to graduation and have my dad trying to hide so nobody sees he is there. And then he is trying to find me afterward, and everybody in the Columbus crowd is saying, 'Look, there is Gary Williams.'" That was the one thing my mom would always say. 'Was it so bad that he could not have lasted three more weeks?'"

Kristin said that her mom went ahead with a planned graduation party for her, and, in an act typical of Diane's generous spirit, she encouraged Kristin to invite her dad. But Kristin declined to reach out to him. "His assistant coaches all came to my graduation party. I didn't invite him," Kristin said. For years, though her father made overtures from time to time, Kristin said she harbored bitterness and shut him out of her life, beginning with the graduation party. Despite advice from her mother and her maternal grandmother to maintain a relationship with her father, Kristin said that due to the "triple whammy," she could not bring herself to do so for years.

"The first whammy was that it happened, that my parents split," she said. "The second was that it happened right before my high school graduation. And the third whammy was that he must have known how bad I felt," given what he had been through himself as a teenager when his parents divorced.

It also bothered Kristin that her dad was heading to Maryland in 1989. "When he got the Maryland job, he and I had an even bigger split," she said. "I don't think I gave him much of a chance to be involved in my life." University officials and boosters at Ohio State were upset too and sought to keep their dynamic, successful coach in Columbus. The school offered him a new contract, and local business executives offered to put up the funds for additional compensation if he would stay. But it was to no avail.

"I don't think it's anything Ohio State did or did not do," Randy Ayers, then Williams's assistant coach, said of Williams's decision to leave Columbus. "I really think it was just the lure of Maryland. A lot of people are going to read a lot of things into his decision, things that aren't there." In a further affirmation of his emotion-laden decision to return to his alma mater, Williams's compensation fell. "People who accuse me of making this move for money are sadly mistaken," Williams said. "I'll make less money my first year at Maryland than I would have made by staying. Maryland is a unique situation in my life, and also something I didn't expect to be available at this time in my career. I looked at my age [43] and realized if someone else went in there and did a good job, I'd be in my 50s and out of contention when it opened up again. I was at Maryland five years as a student and grad assistant and was nearby for four more years as coach at American U. As far as a lifestyle, having roots and truly old friends, that's the place for me to settle down."

On campus in Columbus, there were sighs of relief when star recruit Jimmy Jackson affirmed that he would still attend Ohio State even though Williams was leaving for Maryland. Jackson did say, however, that he wished Williams would have called him with the news, especially since he had received a telephone call every week for several years prior to deciding to attend Ohio State. "I regret that I never did get that team together and talk to them before I left for Maryland," Williams said.

He wasn't the only one who was sorry. Fans and players were unhappy about Williams's decision to depart. He had, among other things, added energy and excitement to the games while restoring the school's ability to recruit the best high school players in the state. His team was winning, too, at least until hot-shooting Buckeye guard Jay Burson broke his neck during Williams's final season, an injury that sent the team into an uncharacteristic tailspin. His coaching had earned the respect of the Columbus media, which covered Ohio State sports extremely closely. "Hating to lose radiates from his sideline style—crouching, roaming, chattering to his players, carping at the referees—and culminates in a unique ritual. It happens before every home game. The Buckeyes run onto the court and receive a hearty ovation. Two beats later, when Williams strolls to the bench, the noise level seems to treble," wrote Mike Sullivan of *The Columbus Dispatch,* a few months before Williams's departure. "What Williams is after is excellence in a game that has nurtured him since childhood."

People think I was dying to come back to Maryland. That is not true. Ohio State was a great job financially, there were terrific people, and my daughter lives there. You are part of the whole Big Ten football consciousness, and Ohio State had won the national championship. The basketball tradition also was there, and we sold out. We were the franchise, and we were the whole social life of Columbus back in the 1980s.

It was great coaching there. That Ohio State team I left in Columbus was a solid bunch of guys. My assistant coach, Randy Ayers, got the job as head coach. I fought for that, though I wasn't in a strong position. I felt better about it then. The players respected and liked Randy. They got to the Elite Eight and one shot away from the Final

Four. I felt so bad about leaving that Ohio State team because I felt we paid our dues the year before. We had a good team, plus we had Jimmy Jackson coming in as a freshman. I was glad to see the team do well. What eased the pain for me was seeing the success they had. If they didn't have success, I would have felt badly.

A week into his new job as head coach of the Terrapins, Williams attended a meeting with University of Maryland officials about the NCAA probe into recruiting violations under Wade. "What law firm are we going to hire?" he asked. "We have people downtown who are big-time lawyers who would do that pro bono for the school."

But the administrators did not want to hear any of Williams's ideas. "We have our in-house counsel right here," one official told the coach. "We know what we are doing."

To the coach, the message from university administrators was unmistakable: "I was told to stay in my place." But from his experience in the Big Ten, Williams had seen how schools dealt successfully with similar investigations, and they all had retained outside law firms. He sensed that doing anything less than hiring experienced counsel was tantamount to inviting the NCAA to treat Maryland like a punching bag. University officials were banking on the notion of goodwill, that their cooperation, coupled with the fact that the school had never been the subject of such a probe in the past, would lead to leniency. But they failed to recognize just how much the death of Len Bias had changed the equation.

Instead of taking a strong stance, Maryland left its fate to the whims and the agendas of others. "The NCAA looked at Maryland as an example of what was wrong with college basketball," Williams said. "The school took the hit from Len Bias dying by not having the confidence to fight the NCAA. Outside counsel would have separated the issues."

In the winter of 1989, after a two-year investigation, NCAA officials came down hard on Maryland, right in the middle of the

ACC Tournament. The sanctions included reduced scholarships and, worst of all, no televised games or NCAA appearances for two years. "I couldn't recruit a good player to play for Maryland under those conditions," Williams said. "They want to play on TV and in the NCAA Tournament. Good players were not going to come."

To *Washington Post* columnist Michael Wilbon, the sanctions against Maryland were unduly harsh and reflected the NCAA's inability to make penalties stick against schools that had engaged in worse behavior but which had fought back aggressively and successfully during earlier investigations. In Maryland's case, the school made itself an easy target for an overzealous prosecutor, judge and jury in the form of the National Collegiate Athletic Association.

The probe took place against the backdrop of the death of Len Bias and unresolved academic questions under former coach Lefty Driesell, even though these were never part of the official proceedings. Maryland officials believed if they cooperated fully, the NCAA would treat the school more gingerly. Wilbon even received a phone call from athletic director Lew Perkins asking him not to write columns criticizing the NCAA.

"The NCAA could never get Vegas or the schools they wanted to get," Wilbon said. "They couldn't get the speeders going 106, so they roughed up the guy going 59. It was one of the great acts of cowardice. You had a gutless cop. The punishment in no way fits the crime. They were the only team ever to be barred from the NCAA Tournament. In the basketball community, people knew Gary got screwed. I ended up thinking, 'This is a crippling penalty. He is not going to stay.'"

I really believed coming into the job that we could be a national power in basketball. Maryland officials had told me there would only be a slap on the wrist by the NCAA from what had happened before. But these severe NCAA sanctions felt more like the death penalty for Maryland basketball. When the sanctions hit, I knew people would think, 'There is Maryland basketball again. Bias died, then this happens—they must be really screwed up.' And here I was, coaching in my first year. There were people out there who thought I was part of the problem. That bothered me. My track record was perfect at three institutions. I thought, 'This isn't fair. Why did I ever come here?' I thought I was left on an island. I didn't feel I was being supported by anybody. I was on my own.

I realized I was going to have to go out on a limb and say things about the basketball program being great in the future. It was kind of the way Lefty came in and said, 'We can be the UCLA of the East.' I thought that was a great statement, and he wasn't afraid to put that out there. I was not going to succeed any other way. We had to change the feeling on campus, and at the university as an academic institution, before we could compete on the national level. We had to get it done on campus first.

I knew what I had to do.

6

A PASSION FOR RED SEATS

High above Byrd football stadium, in a 60-foot tower overlooking the athletic expanse, two groups of men with conflicting agendas prepared to meet. One group had united behind Gary Williams, the other behind Athletic Director Andy Geiger, to review a proposal to renovate the men's basketball locker rooms in Cole Field House. Without an upgrade of the decades-old locker rooms, the Maryland Terrapins would continue to lose good basketball recruits to other schools.

With the Athletic Department budget in a squeeze and apathy on campus among faculty and administrators toward men's basketball in the early 1990s, Williams had looked beyond College Park to find the money and moxie to rebuild the basketball program. In a brainstorming session with a friend, Baltimore insurance executive Terry Arenson, and others in his close-knit circle of supporters, Williams had embraced the idea of raising the $500,000 for the renovation by selling new, high-priced seats on the Cole Field House floor. It would only take a few seasons of selling the courtside seats to raise all the money needed, since the funds earmarked for renovation would qualify for matching funds from the state of Maryland.

Arenson, one of the coach's closest confidantes and friends, outlined the proposal to sell 100 "Gold seats" on the Cole floor surrounding the basketball court to generate money and enthusiasm. The idea may have been new in College Park, but it was hardly radical. Arenson had sold courtside seats in the Baltimore Arena for $100 each when Maryland played games there. And, as he pointed out, the sale of exclusive seats on the floor was a marketing technique that had been used successfully in the NBA.

"How much do you plan to sell those Gold Seats for?" a man sitting to the left of the athletic director asked.

"We are going to charge $1,000 to $5,000 to $10,000," Arenson replied.

"You can't do that. You are nuts," the man snapped back.

"How about if I buy all 100 of those seats for $1,000 each right now? That is $100,000," Arenson said. "I know I will be able to sell them and raise the rest of the money."

Geiger shook his head "No," and the men around him did the same. The athletic director rejected the proposal, saying at best it would sap money from other, more important fundraising efforts and at worst would fail miserably and embarrass everyone. From across the table, their negative reaction felt like a blend of disapproval and disrespect. Sensing that tempers were about to flare and that a clash was coming, Arenson walked over to the door, which was ajar, and closed it tight.

Angered by the lack of support for Terrapin basketball and determined to prevail, Gary Williams glared at Geiger, pounded his fist on the table, and launched into a verbal tirade.

"The problem around here," Williams said, "is that you have no faith."

Geiger shot back, but instead of taking control of the stormy session, he ignited the fires of passion and pride smoldering in Williams. The coach declared that nothing and nobody would stand in his way of making Maryland basketball great. With or without the athletic director's support, Gary Williams was taking action.

"It opened the door," Arenson recalled, "and showed me the strength of Gary Williams. He was quick to jump up and throw all of his support behind the guys like me who had a plan. He knew we were there for him. I saw Gary's spirit and it gave us more determination to succeed. I wanted to prove those guys across the table wrong and show them we could do this."

Mark Turner, a Columbus, Ohio businessman and Maryland grad who flew in regularly to meet with Williams and others in the coach's new inner circle, remembers pitching in to ensure the success of the seat sale. "We all took it upon ourselves to sell those seats and get the word out," Turner said. "The locker rooms were horrendous before they were remodeled. The people at Maryland thought that our plan wouldn't work. Gary battled through it."

Arenson, Turner, and a small group of others quickly sold the courtside seats, raised the funds, and renovated the basketball locker rooms in Cole. One barrier to successful recruiting was eliminated, and in the process, Gary Williams had established himself on campus as a force to be reckoned with.

"That was a very important meeting, and it wasn't just about seats and a locker room,' Williams said. "I think I showed for the first time how I really felt about this place, and the people, and the attitude that had to stop."

The locker room fight was one of numerous battles Williams and his "kitchen cabinet" waged in the early 1990s. The group met regularly, strategizing in restaurants, in offices, at Orioles games and in golf clubhouses after playing a round. Sometimes they would sit with Williams after demoralizing Terrapins games, listening and giving him a safe forum to blow off steam. And win or lose, they always checked in. Arenson and Turner were joined in this effort by Baltimore businessmen Keith Neff and Bill Gaertner, and John

Brown, owner of Bentley's, the popular College Park sports bar and grill just off the Maryland campus.

Williams also wanted to have a sea of red chairs throughout Cole Field House. "The coach came in and saw seats painted four different colors. He detested the patchwork of colors there and wanted the arena to shout 'Maryland' from the moment anyone walked onto the court or into the stands. But again, with budgetary constraints, the university wasn't dipping into its coffers to make things happen. Instead of replacing the seats, Williams got bids, hired the cheapest painter he could find, and repainted Cole's 14,500 existing seats Maryland red.

Neff said the small band of men agreed amid all the adversity that it was their duty to support Williams against the formidable odds he faced. "We wanted to make sure when Gary came to Maryland that he was surrounded by some people willing to help him with whatever he needed," Neff recalled. This included improving Maryland's image. It was immediately clear to this crew that the man they were backing was a focused, tough-minded fighter used to going it alone. However, he was smart enough to recognize that he needed their assistance to turn the program around.

Turner said reaching outside the confines of the campus to this small but loyal group of men was critical for Williams to achieve his goals. "He built a trust with us at a time when the atmosphere on campus was not, 'Let's go get this thing done,'" Turner said. "I helped him on his first charity golf tournament by getting corporate sponsorship and getting people involved. I got motivated by him. It is my school too, and I felt if this guy cared so much about the details of figuring out how to paint seats and fix locker rooms, I wanted to help. He has character and this intense desire to be successful. He just doesn't give up."

We had to have the attitude that we were going to get it done. There were no guarantees we could make it. But it was never going to happen unless people at Maryland changed their attitudes. I had gotten tired of it. I wasn't going to let anybody stop me because I knew I was right.

The typical mindset I encountered here was, 'You can't do it. It has never been done.' There was no real reason, no rule or law against it. They just didn't want it done. We had to make it very clear it could happen. It would have been easier for me just to leave and go coach somewhere else. But I never gave up on Maryland. The biggest thing on campus was for me to meet enough people to make them understand that we wanted to be part of the university. If basketball is outstanding, it helps the school. But after all that had happened following the death of Len Bias, I'm not sure people felt things could be done the right way.

When those NCAA sanctions hit in 1990, the ones who got penalized were the current players and coaches, including me. We were not the ones who did those misdeeds, but we dealt with that for the next three years. And it was not like everything was great again when the sanctions ended. We were not on top, and kids want to go to the best places. We had to fight to get guys in here who would get us up to that level.

During those three years of sanctions, I made up my mind that I was going to stay and see it through. I was not going to win a lot of games then, and I thought, 'I might be fired if people don't remember that we are not on a level playing field.' I was at risk. You get to the point, almost like a player, where you say, 'I will show 'em. I'll show these guys we are going to get it done somehow.' I figured there had to be a way.

The kitchen cabinet offered Gary Williams a base of unconditional support in the state of Maryland, one that served only to further the program and the aspirations of the new coach, and they could provide both ideas and financial resources whenever needed. But as a man recently divorced and struggling to bring Maryland's basketball program back from the ashes, there were times when Williams needed to get away from the pressures of his personal and professional life. In 1990, Dave Gavitt, former coach at Providence, founder of the Big East Conference, and an old friend of Williams, decided to bring together a group of his buddies within the basketball fraternity and organize a golf vacation across the Atlantic to play some of the famous old British links courses. Gavitt invited Williams, who quickly came on board.

The trip was a reunion of sorts for many Big East coaches. Along with Williams and Gavitt, Jim Boeheim of Syracuse and P. J. Carlesimo of Seton Hall both came, along with current Big East commissioner Mike Tranghese. For nine days, the old friends engaged in non-stop competition on the links—36 holes a day, "like a Bataan death march," Gavitt said—and left the pressures of their jobs on the other side of the ocean. The trip soon became a tradition, and the events of past excursions have become collected and traded every year like old war stories. For Williams, especially in the hard early years at Maryland, the trip was a welcome diversion; for someone who had learned the difficult side of celebrity first at Ohio State and now as the defender of College Park, he enjoyed the anonymity that Great Britain provided. Tom Jernstedt, an NCAA men's basketball official and Williams's roommate on the golfing trips, said, "It was comfortable for him to get out of the country and relax and get away from the stress in the continental United States. Although you can imagine with those individuals, there wasn't much break. Those guys like to compete."

Williams has been described by many as a lone wolf, but those who know him best return over and over again to golf as an important, almost vital part of his life. "Golf is a perfect activity to counter the intensity of a professional career like he has. He can still turn on his personal and competitive spirit, but it is with friends, it is social," said tennis Hall of Famer Pam Shriver, a friend of Williams. His buddies are golfing buddies, and it is largely through the competition, they say, that he relates to them. On the course, Williams's intensity sometimes bubbles over. *Washington Post* columnist Tony Kornheiser vividly recalls what happened one day when Williams missed a six-foot putt. "I said, 'Gary, it is only a game.' He ran over and grabbed me by the collar. He said, 'That is what is wrong with you, Tony. It is not just a game! This is the most important thing we are doing right now.'"

In those early years, many Williams supporters worried that the lack of cooperation the coach was receiving to transform the Maryland program might cause him to depart for another job. One way to insure against that scenario was to appeal to his passion for golf and help him put down deeper roots in the community. To that end, friends of the coach who belonged to the prestigious Congressional Country Club appealed to the club's board to grant Williams an expedited membership. Though club policy traditionally had a five-to-seven year wait for applicants, Williams was accepted "faster than anybody ever got in," Marvin Perry said.

When the country club had its cocktail party to introduce its new members, Williams sat at the bar with Perry and told him how appreciative he was. He had never dreamed that he would belong to an exclusive club like Congressional. "Not bad for a poor kid from Jersey," Williams said.

The coach would need all the diversion he could get. Then as now, the best talent in high school basketball wanted to play in the NCAA Tournament and play on television. Because of the stiff NCAA sanctions against his program, Williams could offer neither during his first two years at Maryland. Recruiting against the perennial powerhouses of the ACC, he had little chance of attracting the same level of talent. What was more, the coach faced a possible exodus of current players, most notably star swingman and future NBA first-round pick Walt Williams. After spending two years under Bob Wade, the sanctions promised to wipe out any chance of Walt Williams's playing on college basketball's biggest stage. "I've always wanted to play in the NCAA Tournament," Walt told his new coach. The man students called "The Wizard" could have transferred and played anywhere he wanted; according to Gary Williams, he was recruited to do so by many coaches, including a couple in the ACC. But Walt also had his family living in nearby Temple Hills, and Gary Williams promised his best player that he would play as many minutes as he could remain standing on the court.

Walt Williams made up his mind quickly. "I remember when he came in to see me," Gary Williams said. "He asked, 'What kind of shoes are we going to wear next year?' So I knew he was going to stay."

I will always remember Walt Williams for what he did. That was a big decision for somebody 20 years old to make, since his one big dream in high school was to play in the NCAA Tournament. People have forgotten that period because sports are current. As the coach, I won't forget. As I look back, I remember specifically how hard those guys worked. We won a game down in South Florida where we were down 19 in the second half. When you are not playing on TV and there is no chance to reach the NCAA Tournament, you have different goals. It would have been easy to just give up during that game in Florida. As a coach, it was a great feeling to see guys compete like that, when they are competing to win that one game for self-respect. There was no publicity mill, no playing to make the NCAA Tournament or the Final Four or to look good on television. It was just to win the damn game, and that is what we did.

I'll never forget that after our last year on sanctions, a reporter said, 'I guess next year, with the sanctions off, you guys will play hard since you can go to the NCAA Tournament.' I said, 'There is no way any team I'll ever have at Maryland could play harder than these guys.' They were playing based on pure pride.

With Walt Williams lighting up the scoreboard at Cole Field House, the Terps went on to winning records in Gary Williams's first two seasons at Maryland. But the coach could see that trouble loomed; soon, "The Wizard" and other pre-sanctions recruits would graduate, and without them, the talent just wasn't there. Williams also knew that in big-time college basketball, patience ran thin–even for an alumnus.

As difficult as matters were for the Terrapins on the basketball court, they were no easier for Williams in his personal life following his return to Maryland. After being granted a divorce from Diane in 1990, his daughter Kristin, by then a college student at Miami of Ohio, still wanted nothing to do with him. That hurt.

A new job, a new city, a divorce. The stress on Williams was enormous.

7

PLAYING FOR BALTIMORE

The phone in Terry Arenson's car rang one night; it was Gary Williams on the other end. The Terps were struggling through their rebuilding—the team would go 7-25 in the ACC in its first two years without Walt Williams. Maryland basketball was seen as the enemy in Baltimore, the largest city in its own state, and much of the university believed that the basketball program was a blight upon the school's academic mission. Now, after so much effort, Williams still felt he was getting no respect.

Did you read what was in the paper today, Williams asked his friend. Did you hear what had been said about the program? Arenson replied that he had read it.

"What do you think?" Williams asked.

"Coach, I think there were some things there I agree with."

"He went off like a Fourth of July rocket," Arenson said. "He called me every name. He just went off and I sat there with the phone to my head. He just didn't stop screaming."

Finally, Williams noticed that he hadn't heard Arenson say anything and he wondered whether his friend had hung up on him. "Are you there?" he asked.

"Yeah," Arenson replied. "I'm your support guy. If you go off on me, that's better than you going off on somebody else."

Then Williams dropped the hammer. "You know where I am going? I am heading to Philadelphia. I am so pissed off at this program and getting treated like this. The Philadelphia 76ers called. What do you think?"

Arenson pondered the question and the ramifications—a top-flight coach and a Maryland alum driven from College Park to interview for an assistant coach's position with the Sixers. Finally, Arenson said, "If you are making that trip because of what you read or what other people said, I'm not sure that is a reason to make it."

Williams hung up. "I'm sitting here thinking, 'Did I just piss this guy off so bad?' I had never had a situation with him like that," Arenson said. "He got those emotions out of him, and I've never forgotten that."

A few minutes later, Williams changed his mind, turned his car around, and called Arenson. "I'm coming back."

At a meeting some months later, Gary Williams sat with Keith Neff and Arenson in a small Italian restaurant in Baltimore and talked about what it would take to get the people of that city to trust him and give the University of Maryland a chance. Williams sensed that overcoming the anger toward College Park emanating from Baltimore was something he had to do himself. Yet he also knew that the feelings of hostility toward Maryland were widespread and, in many respects, justified.

No high school coach in Baltimore had been so respected as Dunbar's Bob Wade. But Wade had been unilaterally thrust into the head coaching job at Maryland in 1986 by Chancellor Slaughter, without campus support. Wade's resignation in 1989 made University of Maryland evil in the eyes of the people of Baltimore. Some combination of history and lore supported this perception.

Maryland coach Lefty Driesell traveled far and wide in his recruiting, but he made no special effort to cultivate ties in the nearby city. And more seeds of discontent were planted when one of the greatest basketball players in Dunbar high school history, Ernest Graham, played at University of Maryland from 1978-1981 and then failed to make it in the NBA. As far as many Baltimoreans were concerned, the university was the culprit. Even though many years had passed since Graham's career fizzled, the negative feelings had not.

Graham, who relished the limelight, produced some impressive stats at Maryland, once setting a school scoring record with 44 points in a single outing against North Carolina State, even though he played just over half the game. But his success was overshadowed by talk in College Park that he had a bad attitude and that his inconsistency and hot-dogging made him look like he was playing for himself rather than playing for the team.

There was a racial undercurrent surrounding the perception of his play, with many in East Baltimore convinced the 6'7" Graham was getting a bad rap at Maryland because he was black and viewed as an inner-city player who wore gold chains and didn't conform to the university's norms of behavior. At the same time, he led the team in scoring one year and in assists in two others. "The numbers were camouflaged," Graham said. "Bad attitude—that was something that was said a lot. That wasn't the case at all. The image was different from what I really was." A graduate of Dunbar who led his high school squad to the elite in the country, he appeared to be getting unfair treatment at Maryland. After he was cut by the Philadelphia 76ers and ended up playing ball abroad, the ill-will was reinforced. "I didn't want to be the guy who kept Baltimore players from going to Maryland," Graham later said. "I carried that on my back for years."

Whatever the reality, bad feelings lingered, and the one-two punch of Graham and Coach Bob Wade's disappointing and brief stint at Maryland created a chasm between Baltimore and College

Park that would not easily be bridged. Williams hated seeing so many kids in Baltimore wearing Georgetown or North Carolina T-shirts rather than taking pride in the Terps. From his recruiting experience at Ohio State, Williams knew that to be successful, he needed to be able to recruit well throughout the state; to do that, he could not afford to have his program take on a Washington Beltway image.

With the assistance of supporters led by Terry Arenson and Bill Gaertner, Williams devised a multi-pronged strategy to reach out to East Baltimore, including Dunbar coach Pete Pompay. To increase exposure and as a show of goodwill, Williams decided at Arenson's urging to schedule and play at least one major regular season basketball game in the downtown Baltimore Arena every year. The first year, Gaertner said, "he signed Oklahoma to come and play and he was so excited. We went out and celebrated." Williams also began attending summer basketball league games played in "The Dome," the venue for serious summer hoops in East Baltimore. Williams established his presence. "The Dome is the Sistine Chapel of the inner city in Baltimore," said Gaertner. "That's where everyone goes to make his mark."

Eventually, Williams struck up a key relationship with Jeremiah Dickens, a businessman who organized summer league basketball in Baltimore and was a pillar in the black community. Also, Williams and Arenson, accompanied by a local lobbyist, attended community meetings and gatherings. "He said, 'We are going to get Baltimore back,'" recalled Maryland assistant coach Jimmy Patsos. "And he took the lead."

Rather than defending Maryland or debating what had gone on in the past, Williams connected with those he met one by one and talked about the future. He made sure people knew he was committed to rebuilding and remaining with the program. Through repeated visits, he also showed that he was willing to meet players, coaches and parents in East Baltimore on their own turf. Eventually, Williams started holding basketball clinics in Baltimore in the off-season.

While Williams was working to break into the Baltimore talent pool, he learned about the death of David McMillan, the father of his ex-wife, Diane. While he had not spoken with McMillan in some time, word of his death sparked memories of Williams's childhood and how he had been taken in by Diane's family when his own home life crumbled. McMillan "had a stroke in 1987 and couldn't walk and talk, so when he died, everybody was a little misty-eyed, but there wasn't the traumatic shock of death, except for my dad," Kristin said. "My dad walked in and he was shaking. He had to walk out, and he cried and cried and cried in the parking lot. It said a lot. He had a lot of guilt."

In the early 1990s, one player at Baltimore's Dunbar High School stood above the rest, a high school All-American who also was being recruited by Duke and Kentucky, among others. Williams decided to make a run at him, even though the community in East Baltimore was adamantly opposed to his attending Maryland. His name was Keith Booth.

In considering his choices, Booth trusted his gut and also relied upon advice from his mother, Norma Salmon, as well as Jeremiah Dickens, who had counseled many other Baltimore high school stars before him. Dickens had grown to like Gary Williams and to disassociate him from the things that had gone wrong in the past at Maryland. If Booth went to College Park, he would be noticed and could make a difference. Williams not only talked to Booth about playing a big game each year in Baltimore, he started doing it by playing a game there during Booth's senior year. Also, Booth's high school coach, Pompay, had grown to like and trust the straight-talking Williams.

Booth just couldn't see himself at Duke. It didn't feel like a good fit. That left Kentucky and Maryland.

"Norma Salmon wanted to watch him play. And she understood that if Keith went to Maryland, he was going to be a big man in Maryland history. Norma also liked Gary," said Maryland assistant Patsos. "Jeremiah Dickens had a vision that Keith was the one who should go to Maryland," Gaertner said. "He was an ace. Jeremiah was his own man. He kept Keith Booth's head straight."

Back at Maryland, the full effect of the NCAA sanctions was being felt on the basketball court during the 1992-1993 season. The team finished with a losing record and a worst-ever 2-14 regular season ACC record. Then, in the ACC Tournament, Maryland and its proud coach were embarrassed by the 102-66 shellacking they took from North Carolina.

For a coach who hated losing, getting hammered from start to finish was torture. A brooding Williams came back to College Park in a funk, demoralized over the beating his team had taken and uncertain about his own future. "We could have gotten fired," Patsos said. "Who knows? Gary felt like it could be the end of his career." After the loss to North Carolina, Williams returned to Cole Field House. Then, within a day, he learned that Keith Booth had decided on Maryland.

The next time Jimmy Patsos saw Williams, the coach looked like a different man. He was sporting a wide grin as he walked out of the tunnel onto the floor at Cole. "For Gary to get beat by 30 and smile within 36 hours is unheard of. He went from the lowest of the lows to the highest of the highs," Patsos said.

"We are going to turn this thing around," Williams said. The coach, surviving the sanctions and other obstacles, had landed a national recruit, one of the most coveted players in the country and a Baltimore guy who could help the team win games immediately in his freshman year. Said Patsos, "Gary handled that recruit. Keith was his guy."

After encouraging Williams to make himself known in Baltimore, Terry Arenson and Bill Gaertner were elated. The kitchen cabinet had triumphed. And the coach who had risked it all, and suffered in the process, knew better times were ahead. Still, not everyone was happy. "When Gary got Keith Booth, that was to the chagrin of half of East Baltimore," Arenson recalled. At the same time, the positive vibes Williams gave off were beginning to change attitudes in Baltimore. Joe Green, a self-described "ghetto guy" and shoeshine man in downtown Baltimore, said it this way. "Maryland ought to be able to get the best players from Dunbar and DeMatha," he said, noting that a decade had gone by since the problems with Ernie Graham arose at Maryland. "But to the people in East Baltimore, they didn't see the change. Gary stopped the problems with Baltimore around the time he recruited Keith Booth."

Back in College Park, Keith Booth's decision signaled the end of a drought and the beginning of the kind of potential success Williams had returned to his alma mater to achieve.

"Keith Booth," Gaertner said, "was the turning point."

No recruit was more important than Keith Booth. You never know what it is that builds a program. You can be talented and good, but you have to be tough too. Keith allowed us to get tough as a program. Keith had to be very tough mentally because there were people very upset about him coming to Maryland.

To be successful at Maryland, you have to recruit successfully in the entire state of Maryland, as well as Washington, D.C. and Northern Virginia. This area gets recruited more heavily than most areas of the country, and there are a lot of potential Division I players. The region is just a couple of hours, at most, away from coaches in the ACC, Big East and Atlantic 10. Coaches like to get players out of D.C. because they know they can play. Baltimore, too. You know you are getting a guy who has gone up against good players. You worry about recruiting a guy from an isolated area. You worry that he hasn't played against consistent quality.

Going to Maryland was not an easy decision for Keith. Once he was here and playing ball, he would throw his body at people. He was not a great shooter, but he would get knocked down a lot. Keith would bother some people so that they would try to knock him down. He liked that, and he would make two free throws and hammer the guy again. He put his toughness into our program for four years.

The Maryland team Keith Booth joined in the fall of 1993 may have lacked a fearsome leader, but it was not devoid of talent or personality. The squad already included one of Gary Williams's favorite players, Johnny Rhodes. Like Booth, Rhodes reflected the coach's desire to recruit locally. A fun-loving, multi-faceted player from Southeast Washington with deceptive quickness, Rhodes set the ACC career and single-season records for steals. "I was one of those people who was always roaming on defense," Rhodes said. Williams fondly remembers that in addition to his hustle, smarts and uncanny anticipation on defense, Rhodes had an easygoing personality that, with a dose of winning, had the potential to make basketball at Maryland fun again.

"He's such a good guy. He was always acting crazy in the locker room. Johnny liked everyone. There wasn't a player he didn't have time for," Williams said. An outspoken leader, Rhodes shared his coach's combination of passion and instinct for the up-tempo style of play. "Johnny's big thing was that he loved the game," Williams said. "He knew how the game should be played." It also helped that Rhodes didn't come to Maryland alone; he had decided to attend College Park with two of his buddies from the Washington area, Duane Simpkins and Exree Hipp. Though they struggled for a season on the court before Booth's arrival a year later, their presence reinforced the coach's strategy of tapping local talent.

Ironically, Keith Booth nearly failed to get to play alongside the record-setting Rhodes. Just two weeks into his freshman year, Rhodes walked into Williams's corner office in Cole one Friday afternoon and declared that he was heading home. Knowing that Rhodes's family lived only about a dozen miles away, the coach wished him a good weekend and said he would see him on Monday.

"Be careful," Williams said, recalling that Rhodes had been shot during high school and had seen others shot.

"No," Rhodes replied. "I'm going home, and I'm not coming back."

"You can't leave like this," Williams said. "This is your freshman year. You are part of our first good recruiting class."

But Rhodes felt out of place in College Park.

"I come here, I don't dress like these people, I feel completely out of place. I don't have their clothes and money."

Williams empathized with Rhodes, recalling his own feelings of alienation as a player at Maryland when he arrived without the kind of money that others had. "It doesn't give you confidence you can be successful," Williams later said. "Even though Johnny was 12 miles from home, he might as well have been 12,000 miles from home. I pleaded with him to give it a chance."

"You are not going to feel comfortable for awhile," Williams told Rhodes. "There are people here you are not used to being around. You are too good a person not to give it a chance."

Williams wasn't sure that Rhodes would return, but after a long weekend of wondering, his pleas paid off.

"On Monday," Williams said, "he came back."

Rhodes went on to stay all four years in College Park, playing a vital role on Gary Williams's teams. Throughout his years with the Terps, Rhodes and Williams developed a close relationship that continues to this day. "It was so good to have a head coach you can talk to," Rhodes said, recalling those rough early days at his new school. "That is the type of person he was to me. He was a 'Come on in and grab a seat' type of person." The effect that the player had on the coach was just as profound. Rhodes was the player who reminded Williams most of himself. "There was something about Johnny where you started to see Dad being more positive," Williams's daughter Kristin said. "Johnny really changed Dad."

Keith Booth and Johnny Rhodes were not the only important young players on that Terrapins team. Williams landed one other recruit before the next season began who in his two years in College Park would outshine everyone in the ACC. Down in Virginia, the other major local area where Williams and his assistant coaches had been scouting for talent, a young man in Norfolk had come to their attention, as recruits often do, by accident. While going to watch another player, a long, lean kid named Joe Smith caught their eyes. Largely overlooked by major universities, Williams suggested to his assistants that they keep tabs on Smith, joking that that shouldn't be too hard since he had such a common name.

Joe was really under-recruited. He went to the Nike Camp before his senior year of high school, and Joe was in the sixth or seventh All-Star game. Joe was a center in high school, used to playing with his back to the basket. Guards dominate those all-star games, and they are not looking to pass. Joe ended up as the leading rebounder, and we hoped nobody would say anything. I had no idea he would turn out to be a scorer. He played AAU ball and averaged 10 points a game. Allen Iverson was the guard on that team, and Joe would score on follow-ups. We got to Joe's senior year before people realized how good he was.

The amazing thing with Joe was that from his first day of practice, he was a great player. I had no idea how good a shooter he was. He came to practice, and we were doing shooting drills. He was a great jump shooter, with great timing, who could run the court, fast break and follow-up. Anytime big guys can run, I like that because of the way we play. It was just great to see.

Joe Smith. Keith Booth. Johnny Rhodes. Duane Simpkins. Exree Hipp. After four years, Gary Williams finally had assembled a talented team at Maryland. And the coach was ready to find out just how high his guys could fly.

8

WINNING BIG

The struggle between coaches Gary Williams and John Thompson began even before the Terrapins and Hoyas dueled on November 26, 1993, the day after Thanksgiving. It had been 14 years since they played during the regular season, and the underdog Maryland Terrapins and the highly touted Georgetown Hoyas were set to square off in a local battle of national interest. But days before the game, when a photo crew wanted shots of Williams and Thompson walking onto the basketball court together, the coaches couldn't agree on where to meet. Williams refused to do it at USAir Arena, Georgetown's home court, where the game would be played. Thompson wouldn't come to College Park and pose on Terrapins turf at Cole Field House. Ultimately, two of America's most stubborn and successful basketball coaches compromised. The duo met for the photo shoot at D.C.'s Catholic University.

Williams had wanted to play Georgetown since returning to coach the Terps in 1989. Having grown up watching games at the Palestra in Philadelphia, where the city's "Big Five" schools battled each other for supremacy, he knew the energy and excitement that a local showdown could fuel. But Thompson's team had been dominant in the region for more than a decade, and this was just the kind of highly charged rivalry he vigorously and purposefully sought to avoid. From coaching against Williams when the latter was at Boston College, Thompson also was aware that the Terps coach was possessed of a boundless intensity. Talented or not, his teams always showed up ready to play, and that made them dangerous. Knowing, as well, that there were far more Maryland graduates in the area than Georgetown alumni, Thompson didn't like the tilt in the stands. He finally gave in and scheduled a single ballgame, but only after a promoter put up a guarantee of $125,000 for each school and other early-season options for the Hoyas didn't fall into place.

The last time the two teams played in the regular season was in 1979, and Georgetown prevailed in a game notable, for, among other things, a shouting match between Thompson and Maryland coach Lefty Driesell. Until that game, Maryland had bragging rights in the D.C. area. Since the conclusion of that season, Georgetown had been the hottest program in town. Now, Williams was hoping to surprise everyone with his talented young Terps and knock off D.C.'s premier team.

In his quest to build a championship program at Maryland, Williams believed the chance to play Georgetown was big. He had overcome the Baltimore problem by recruiting Keith Booth. He had top local recruits from D.C. and Virginia in Johnny Rhodes and Joe Smith. Now, the Hoyas, led by sophomore sensation Othella Harrington, were next on his hit list. And with his collection of hungry local stars playing before their families and friends, Williams believed he had a shot at pulling off an upset with millions watching on national television.

Although the game was played at USAir Arena, the Hoyas' home court, the arena in Landover, Maryland was far from the Georgetown campus, and many of its students had gone home for the holiday weekend. Maryland fans drowned out the Georgetown supporters during the game. Leaving little to chance, Gary Williams had his team practice on Thanksgiving; he sensed this could be the opportunity he had been waiting for, the end of that awful phase of struggling under NCAA sanctions, and the beginning of a new era at Maryland.

But Williams also knew Georgetown's rugged style of play could rattle his squad early if the Terps didn't get off to a good start. He was nervous but focused as he delivered the pregame message to his team. "They will try and push you around, and you can't be intimidated," he said in the locker room before the game. "You've got to match 'em early and be ready to take it to 'em."

The conventional wisdom before the game was that Thompson's bunch were bigger and stronger and ultimately would be too much for the Terps to handle. But Keith Booth was not intimidated by the predictions, and though just a freshman, the rough-and-tumble Hoyas didn't faze him; he had been playing at The Dome against Baltimore's best since he was 15. Once you had played The Dome, you knew physical ball. "Walking out behind Boothie, you knew you had a chance," Jimmy Patsos said. "Boothie was like, 'Fuck these guys. I'm Keith Booth from Baltimore.'"

Booth's confidence carried over to the rest of the team, and from the opening minutes, it was clear that the Terps had come ready to play. With the combination of Booth and Joe Smith, Maryland was able to hang with the Hoyas on the inside. And meanwhile, Georgetown was having a hard time handling the quickness of the young Terps.

It was soon evident to everyone watching the game that Maryland had a star freshman in Joe Smith, who had so much speed and talent on both ends of the floor that he made Georgetown's Harrington look flat-footed. With the strength of Keith Booth and the athleticism0 of Joe Smith, Maryland had firepower inside. At one point, John Thompson stood on the sidelines, arms crossed, trademark white towel over his shoulder, shaking his head while watching Joe Smith blow by Harrington for a thunderous dunk that shook the rim and the Hoyas with equal force. But Georgetown had plenty of talent too, and they had Big East, Final Four and national title banners hanging from their rafters. They hadn't gotten those by buckling under pressure to younger, less experienced teams.

Maryland jumped out to an 18-11 lead nearly eight minutes into the game. But then the Terps went cold, and Georgetown kicked into gear, moving out to a 38-28 halftime lead. Maryland's poor shooting continued in the opening minutes of the second half, enabling Georgetown to stretch the lead to 51-37. Williams knew he had to shift strategy to shake things up and alter the flow of the game, so he took starting guard Duane Simpkins out and went with a taller lineup and a full-court press. The new approach worked, and Maryland began mounting a comeback as Georgetown's offense all but shut down. Still, with just under nine minutes left to play, Maryland trailed by 10 points. Under relentless pressure from Maryland's defense, the Hoyas hit only one bucket from the field during the remaining stretch, and Maryland surged to a 73-69 lead with 2:40 left in the game. But the battle didn't end there. Georgetown hit a three-pointer that sent the game into overtime and seemingly shifted the momentum back to the Hoyas.

The lead swung back and forth throughout the five-minute overtime. The Terps jumped ahead 80-76 after Joe Smith hit a basket and two free throws. But a Maryland turnover gave Georgetown new life, and before they knew what happened, the Hoyas had put seven points in a row on the board to take an 83-80 lead. Booth hit two free throws to cut the margin to one, and with the clock ticking down, Maryland had the ball and called time out with 13.7 seconds left.

Williams carefully diagrammed a play in the huddle that called for guard Duane Simpkins to receive the in-bounds pass near midcourt, drive the lane, and dump the ball off to Joe Smith or someone else if a Hoya stepped in front of him to help out on defense. Simpkins took the in-bounds, drove past Joey Brown toward the basket, and kept his eyes on the rim. Instead of following the coach's plan and feeding Smith, Simpkins took it to the hoop himself and with three seconds left in overtime shot a running layup over the outstretched arm of Othella Harrington, sealing the dramatic come-from-behind victory, 84-83.

Terps fans poured onto the floor of USAir Arena, mobbing the victorious Maryland players. Simpkins ran from the court to the press table, where he high-fived Terrapins announcer Johnny Holliday, jumped up on the table, and raised both fists high above his head in triumph. En route to victory, Smith had set a new scoring record for a Terrapins freshman in his first game, tossing in 26 points with an impressive array of turnaround jumpers, strong follow-ups and dunks.

For Gary Williams, the triumphant victory over Georgetown was his sweetest moment since returning to College Park four years earlier, and he let loose, showing his players, the fans and everyone else just how he felt. In what would become a trademark gesture, he pumped his fist toward the Maryland partisans. He hugged his players. The man with the serious demeanor couldn't stop smiling. "Gary was jumping up and down," Patsos said. "It was the most excited I have ever seen him after a game. It was euphoric. It was out-of-control happiness."

Johnny Rhodes has an image of an ecstatic Williams he will never forget. "He did a 360 off one leg with his fist in the air."

The victory confirmed that Williams and the Terrapins were on the path back. The Maryland alumnus who feared he had made the biggest mistake of his life when he returned to Cole Field House was now the happiest he had been in years, convinced this magic moment would have lasting significance. "This was one of those you remember your whole life," Williams said.

The next morning, there was a photograph of the Maryland bench and Williams "about to erupt" on the front page of *The Washington Post* just before Simpkins hit the winning shot. Since the death of Len Bias in 1986, there had been numerous negative Page One stories and references to the university and its basketball program. But since that tragedy and the years of fallout, this was the first time the Maryland program had hit the front page of *The Post* because of good news.

"I want everyone associated with Maryland basketball to enjoy this," Williams said. "As an alumnus, I've watched everything that's happened. It's been tough. But I haven't lost the faith that this program can be excellent or that I can coach. I've had doubts. It's no fun getting hammered. And there are still some tough times ahead. This shows what we can be. For a long time, we haven't known what we can be at Maryland."

That Georgetown game was the most important game we played until the national championship final against Indiana. Nobody thought we were any good. You need a breakthrough game. Back then, if you could beat Georgetown, it meant you were pretty good. It gave Maryland fans a belief we could be good. You need that one game, like the game after Lefty came here and beat South Carolina using the slowdown offense. The Georgetown game made people believe we could turn this program around.

We were the only basketball game on nationwide TV that afternoon. A lot of people saw it and saw Joe Smith. He had 26 points and nine rebounds against Othella Harrington, an All-American. I'll always remember John Thompson standing up there and watching Joe with the ball, about 20 feet from basket. Harrington came out on him, and Joe took one dribble, went up and dunked the thing. Thompson just shook his head a little bit. When Joe made a great move like that, there was a big buzz. That was the one where people realized how good Joe was and the fact we could play. The big thing was that we had to come from behind to win it. That gave our players confidence all year. Nobody in the ACC was younger. We had two freshmen and three sopho-

mores starting, so we needed a confidence boost in that situation, and we got it.

There were a lot of happy Maryland people across the country who sent me letters after that game. And we played well as the season progressed too. We had turned it around.

After winning only two games the previous year in the ACC, the Terps went 8-8 in the conference and 16-11 overall in the regular season, including the win over Georgetown. The team had been 7-8 in the ACC going into its last home game against Virginia. If the Terps lost that game, the season was over. But Maryland prevailed, giving them a fourth-place finish in the ACC and an equal number of wins and losses in the conference. The team then turned around and lost to the Cavaliers in the first round of the ACC Tournament. Now, the coaches and players wondered what would happen when the NCAA selection committee met. Williams believed the Terrapins deserved a bid. "We were nervous as hell. With so many solid programs and the need for geographic diversity in the tournament, Williams knew Maryland was a "bubble team" and that the decision could go either way.

Williams and his players gathered in Cole Field House to watch the draw on TV in the team room. Maryland hadn't played in the NCAA Tournament in seven years, and the tension built as the selection committee kept naming teams without mentioning the Terps. Finally, with only a handful of chances left in a field of 64 teams, Maryland was picked for the NCAA Tournament. Williams cried and hugged Johnny Rhodes as the celebrating began. "The Man broke down and started crying. It was the first time I had seen him cry," Patsos recalled. The Terps were headed for Wichita, Kansas to play St. Louis in the first round, but at that moment, the details didn't matter.

The Terps were Dancing.

Coming into the tournament as a No. 10 seed, Maryland faced the St. Louis Billikens in the first round. The young squad was not sure how it would match up to March Madness competition. Although the Billikens were the higher seed, as the teams ran through their warmups, "I could see our guys looking at St. Louis and saying, 'We are better than these guys,'" Williams recalled. The Terps proved it, advancing with a 74-66 win.

Next up for the Terps was John Calipari's No. 2-seeded UMass squad. The Minutemen were led by one of the best post men in the college game, Marcus Camby, and few expected Maryland to give them much more than a scare. In the locker room before the game, Williams challenged his players. "I don't want to see the season end, do you?" he asked.

"Hell no, Coach!" the players shouted.

Williams tried to get the ball inside against Camby, hoping that the physical combination of Smith and Booth would fluster the lithe seven-footer. The Terps were also able to execute their fast break, and with hot shooting in the second half and great play in the last five minutes of the game, the Terps managed to pull off one of the upsets of the Tournament, getting to the Sweet Sixteen with a 95-87 win.

To get into the NCAA Tournament was such a big deal. Maryland hadn't been in the tournament since 1987. To finally get there was such a great feeling. To go to the Sweet Sixteen the first year we made the NCAA Tournament was a great thing. That win over UMass gave us a preview of what we could be.

That was a big turnaround. We didn't have a lot of confidence after going 2-14 in the ACC the prior season, even though I thought we now had good players for the first time. You have to go prove it, and you have to prove it to yourself. The coach can say it, but you have to get the wins. We did, with the Georgetown game and those two NCAA victories, and that alerted Maryland fans here and across the country that maybe we could have a good program.

The players enjoyed every minute of the glory of making it to the Sweet Sixteen of the NCAA Tournament. A fancy hotel, boxes of new shoes from Nike, media attention and pride in the program propelled them all to dizzying new heights. The Cinderella run ended in Dallas when Maryland ran into a stellar Michigan team and lost 78-71. But overall, the season had been a successful one, and no one was too upset after the game. The players also knew, from the time he devoted to counseling them one on one about problems on and off the court, that they had a coach who cared about them. In the locker room, an upbeat Williams talked to his team about the incredible journey they had enjoyed together by making the NCAA Tournament and achieving their goals. "We got here," Williams said. And to the players gathered around him, that was what truly mattered.

Gary Williams had one piece of unfinished business from the 1993-1994 season to take care of, and it had to do with *The Washington Post.* When Georgetown successfully recruited Othella Harrington, one of the nation's most sought-after centers, the story made a big splash on the front of *The Post's* sports section. Not so for Joe Smith. After Maryland signed Smith, *The Post* buried the news inside.

Williams knew Smith was the kind of dominant player who could make an immediate difference for the Terps. In addition, Smith was from Virginia, which made it even more of a local story. Williams, outraged that *The Post* seemed to be pandering to Georgetown and treating Maryland like a stepchild, called sports editor George Solomon and gave him a piece of his mind. Solomon listened and then defended the newspaper's play of the stories. "It's some guy named Joe Smith," he said.

After Smith received national Freshman of the Year honors, Williams, a careful newspaper reader with a quick wit, knew exactly how to handle Solomon. "He reminded me of what I had said every time I saw him for the next five years," Solomon recalled. "'Some guy named Joe Smith.'"

9

WHERE IS THE MAN?

I wasn't sure, for the first three or four days, if I was going to live. I didn't care. They had all this crap in my arms, oxygen up my nose, and I couldn't breathe right. I just thought, "Well, if this is it, it has been good, I don't have any complaints." I had no resolve to get well—and this was during basketball season.

As he took the flight home with his team after defeating the Cincinnati Bearcats on February 19, 1995, Gary Williams didn't feel like himself. Fighting through what he believed to be a cold, Williams won his 100th game as head coach at Maryland three days later, 84-71 over N.C. State. "We were rolling," assistant coach Jimmy Patsos said. "That was when Gary got sick."

Before the team's March 1 game against Duke, it was clear that Williams was ill. As the coaches left the offices in Cole after practice, Patsos noticed that Williams had zipped his jacket all the way up. "He didn't look right," Patsos said. "He looked weak and it was like you were talking to him, but he wasn't listening. I said,

'Coach, we gotta do this,' and he was like, 'Yeah, whatever, see you tomorrow.'"

Players and coaches thought he had a bad cold, and Williams was not about to call a doctor for that. The night before the team was to leave for Duke, Williams went straight home and pulled the covers up to his head. He knew something was wrong, but he hoped he would be able to sleep it off.

The next morning, the assistant coaches began to worry about Williams when he didn't show up as scheduled. "I remember going in the next day, and after a half-hour, I was like, 'Where is The Man? Has anyone heard from him?'" Patsos said. Trainer J.J. Bush had heard from Williams and took him to the infirmary, where they summoned an ambulance immediately. Because he had been trying so long to sleep or work through his symptoms, Williams had allowed a great deal of fluid to build up in his lungs. He was very, very sick. As Bush was preparing to leave Williams at Adventist Hospital and return to the team for its trip down to Durham, the coach gave him a message: "J.J., tell 'em to take care of business."

I don't know if it is adrenaline, but I normally don't get sick during the season. This all started when we played Cincinnati. I remember feeling cold and happy we won. I didn't think much about it. I got on the plane, and I couldn't get comfortable.

After we landed, I came back to Cole, got in my car and drove home. And then it was a gradual thing. I think a week or so went by. It started to get worse. I was losing my voice and things like that. And then, I remember the last night before I went into the hospital, I had to speak to sponsors. It was a pain in the neck to do. I remember feeling really tired. I couldn't believe how tired I felt. I can't remember how I drove home. It was cold outside, and I couldn't get warm. I remember going home and not eating, and I had my parka on under the covers. I tried to get some sleep, and when I woke up the next morning, I couldn't do anything.

I didn't want to miss the next game, and I was thinking, 'I will get some penicillin and be all right.' I spoke to J.J., and he told me, 'I will see you when you get in.' I said, 'I don't think I can come in.' J.J. came over and drove me to the infirmary. They called an ambulance and took me to the hospital from there. The next couple of days, I didn't know what was going on. They were not sure if this was viral or bacterial pneumonia or possibly even Legionnaire's Disease. It turned out to be pneumonia. There were probably a good five or six days where I just didn't care about anything.

Earlier in the 1994-95 season, before Williams's near-death experience, his Terps seemed to have arrived. From the depths of despair and in the face of a sometimes hostile administration still wary of the scars left by drugs and scandal, Williams had turned the basketball program around and given back to his alma mater a measure of pride in its team. More than simply improving a losing team, he had revamped the culture of Maryland basketball. His Sweet Sixteen finish the previous year matched his best performances in the NCAA Tournament with Boston College and Ohio State, and with his landing of Keith Booth and Joe Smith in the same year, no one could say that he was unable to bring top-notch talent to College Park. Students came in droves to support the team that was back on the national scene, packing Cole Field House to capacity to watch Midnight Madness, the first official practice in the fall. Just a few weeks later, the university administration showed its appreciation in the form of a seven-year contract extension.

Maryland's turnaround was a testament to Williams's coaching style and overall philosophy. At its core was an extraordinary passion for the game and a quest for excellence at his alma mater, which had disappointed its alumni, fans and players as much as any major college program. He remained determined to make a difference.

I don't think you can be a basketball coach without really loving the game, because it's more than a job. It requires more time than a normal job, and the stress of the job, especially at the ACC level, is something that you might not want to put yourself through unless you really enjoy what you're doing. And you know I certainly like coaching—the teaching part of coaching, for me, is the best part. Practices are something that's hard to describe, because it's just you and the players. There are no fans, there are no other people involved, and you get a chance to teach.

When I came here in 1989, it was probably as low as any basketball program because of some things that happened previously. We weren't very competitive, and we've had to become that way in a very good basketball league. It wasn't like the teams in the ACC came back to us. We had to go get better. And that's probably, in terms of my personal feelings, my greatest achievement. And it came as a gradual thing; it wasn't an overnight change that we made. We just had to do a lot of things, in a lot of different areas, to make this a good basketball program.

With the building of a better basketball program came new and loftier goals. Williams had brought together one of the most talented young teams in the country, and together, they had gained valuable NCAA Tournament experience in their surprise run to the Sweet Sixteen the prior year. Alongside the glow of unexpected success came the longing from Maryland alumni and fans that had dogged Lefty Driesell for years—the Terps had never made it to the Final Four. Williams had proven time and again that he could take a struggling team and make it better. But he also knew that the leap from good to great was much more difficult, especially if the litmus test was the NCAA Tournament. Its single-elimination format could send any team home early. The climb was steeper still in the rock-solid ACC, where Duke and North Carolina were firmly entrenched as national powerhouses, and away games against any conference school presented a challenge.

Williams redoubled his efforts, especially in practice, which, Johnny Rhodes said, were "not anywhere near a fun time." Rhodes and others recalled how Williams's penchant for punting basketballs remained alive and well. "He kicked a few [basketballs] off into the stands. He got more than a few off. A slight anything could lead to a basketball on the track in Cole. He probably kicked one of the lights out. It all depends how it came off his foot."

The coach's no-nonsense approach produced results. The Terps surged to an 8-2 record to open the season, including 120 and 138-point efforts in back-to-back games going into Christmas. And on December 26, 1994, Maryland found itself back among the elite in college basketball, ranked No. 9 in the weekly Associated Press poll. It marked the first time that Maryland was ranked in the top 10 since the 1984 season, the days of Len Bias and Lefty Driesell. The Terps ran off three more wins before heading down to Chapel Hill and running into Dean Smith and his loaded Tar Heels squad. Maryland fought hard and kept the game competitive, but Carolina had too much talent in the end. The 100-90 loss was an impressive performance and did nothing to quell suspicions that this year's Maryland team was for real. But Williams and the Terps left town unsatisfied and prepared for their rematch in College Park.

Exactly one month later, they got their chance, as North Carolina came to Cole Field House ranked No. 1 in the nation. The Tar Heels were led by sophomores Rasheed Wallace and Jerry Stackhouse, one of the best inside-outside combinations in all of college basketball. But the Terps had their own go-to guy in Joe Smith, who had outshone Stackhouse and Wallace in his freshman year and was on his way to becoming the best collegiate player in the land. When Smith, the man with the common name and a most uncommon game, led his team to a convincing 86-73 victory over the Tar Heels, it marked another major coup for Gary Williams in his efforts to take Maryland basketball to the top. Students poured onto the court following the win; the Terps had proven they could play with anybody, including the top-ranked Tar Heels, a team that would advance to the Final Four that season.

But none of that mattered to Williams weeks later as he lay in his hospital bed, missing the first game of his coaching career. "If I had tried to travel to Duke that day, they said I might have died." The assistant coaches told the players Williams was sick and would not be able to coach. Assistant coach Billy Hahn stepped into the coach's box in place of Williams and helped make a bit of ACC history. Mike Krzyzewski had taken a leave of absence from Duke that season due to a chronic back problem and had turned the reins of his team over to assistant Pete Gaudet. The Hahn-Gaudet coaching matchup was the first in conference history in which neither of the two teams' head coaches had been on the sidelines for the game. The Terps, led by a dominant performance from Joe Smith, prevailed against the Blue Devils and spoiled Duke's Senior Night.

I didn't watch the Maryland-Duke game, and we played Virginia next. And then the ACC Tournament was that next week. About six or seven days later, I don't know if the medicine kicked in, or the disease had run its course, but I remember at 10 at night, all of a sudden, starting to feel better. That night, it was like, 'I think I am going to be all right.' I went from not caring to starting to feel better in half an hour.

Once I started to feel better, the fight in me returned. I was out of the hospital a day after that and had portable oxygen with me. I remember coming in and talking to the team. We were going to play in the NCAA Tournament at the University of Utah against Gonzaga. The doctors didn't want me to go due to the elevation out there. I had to sign some release or waiver. I had oxygen behind the bench. I felt really weak.

I had lost 20 pounds. I didn't eat at all for a week. Once I started feeling better, I could eat anything. The first thing that tasted good was a lemon water ice. It wasn't great because it wasn't from Philadelphia, but it was the one thing I started to eat first. Once I started feeling better, I ate two cheesesteaks. It was great. I got the weight back really quickly, but it took months to get my strength back.

The absence of their coach had a profound effect on the team and the season from that point forward. "We were missing our leader," Patsos explained. "Billy did as good a job as he could do, but we lacked toughness. We went to Virginia and got our ass kicked big-time." Instead of winning the ACC regular season championship outright, the Terps ended up tied for first.

The Terps' disappointments continued when they were bounced in the ACC Tournament semifinals by the Tar Heels in overtime. Williams returned for the NCAA Tournament, where Maryland had been given a No. 3 seed in the West Region, but he was by no means healthy. At halftime of the Terps' second-round game against Texas, Williams was being treated with oxygen. "We were walking around on pins and needles," Patsos said. "We lost a little of our edge. That will cost you."

It all caught up to the Terps in a regional semifinal loss to the Connecticut Huskies, 99-89. For the second year in a row, Maryland had bowed out in the Round of 16, but this season's end had a melancholy feel. The team had finished 26-8, by far its best record under Gary Williams, and was ranked No. 10 in the final AP poll, its highest finish in 15 years. Yet, according to Patsos, it was anticlimactic.

"Last year, we made it to the Sweet Sixteen and we were happy as hell. This year, Gary wasn't at all himself, and it was a real strange feeling."

In addition to Williams's illness, part of that feeling emanated from the breakup of a talented team. One day after the Terps lost to Connecticut, Joe Smith was all but a memory on the Maryland campus. The barely touted high school prospect had in two seasons become the national Player of the Year in college basketball, and he had decided to go pro. Williams knew Smith might leave early, and at the beginning of the season during the Maui Classic, he had seen him walking the beach in Hawaii with an agent. The presence of agents lurking had become a distraction for his players, but beyond yelling, cajoling and trying to reason with his team, there was little Williams could do.

When Smith was selected as the No. 1 pick of the NBA draft by the Golden State Warriors, it signaled future recruits that the Maryland program was capable of preparing them for the NBA. But at the time, it was small consolation to a team losing its most potent weapon that had to find a way to rebuild.

That's the great thing about college coaching—it does change year to year. Even if you have your players back, they're a year older and they change a little bit, so you have to keep trying to find out what makes those guys go and just have the right buttons to push. You don't always do that, but you're constantly trying. I think your team is always changing. One of my goals each year is to keep improving all the way through the season. What you see in December hopefully won't be as good as what you see in March. But it doesn't always work out that way. You try to make it happen, but sometimes it doesn't happen.

The 1995-96 season, following Smith's early exit, was one of the most challenging in Williams's career. The team struggled to a 17-13 record and went 8-8 against conference opponents. Williams's tirades in games had become legendary in the ACC—his manner on the sideline prompted students at Duke to chant, "Sweat, Gary, sweat!" whenever the Terps visited Cameron Indoor Stadium. Meanwhile, Williams felt angry and frustrated with the attitudes of his players. His team wasn't hungry enough; they had been fed too many stories of their own greatness. And for the first time since his return to Maryland, Williams's players were rebelling against his hard-driving coaching style. After one particularly dispiriting loss to Wake Forest, Williams came back to the locker room and confronted his players. "By the way," he asked, "have you guys seen any of those agents who were your best friends last year around here lately? I wonder where they went?"

The barb cut deep, and Williams knew it. Though he believed every word of what he said, there were also moments when he wondered if it would have been better to keep some of his thoughts to himself. But with the exception of senior guard Johnny Rhodes, Williams felt his team stopped giving its best every time out. So infuriated was Williams by his team's lack of determination that by February, he had inserted three freshmen into his starting lineup, a huge statement from a coach who believes in experience and leadership on the floor.

Sent to the West Region again for the NCAA Tournament, Maryland suffered its final insult at the hands of Santa Clara, a No. 10 seed that few expected would even make the tourney. Steve Nash, a talented senior scoring guard from British Columbia, led Santa Clara to a 91-79 victory, putting a mercy bullet into the Terps' disappointing campaign. "They got me back," Williams said later, referring to his seniors. "Their way of getting me was not to play hard, which is sad, because I'll be coaching for a long time. It was their last chance as college basketball players."

Williams came into the 1996-97 season rejuvenated, and so did his team. Although it was Keith Booth's senior year, Maryland had been picked to finish eighth in the ACC. But from the first day of practice, Williams saw a renewed commitment from his players. Walking toward the floor of Cole Field House, Williams stopped in the tunnel in front of the locker room and noticed, a full half hour before they were scheduled to begin, his players dressed, stretching and getting ready to go. "Last year, we had guys getting to the locker room most days five minutes before practice," Williams said. "These guys are ready to go. Eager to go. It makes me feel good."

The Terps defied the projections and tore through their early-season schedule, winning their first 11 games and six of their first seven conference games. And on January 8, 1997, the Terps silenced any remaining doubters by heading down Tobacco Road and overcoming a 22-point second-half deficit to defeat No. 13-ranked North Carolina, 85-75, in Chapel Hill. Just over a week later, the Terps went to Winston-Salem and pulled off an even bigger upset, a 55-51 win over No. 2 Wake Forest and the most dominant player in college basketball, Tim Duncan. The Terps' trio of sophomores, Laron Profit, Terrell Stokes and Obinna Ekezie, were playing well. And with continued strength and leadership from their sole senior starter, Keith Booth, the team picked to finish next to last in the ACC rose as high as No. 5 in the national polls. Gary Williams had his guys rolling again.

But it didn't last, and the Terps stumbled badly at the end of the season. They lost their last three regular season conference games, and as a five-seed in the West Region, they were ousted in the first round of the NCAA Tournament by the College of Charleston. As reporter David Nakamura described it at the time in *The Washington Post,* "There certainly are two very different ways to look at the 1996-97 Terrapins. On one hand, they are a team of overachievers who shocked most observers by reaching the nation's No. 5 ranking on Jan. 27. On the other hand, they are a team that lost its focus and drive when it counted most, at tournament time, and failed to live up to the overachieving image it had created."

Williams also noted the stark dichotomy between the way the season began and ended. "What made us good was that we did not become satisfied with someone telling us 'You're eighth place,' or, 'You stink,'" Williams said. "We didn't accept that. But when we beat those top teams, I think we became comfortable. With all the guys we have coming back next season, hopefully we'll learn. We've got to stay hungry."

As he prepared to head into the off-season, Williams denied rumors that had him fleeing College Park for the head coaching job at Rutgers, in his home state of New Jersey, or returning to Columbus to coach Ohio State. His instincts told him the Terps had promise. They had four returning starters and a promising new wave of recruits. And Williams believed that the tradition of success he had been building at Maryland was on track.

He had been head coach in College Park for eight seasons and survived a near-death experience. His tenure could be defined by pre- and post-Keith Booth. Before the Dunbar High standout came to Maryland, Williams had suffered through four lean years. But in Booth's four years at Maryland, the team had produced four NCAA tournament appearances, two Sweet Sixteens, and two 20-plus win seasons. And most importantly, the door to the vast Baltimore high school basketball talent pool had been reopened. Next season, Williams and the Terps were going to find out just how important that Baltimore reservoir would be.

10
DISCOVERING DIXON

Gary Williams walked into a small gymnasium in Georgia on a hot summer day in 1996. He had come with assistant coach Dave Dickerson to the Deep South to scout high school players in an AAU summer league tournament; he didn't know that on that day, he would see a pint-sized guard who would become the most important player in the history of Maryland Terrapins basketball. But as the sun beat down through the roof of the gym and slowly turned the floor beneath into a hardwood griddle, Williams's eyes turned to that very player, who charged and scraped and dove in a vain and glorious effort to bring his team back.

"It was 100 degrees in the gym and Juan's team was losing by 20, and there were two minutes left in the game," Williams recalled. "And there was this one guy on the court, he was still diving on the court for balls, trying to win the game, to somehow come back from 20, and it was Juan."

Juan Dixon, Williams learned that day, played basketball like it was a matter of life and death. The second son born to Phil and

Juanita Dixon, Juan exuded the spirit of the coach who sat scouting him. Growing up in the Garden Village section of East Baltimore, with the support of a collection of aunts, uncles, and grandparents, Juan learned early how to struggle and persevere as the specter of hard drugs beat a path to his doorstep.

Phil Dixon, Jr. and Juanita Graves had met while going to the same high school in Baltimore; in many ways, theirs was an odd match, the daughter raised as a strict Jehovah's Witness and the wannabe street hustler whose intelligence was betrayed by a need to fit in with a fast crowd. Ridiculed for his light skin, Phil would often get into fights growing up. He began sniffing glue in high school. From there, it was not long before he moved on to harder drugs and more intense highs. "Phil was a very smart guy," Juan's uncle Mark Smith said. "He was smart in a variety of ways. He was street-smart. That was his downfall. What hurt him was his intelligence. He knew that he could hustle; with glib talk and personality, he could hustle his way through life instead of doing it through legitimate ways."

"He felt like he needed to be accepted, and I think that's the downfall of where he got involved with drugs," Phil's sister, Sheila Dixon said. "It was like he had to be accepted in a certain group."

Juanita, known as "Nita" to her friends, experimented a bit during her high school years, but, Sheila recalled, it was not until after graduation when she became involved with Phil that she, too, started doing harder drugs. "She was a nice person," Smith said. "She had a lot of personality—very loving, outgoing, family-oriented. They just got caught up in that web."

Phil and Nita grew closer after graduation, to each other and to the chemicals that were taking an ever stronger hold on their lives. They were married and soon after had their first child, Phil III. And five years later, on October 9, 1978, the Dixon and Graves families welcomed Juan into the world.

Juan's early childhood was a struggle, as he shuttled from home to home with his parents. But it soon became clear that Phil and

Nita, who were themselves shuttling in and out of jail as a result of their addictions, could not care for their children full-time. So when Juan was four years old, the kids—Phil III, Juan and younger sister Nicole—moved in with their maternal grandparents, Roberta and Warnick Graves. While the move gave Juan and his siblings a measure of stability and brought them even closer to their warm and loving extended family, the absence of their parents cast a pall on even the happiest of days.

"I remember them being in my house for Christmas," Juan's aunt, Janice Dixon said, noting that as a Jehovah's Witness, Roberta Graves did not celebrate holidays of that sort. "I always asked my mother, every time [their parents] would call on Christmas Day, I asked her, 'Why do these kids keep telling these two crazy people they love them?' All three of them come in there telling them that they love them, and they're in jail on Christmas Day. But that's why they're a little different than me. That's the kind of young people they are."

When their parents were out of jail, the children learned to step lightly, so as not to be reminded of the drugs that had become a daily terror. "They knew not to go into the bathroom when their mother was in there, because she might be in there shooting heroin, and they didn't want to see that," Smith said. Whenever Juan found needles and other drug paraphernalia hidden in the basement or behind the ceiling tiles, he would quietly throw them in the trash and say nothing of it afterward. "The worst thing we had to do was sit in the car and wait for them to go buy their drugs and come back," Juan's brother, Phil, said. "Sometimes, it'd be two hours and I'd take it out on Juan and Nicole. I'd cuss at them. I mean, sitting in one spot for so long can be annoying. But they wouldn't have left us alone if we couldn't handle it."

As Phil adamantly argued and as Juan has fervently echoed, "Yes, our parents were addicts, but they weren't bad parents." Heroin did not keep the Dixons from demanding order and discipline in the house and respect from their children for elders. Phil, in particular, was compulsively neat—a trait that family members are quick to note has passed on to both Phil and Juan—and he demanded that his children fold all their clothes, do their homework on time, and stay off the couch in the living room. And he insisted above all that his children do things the right way. "Their father was a baseball man," Smith said. "In one game, Phil [the younger] hit a double, and the third base coach told him to slide. But Phil didn't want to get his uniform dirty, so he overran the base and got tagged out." Smith was coaching Phil's team. "I told him, 'That's why I want you to slide. You've got to listen to me.'" For Smith, the matter was over and done with, but Phil's father promptly took the young boy and gave him a spanking. "I would have never made it such an issue had I known," Smith said. "But that's what happened if his children didn't listen to an adult."

"We never disrespected my mother or my father, trying to get into their business, because they would have whipped us," Phil said. "They loved us, but they also demanded respect, no matter if they were high, or anything."

Try as they did to stay in their children's lives and away from the dealers, the streets would always find Phil and Nita, and sooner or later, they'd be sticking themselves again, pushing more junk into a vein. It was the era of the Reagan Revolution, and while the First Lady was telling America's children to "Just Say No," in East Baltimore and in cities around the country, children like Juan went through life with parents who couldn't. Juan was just seven years old when Len Bias was found unconscious in his dorm room, introducing the nation to the deadly effects of cocaine. But even at that tender age, no one needed to tell him about how drugs could ruin lives or make a slave of one's body and mind. The dark recesses — the ones that so many people made passing mention of, but few paid attention to at that time—never left Juan's world. They camped out at his house.

Faced with long odds, Juan made the best of his situation and benefited from a strong support network that included his grandparents, aunts, cousins and uncles. Sheila Dixon, who went on to become president of the Baltimore City Council, was just one of the many family members who emphasized discipline and the importance of education. And her husband, Mark Smith, became a strong male role model for both Phil and Juan, taking them on weekend outings with friends from the neighborhood, teaching them to swim, and when he was old enough, taking Juan to get his driver's license. Smith stayed involved in the children's lives even after he and Sheila divorced and both remarried. Juan once told a friend that it was Uncle Mark who introduced him to anything interesting or new in his life.

"I didn't realize that," Smith said. "I just enjoyed their company. They were great kids, always very polite. I didn't have an ounce of trouble or disrespect. They were very respectful, always. I used to take him out of school to go to Opening Day. Sheila was on the city council at the time, so she got free tickets. Juan used to tell me he loved it. We went on family trips, and they'd drive in my car because I drove fast and so we got there quicker. We took Phil and Juan go-karting, and I had to fight them to get them out of the car. They were so competitive with each other driving. They were racing and had to be warned several times not to hit people. I really did it because that's what my father did with me and with the neighborhood kids. He would take us, and as many kids as he could fit, and take us to the park. So when my brother was taking his kids out, I'd bring Phil and Juan. At the time, their father was in jail."

But no one had a greater effect on Juan Dixon than his own brother, Phil. One of Juan's high school teammates, A.J. Herbert, remembered, "I heard Phil's name every single day. 'Phil this, Phil that, Phil told me this.' So without Phil, I don't know where Juan would be." Five years Juan's senior, Phil engendered a loyalty from his younger brother that bordered on idolatry, and in turn, Phil wore the title of older brother with pride and conviction, shepherding Juan through childhood and always pushing him to exceed his own expectations. As a young child, Juan followed his older brother everywhere, so when Phil started playing sports, it was natural that Juan would get involved, too.

While Phil starred on the Little League team coached by Uncle Mark, Juan would come around and serve as the batboy. One day in batting practice, a boy pulled a hard line drive that hit Juan square in the eye. "I'm like, 'Oh, my God. I've got to get this boy to the hospital right now.' But he didn't cry," Smith said. "He was like seven years old, and he ran over to me and hugged me, but he didn't cry. I'm thinking hospital, surgery, but he didn't cry."

Eventually Juan followed Phil onto the fields where they both excelled in baseball and as quarterbacks in football, and Juan learned important lessons that would help him in later years. "Quarterback builds leadership," Phil said. "It puts you in the position where you got to lead, you got to be focused and you got to have heart, you got to know what decisions to make." And before long, Juan began to follow his brother out to the basketball courts, where Phil was becoming one of the city's most talented young players. The game was perfect for the Dixon brothers. They both had the quick and agile bodies needed to excel. But more importantly, basketball could be a solitary pursuit. If there were problems at home, if their parents were using again, if they were in jail, if they were sick, the game would always be there. They didn't need to gather a team or equipment. All they needed was a ball and a hoop to work it out. "That was our medicine," Phil said. "Whenever something was going on, man, take it up to the court and deal with it."

There, on the basketball courts in Garden Village, they would play, working on their games until their feet could take no more. They played over and over for the only thing that really matters when you're playing your brother—beating the other guy. Every night, Juan came home beaten, but every morning, he came back to try again. "I remember the days when he was just growing up; he was a skinny kid," Phil said. "He was so weak and so slow. He could never beat me. I was just pushing him, pushing him, to the point where he was disgusted with me, to the point where he was crying because he couldn't beat me. But he would just get better and better, hungrier, hungrier, hungrier."

Eventually, Juan scored an "upset" victory. "I call it an upset," Phil said. "I was just playing with him and playing with him," letting Juan stay in the game early, "and he got to the point where his confidence was built up. And he hit a couple shots in a row, and he beat me. I remember he made the noise of a 75,000-seat packed arena. That's how loud he was. That's one thing about our family. You get that family respect, you feel like a king, because our family's so big and we're competitive. We could be in Chucky Cheese's shooting on baby rims and we're still competitive."

As Juan began to excel in organized basketball, Phil, who aspired to playing basketball at the next level himself, made time to come with his family and watch his brother's games. The Dixon cheering section was consistently the largest and loudest in any gym they entered, but they set high expectations for Juan, even at an early age. When he was 11, a youth league coach began to yell at Juan during a game, and the young boy broke down in tears. Rather than going after the coach, Phil came out of the stands and smacked his brother in the chest. "Come on, boy!" he shouted. "You gotta be tough! No fear, man! What are you crying for?"

"That made me tougher," Juan said.

That day, Phil gave his little brother a piece of advice that would serve him well later under Gary Williams: "Look," he said, referring to the youth league coach, "you listen to the words he's saying, but ignore the hollering, because the man knows what he's talking about."

Juan took his brother's lessons to heart, and he continued to work on his game, quietly becoming one of the best schoolboy players in Baltimore. One of the earliest indications that Juan had a future in the game was when he joined the Cecil Kirk recreation center team to play AAU ball. "They come from all over the state, sometimes, to play there," Mark Smith explained. "But it's *the* place. If you play on Cecil Kirk's team, you have *arrived*." Playing with Cecil Kirk, Dixon teamed up in the backcourt with future Georgetown guard Kevin Braswell. The two formed a close friendship, forged by grueling workouts that the coaches created for the two of them, in which they often ended up shooting 500-1,000 shots a day.

Dixon also found a mentor in Anthony Lewis, the director of the Cecil Kirk center, who constantly stressed academic as well as athletic excellence to the boy he nicknamed, "World," due to Juan's big head and skinny body. Lewis "would sit out front of my house for hours, and just talk about my grades, my grades, my grades," Braswell said. "Then he would take Juan out of his house, and yell at him for hours. And then we'd call each other and talk about it like, 'Man, we got to stop messing up, because if this guy cares about you this much, we got to listen to him.'"

Juan went to Lake Clifton High School, a public school in Baltimore, for his freshman year, but the family quickly soured on the educational experience he was receiving there. Around the same time, Mark Amatucci, head basketball coach at Calvert Hall College High School, began recruiting Juan to come and play on his team. The family appreciated the academic rigors of the all-boys Catholic school. Juan would not be allowed to slide on his schoolwork for the sake of athletics, but they worried about the financial burden.

"Amatucci had come down to where I work and asked me, 'Can I help him go to Calvert Hall?'" Janice Dixon said, "and I'm like, 'How much does Calvert Hall cost?'" The school assured them that issues of tuition would be worked out, and they were, through established scholarships and alumni sponsors. Meanwhile, Juan left his grandparents' house and moved in with an older cousin, Sherrice Driver, who lived closer to Calvert Hall and had children of her own. "He fit right in," Driver said. "It was just like he was a part of my family. It was me, my son and my daughter. ...They looked up to Juan." And so, in the fall of 1994, Juan Dixon enrolled as a sophomore at a new school, with the same determination to make his presence felt on the court.

Dixon thrived with the Calvert Hall Cardinals under Amatucci, and was named First Team All-Metro by the *Baltimore Sun* for two of his three years there. College scouts worried about his size, but the wiry, wispy guard displayed quickness, tenacity and shooting range that was second to none in all of Baltimore. But more than anything, Amatucci was struck by Dixon's feel for the game and his tremendous work ethic. It was not uncommon for Dixon to call the coach at his home, on weekends, in the summertime, and say, "Hey, 'Tooch, can you open the gym? I want to shoot for a while." Amatucci was a fiery leader on the sidelines, known to tear into one of his guys when he noticed sloppy or lackadaisical play. But Dixon, who had already come well trained by tough love and hard knocks, never withered under Amatucci's tirades, and before long, the two had established a personal bond that went beyond player and coach. "We had lots of heart-to-heart talks," Amatucci said. "We talked about school, we talked about college, we talked about his relationships outside of school. But when it came to mom and dad, he was guarded and didn't show his hand a whole lot."

Juan's reticence hid an unfolding tragedy within the Dixon family. In recent years, both Phil and Juanita had taken steps to get themselves clean. During Phil's most recent stint under incarceration, he had gone through detox and enrolled in school, getting an associate of arts degree in sociology from the University of Maryland while in prison. "We would sit down and discuss sociological theories," Smith said. "And he would know the names of all the theorists and all about their theories." With help from his sister Sheila and her political contacts, Phil was able to get a job at the sanitation department. He even found a home of his own, for a time, and finally had a steady job on a road crew, cutting grass or shoveling snow for the city. Juanita, meanwhile, had enrolled in a drug treatment program and was looking forward to starting her life over with the help of family and friends.

But in the end, the two could not shake loose from the consequences of their longtime drug abuse, even if it seemed they finally had gotten rid of the drugs themselves. Before he transferred to Calvert Hall, Dixon's mother, Juanita, was diagnosed with HIV, contracted from sharing infected needles. She accepted her fate with the same kindhearted spirit that had characterized her life—"She would stop and see my mother on her way to the hospital for whatever kind of treatment she was getting," Janice Dixon remembered—but also with the resignation of a woman who had seen so many other obstacles, self-made and otherwise, thrown in her path. At the beginning of Juan's sophomore year, Juanita Dixon died of complications due to AIDS.

"Not too long after that," Dixon's friend Braswell said, "He told me, 'Man, I know my father's going to end up dying.'"

Shortly after they buried their mother, Phil, Juan, Nicole and their younger brother, eight-year-old Jermaine, learned that their father was HIV-positive, too. "He kept it hidden for a long time," Janice Dixon said. "I think my sister was the only one who knew, and that was only because he had to have tests and things done to see why he was losing weight. So she called his boss and told him why." As his body was ravaged and withered away by an unyielding disease, Phil turned one last time to the needle. "He stayed clean until a couple months before he died, and at that point I guess he knew he was dying and he got himself some," Janice said. "He got pneumonia and the doctor said that it was going into the final stages, and he said, 'What the heck?' My sister tried to detox him in the last couple months, but he just refused to go."

In December of 1995, sixteen months after Juanita succumbed to her illness, Phil Dixon, Jr., took his final breath and ended a hard life lived hard. But before he did, he made some final requests of his family on his deathbed, that Uncle Mark continue to look after his children, and that his children get their education and graduate. Phil did not need to tell them to avoid the road he had traveled. Seeing him on that hospital bed was caution enough.

A few days after his father died, Dixon went to Amatucci's office and told his coach that he had lost his sole remaining parent. Amatucci was shocked by the news, but not surprised that this child who had endured so much tragedy would hide his pain beneath a stoic façade.

"Do you need some time off?" Amatucci asked.

Shaking his head, Dixon replied, "No, I'm all right." But it was two days away from a league game, and he was worried that under Amatucci's "no practice, no play" rule, he would miss the game if he went to his father's funeral. He couldn't miss that game. He had to play.

"Juan, it's okay," the coach said. "Go to the funeral."

Dixon went, and then he came back to have one of his best games of the year. Like he had so many times in his life, Juan took his pain, his frustration and his anger at the world and unleashed it all on the court.

Juan Dixon first came to the attention of Maryland basketball coaches when then-assistant coach Billy Hahn went to watch his son's Atholton High School team play against Calvert Hall. Though he sat out the entire first quarter, Dixon ended up with 25 points for the game. After hearing back from Hahn, and from Amatucci about how his young guard "shoots threes like other guys shoot layups," Williams decided he'd better take a look at the kid. But it wasn't until that hot summer day in Georgia that Williams began to see what Dixon could be. He saw all the dynamic yet undersized perimeter players—Michael Adams, Jay Burson—that everyone else said could never play major college ball but whom he helped turn into stars. Though Dixon was a better shooter, he saw parts of himself in Juan, similarities in the way they drove themselves by the force of their court savvy, guts and heart.

"Juan and Gary are both killers on the court and great people off the court," assistant coach Jimmy Patsos said. "Both are misunderstood. You look at Juan and he is a delightfully nice kid to be around. Put him in suit and tie and you wouldn't think he was a basketball player. But he's a total competitor. He does whatever it takes to win."

Maryland joined George Washington University, Providence, and Xavier University of Louisiana, a historically black college in New Orleans, in the pursuit of Juan Dixon. But from the outset, Dixon knew where he wanted to go. He wanted to play close to family and friends. He wanted to play on TV. And he wanted to play with the best. Other factors made the decision easier. George Washington coach Mike Jarvis told Juan that he would first have to go for a postgraduate year at prep school. And on his recruiting visit to Providence, some Baltimore-area players on that team told him to stay away from the school. Mark Smith remembered that when he came home, "Juan said, 'They told me not to come up here because it's so boring.'"

By his senior year, Juan also knew that his girlfriend, Robyn Bragg, was attending Maryland starting that fall. The two had met one year before, in the halls of McDonogh High School, where Bragg was a student and which Calvert Hall had come to play in a league game. They had seen each other several times before Dixon ever went up to talk to her. "We probably first made eye contact in November, and we saw each other a couple other times in January and it got to the point where he kept looking at me," Bragg said. "You know how you can tell when someone just keeps looking at you when they're walking by? I thought, 'What is this guy staring at?' So finally that day, he came up to me, and actually his first line was 'Don't I know you from somewhere?' It was a pretty cheesy line, but I kind of gave him a chance."

After a first date that included Juan falling asleep in the theater watching the movie *Dead Man Walking*, their relationship grew to where "Robin's family basically has adopted Juan," according to Mark Smith.

Maryland assistant coach Dickerson took the lead in recruiting Dixon to the Terps, staying in close contact with Dixon, as well as with many others in his extended family, through the summer and into his senior year of high school. Williams went to Dixon's home and met with the family during Juan's senior year. Aunts Janice and Sheila, cousin Sherrice, Uncle Mark, and brother Phil all joined Juan. They questioned Williams thoroughly on all aspects of his program and paid particular attention to a recent article that had been written about poor graduation rates on the University of Maryland basketball team. They had all lived in Maryland and seen the fallout from the Len Bias ordeal, and they did not want to send Juan into a situation where he would learn only "basketball and basket weaving."

"He explained it to my satisfaction and to everyone's satisfaction," Smith said. "He was totally honest about the statistics. He said he saw things in Juan that he loved. He liked his hustle on the court. He thought Juan would be a good student at Maryland."

Few who attended that meeting came away thinking that this was the beginning of a beautiful friendship. "It was just like another coach coming in, but I knew he had his best interests at heart," Phil said. "He was interested in Juan's skills and him as a person. But he didn't seem much different from the other coaches. Time [would] tell all that." But it was clear from the outset that Williams saw in Juan qualities that few other coaches or fans noticed. When the announcement was made that Williams was using one of his scholarships on the skinny shooter from East Baltimore, many Maryland supporters greeted the news with nervous resignation. "When Maryland was recruiting him, they were also recruiting Albert Brown and Albert Mouring, and a lot of people were disappointed that they got Juan instead," Bragg said. "They really wanted Albert Brown. I know they were kind of like, 'This kid is 6'3", 160. He's too small.'"

Juan was all set to go to College Park and play college ball for his home state, but one obstacle remained: the SAT. Juan had struggled on his first attempt, and his score of 840 was too low to get into Maryland. On his second try, his score fell to 690. Dixon grew nervous; having come so far and nearly accomplishing a dream of playing college basketball, he could not let one test stop him. With the help of Robyn's mother, Gladys Bragg, who had been a teacher at Morgan State University, Juan spent the summer and fall after high school studying for his third attempt. His aunt Sheila helped him get a minimum-wage job docking boats and distributing passes to the wealthy sailors who had brought their vessels into Baltimore's Inner Harbor. And all the while, according to his brother Phil, Juan called Coach Dickerson, pleading with him, "Don't give my scholarship away. I'm going to get the scores."

He did get the numbers in the fall of 1996, scoring a 1060. But his leap was so precipitous that the College Board could not believe it. They alleged fraud and discarded the score. The Dixons and the Braggs filed reinstatement petitions, but Juan was used to proving himself to doubters, and he had a different plan. "Miss Gladys," he said, "I'll just take the test again." And though the Board eventually reversed itself and reinstated his third score, Dixon first went ahead and took the SAT a fourth time and received a nearly identical score of 1010.

In the winter of 1997, Juan Dixon enrolled in the University of Maryland, one semester late, but worth the wait. Though by no means a finished product as a basketball player, Juan Dixon was on his way. Sheila Dixon said, "I guess the key is a term that's used—it's part of the Kwanzaa principle—and that's 'Kujichagulia,' which means self-determination. They all had self-determination, and what helps that is other people believing in them."

Gary Williams believed in Juan Dixon.

11

A BITTER DEFEAT

In January of 1998, Juan Dixon stepped onto the Maryland campus as a small, baby-faced freshman for the start of the second semester. As a redshirt, he would not play a game for the Terps that season, but he immediately made his presence felt in practice. On a team in which every player had a nickname, Laron Profit dubbed Dixon, "the Kid," due to his playful personality and the braces on his teeth. But his work ethic, refined on the courts in Baltimore and at Calvert Hall, was that of a veteran, and he immediately impressed both teammates and coaches. It was also clear to Dixon that he had found a kindred spirit in Gary Williams. They got along so well that Dixon told his uncle soon after his arrival, "Boy, Coach really loves me."

"I wasn't afraid of Coach Williams," Dixon explained. "I had the same type of coach as Williams in high school, an intense motivator and a guy who goes crazy on the sidelines, but off the court, he's a great guy and you can get along with him easy. Because of his coaching style, people were intimidated by him." In contrast, Dixon, who relished being close to his coaches, sought to build a personal relationship with Williams. "My redshirt year, our relationship grew stronger," he said.

Dixon made the most of his first semester at Maryland, pushing the starters in practice and being a vocal cheerleader on the sidelines during games. His habit of riding the referees, while sitting on the bench in street clothes, sometimes got him into trouble. During one crucial game, "Gary told him to shut the hell up or he was going to send him home," Patsos said. "The ref said, 'I don't mind hearing it from you, but not from that guy.' Both guys were trying to win and compete."

Before long, the team realized that Dixon was not only a smart player with hustle, but also talented and ready to excel once he was ready to play in games. "He was killing them in practice," Mark Smith said.

Juan loved to play. I saw that immediately. He was always shooting extra after practice, trying to get better, in part by increasing his range. He went from 17 feet to 19 feet to 22 feet. It was a gradual thing. You take thousands of shots and get your legs stronger in the weight room and all of a sudden, it happens. It is one thing to be able to put it up from out there, but it is another thing to be able to make it. Every great shooter I've ever coached takes more shots after practice. They come back at night or stay and just keep shooting. You have to dedicate part of your social life to becoming a great shooter. Not many guys want to do that.

Our relationship grew from being honest with each other. Juan wasn't perfect and would take some bad shots at practice. I would get on him hard sometimes. I could tell he didn't like it. That's part of being a great player. Nobody likes to be criticized. But Juan understood I was trying to make him a better player. I could see how much he wanted to play, how hard he wanted to play, and how much he wanted to win.

I think we both used basketball to get through some things growing up. At the time, you don't really look at it that way. But by the time I was in high school, I spent all my time when I wasn't in school playing basketball.

Sports played a big role for him when his parents died. My parents got divorced, and divorce was a bigger deal back then. I can't equate it to what Juan went through, but we both handled it with basketball. I think there is a tendency to blame yourself a bit when your parents get divorced or your parents get messed up. 'Did I do something that caused this?' There is no answer, so in that situation, you spend time on what you are good at. We both spent time playing basketball, where we knew we were successful.

Just prior to Dixon's arrival at Maryland, the Terrapins had begun the 1997-98 season as a nationally recognized program loaded with talent: juniors Profit, Stokes and Ekezie all returned with a wealth of experience, as did local stalwart Rodney Elliott and European product Sarunas Jasikevicius. The squad also included a 6'9" recruit from Frederick, Maryland named Terrence Morris, who generated much of the buzz in scrimmages and a pair of preseason games.

The Terps had a number of chances to show just how good they were as a team, playing tough games against No. 5 South Carolina and No. 17 Clemson early in the season. In both contests, Maryland gave their opponents all they could handle, found themselves ahead late in the game, but ultimately lost in overtime. So when No. 2-ranked Kansas came to town on December 7, Williams was careful not to do anything that might show a lack of confidence in his team. He pushed the tempo, employing a pressure defense in the first half that challenged the Jayhawks' high-powered attack. The strategy worked, as Maryland went on an 18-0 run to take a 54-41 lead into the locker room at halftime. In the second half, the Terps went without a field goal in the last four minutes of play. But their strong defense, sharp shooting from the foul line, and 21 points apiece from Elliott and Jasikevicius were enough to allow the No. 23-ranked Maryland squad to hang onto a huge 86-83 win.

The win over Kansas after a pair of heartbreaking losses boosted the team's confidence, at least temporarily. But the Terps soon found themselves on the wrong end of a 32-point pounding from the Duke Blue Devils, which by then had risen to No. 2 in the nation themselves. Williams chalked up the blowout to an aberration. When asked later in the season if he had watched the game again, Williams said no, "that tape's still in my trash can." He concentrated instead on the future and steered his team to wins over conference opponents Florida State and N.C. State before No. 1-ranked North Carolina came to town.

Prior to the start of the season, the Tar Heels faced a huge loss with the retirement of Coach Dean Smith. But in the hands of longtime assistant and new head coach Bill Guthridge, Carolina had not missed a beat, going undefeated in its first 17 games and rising to the top of the college basketball world on the backs of star forwards Antawn Jamison and Vince Carter. But that winning streak ended at Cole Field House as the Terps pulled off another upset of a top team, winning 89-83 in overtime. It was the second time in three years that the Terps had beaten a No. 1-ranked Tar Heels team, knocking them from their lofty perch. And for all the talk of Carolina's high-fliers, this game belonged to the Terps' young guns, particularly Morris, who came off the bench to score 10 big points, and Mike Mardesich, who filled in admirably at center when Ekezie fouled out. Both players were on the floor for crunch time, and after the game, Williams said, "I thought [they] were sensational. You could see it on their faces—they wanted to be in there." The focus of enormous attention from both Maryland fans and the media after the game, Morris got top billing. The next day, Michael Wilbon summed up the popular thinking of the time in his *Washington Post* column, writing that Morris "is in the same raw talent class as Jamison and Carter."

While Maryland went into the NCAA Tournament with a 19-10 record after being knocked out in the ACC Tournament semifinals, they were given a No. 4 seed because of their wins over top teams. Again, the Terps were sent packing to the West Region, where they shone in their opening games to advance to the Sweet Sixteen for the third time in five years. But once again, the Terps could not break through that third-round ceiling, this time falling to the talented Arizona Wildcats, 87-79.

Despite the loss, Maryland was enjoying success under Williams by making it to the NCAA Tournament year after year, a feat matched by few other schools. At the same time, it was Williams's fifth-straight loss in the Sweet Sixteen. Despite all his efforts and high expectations, the coach began to question whether he and his alma mater would ever reach the Final Four.

Every team came in here to Cole during the regular season and we kicked their asses. The question was always, 'Can you go further than the Sweet Sixteen?' We were always measured against Duke or North Carolina since they got to the Sweet Sixteen or past it. We were always talking about those two teams since they were in the ACC. But those are two of the top five teams in country over the last 50 years. That skews things out of perspective. There were times when all I heard was, 'Maryland can't beat Duke.' Well, during some of those seasons, nobody could beat Duke.

It was hard only because I thought we were gradually getting in position to beat anybody. We seemed to always run into a good team in the Sweet Sixteen and lose. That Arizona team we played had three guys going to the pros. We were shipped to the West Regional to play most years. I wondered if we would ever stay in the East and get the right draw for us to be favored.

At the end of the 1997-98 season, Williams followed his yearly custom of meeting one on one with each player to share expectations and talk about how each man could improve over the summer. When it came time for Dixon to meet with the coach, Williams knew exactly what he wanted to say. "Before I got to Maryland I used to shoot threes and a couple of mid-range shots," Dixon recalled. Williams loved the kid's outside game, but he told him that in order to become a great player in the ACC, Dixon had to take, and make, more shots from closer range. "Williams is one reason I developed my mid-range game. He is the main reason for that," Dixon said. "That is my bread and butter now, and that is because of him."

Dixon was half right. Williams had conducted meetings with hundreds of players over his two decades as a college head coach. Some players took his advice to heart and worked hard to improve their games. Others listened but didn't follow through. Dixon walked out of that meeting determined to come back with a mid-range game, and he worked feverishly to get it.

That summer, Dixon returned to Baltimore, and each day, he went to an outdoor court, carrying only a ball and a ladder. He set up the ladder in the lane, between himself and the basket. And for hours every day, he dribbled into the lane, stopped and popped jump shots over the ladder until he could shoot no more. Dixon came back in the fall a vastly improved player, just in time to test his skills against a new junior college transfer, Steve Francis, who would quickly become one of the nation's finest backcourt players.

Steve Francis swept through College Park like a tornado, touching down on campus for only a short time but leaving a lasting impression on the program and on those who played with him in his one and only season as a Terp. Francis grew up in the shadow of Cole Field House, in Silver Spring, and honed his game on the playgrounds in Tacoma Park. He was, by all measures, a diamond in the rough, the most heralded junior college transfer ever to come to Maryland, but one who had started only one game of high school ball. Like Dixon, Francis could have become a sad story of a young man whose obstacles overcame him. He floated through three high schools, enduring the heartbreak of his mother's death from a heart attack and struggling with his grandmother, Mabel, to make ends meet. But Francis had transcendent skills on the basketball court, and they were put on display in an AAU tournament late in his high school career, ultimately helping him secure a junior college scholarship. It was at San Jacinto Community College in San Antonio, and later at Allegheny Community College in Maryland, where Francis blossomed into a basketball phenom. He led both teams into the National Junior College Tournament undefeated, a first in junior college history. He could have gone straight to the NBA, where his talent would have made him an instant millionaire. But instead, he chose to accept a scholarship from Gary Williams and his hometown Terps.

The buzz among college insiders was that Williams had landed a prize. But no one could have been prepared for Francis's coming-out party at the Puerto Rico Shootout in November of 1998, when he became a one-man highlight reel, scoring 18 and 19 points in two convincing wins over UCLA and Pittsburgh. Though Laron Profit was named tournament MVP, it was Francis who became the breakout star and what looked to be the last missing piece in the Terps' Final Four puzzle.

S*teve Francis was a junior college player we thought we would have for two years. He had that great impact early in his junior year, and we got to Puerto Rico and he was the best player there. And with the NBA on strike, Steve was the highlight on ESPN* SportsCenter *that whole week. He was immediately considered one of the great players in the country. I've never seen a guy just take over that way in a week.*

The Terps went on to win their first 10 games, and on December 1, they rose to No. 2 in the national polls, matching the highest ranking in the history of Maryland basketball. Meanwhile, Francis continued establishing himself as one of the best and most explosive guards in the country. But as the local and national media focused on the man they were now calling "Stevie Franchise," the coach quietly but unabashedly said that there was a kid playing behind Francis who would soon garner some attention of his own. "I was up at Cole watching preseason practice. He was shooting at one of the far baskets while practice was going on, and Gary came over to where I was sitting at the scorer's table area . . . and I said, 'Who is that skinny kid over there?' And he goes, 'His name's Juan Dixon and he's just like Johnny Dawkins,'" said Jay Bilas, a former Duke player and coach and current ESPN college basketball commentator. "Gary knew I played with Johnny for four years. To me that's pretty high praise, because I think Johnny's one of the top 10 players who have played in the ACC."

As Dixon got his first taste of ACC basketball, he benefited greatly from being able to go up against Francis in practice every day. Steve recognized Juan's abilities and his potential. "They both admitted that playing against each other helped them," Mark Smith said. Francis had a tremendous effect not only on the younger guards, but also on a freshman center named Lonny Baxter, who was also a native of Silver Spring.

One of the things that helped Juan was that Steve Francis was here and Juan played behind him. Juan played head to head with Steve every day in practice. Steve was a little guy, and Juan is still considered a little guy. But if you are smart like Juan, you pick up things that can help your game. You watch Steve Francis shoot an extra 200 jump shots after practice and see how he comes at night and shoots on his own. If Juan needed any convincing, seeing that convinced him that was the way to go. So those became things Juan did too.

We have been fortunate to have players who have helped the younger players in our program. Steve was like Lonny's mentor. He and Lonny talked a lot. When Lonny had a tough game, Steve was there to pick him up. Steve has given back to the program. He was one of the program's greatest players. Even though he played a different position, Steve really helped Lonny Baxter in terms of his attitude. Steve was very unselfish. He only averaged about 12 shots a game. And he put that extra work ethic into Lonny, Juan and other young guys.

The Terps finished with a school-record 13 conference wins, including a sweep of the Tar Heels during the regular season for the first time under Williams. Despite losing to North Carolina in the semifinals of the ACC Tournament—a game in which Maryland trailed by 23 points—the team's 26-4 record still was good enough to secure a No. 2 seed in the South Region of the NCAA Tournament. Finally, it seemed that Williams was in prime position to take the Terps to the top.

He had an All-American in Francis. In Terrence Morris, he had only the fourth Terp ever to be named All-ACC as a sophomore. Ekezie and Mardesich provided front-line strength, Profit was a scoring threat who offered senior leadership, and Dixon and Baxter rounded out a solid, hustling bench. But for all the talent on the Maryland team, Williams and the Terps could not break through the Sweet Sixteen ceiling.

In the most bitter defeat since his return to Maryland, the talented Terps fell to St. John's in the regional semifinals, 76-62. The problem wasn't just that Maryland lost; it was the way they lost. They panicked, played tentatively and lacked the kind of all-out effort teams coached by Gary Williams typically displayed. During a 10-minute period after St. John's went to a zone defense, Maryland was outscored 20-0.

During that stretch, Williams called a timeout and told his squad they were not playing tough enough. The players, including Francis, remained off their game, playing badly and struggling to score against the 1-3-1 and 2-3 zone defenses that St. John's was using against them. By halftime, with the score 38-19, the Terps had almost twice as many turnovers as baskets. "It's the worst half of NCAA tournament basketball I've ever seen Maryland play," said columnist Michael Wilbon of *The Washington Post.*

Things got worse, and before long, the favored team from College Park trailed St. John's by 26 points. The Terps went cold from the perimeter but repeatedly tried shooting over the zone defense rather than sticking with their plan to pound the ball inside. "Williams—and I can understand his extreme annoyance at the way his team was playing—met them coming off the court for a timeout and roasted them," according to Wilbon, who added that NBA scouts sitting near him were shocked at the way Maryland crumbled.

After the game, a dejected Williams sat with his closest friends—Terry Arenson, Keith Neff, Don McCartney and Mark Turner—at a table in a private hotel dining room and grew increasingly angry after learning that questions about his coaching ability were running through the Maryland alumni and fans seated near his daughter Kristin. "Gary was hurt because Kristin told us at the table that a number of alumni had said bad things about her father that they knew she could hear," Neff said. Even though the Terps had gone 28-6, winning more games than in any other year in the history of the program, there was an abiding sense of frustration.

"It was a suicidal night after we lost to St. John's in Knoxville. It was a very ugly time. We had been embarrassed nationally. The pain that went through that man in Knoxville was like I had never seen before. Gary caught a lot of crap, and it built up and built up. There was a degree of negativity that ran through our program that night that was really bad, about not being able to recruit and make it to the Final Four," said Neff, who was among those who stayed with Williams in the hotel dining room until 5 a.m. "There were long periods of silence where nobody would say a word or leave the table. It would have been too brutal to leave."

12

KRISTIN'S WEDDING

The separate worlds of Gary Williams came together at his daughter Kristin's wedding in Columbus, Ohio. On one side, there was his ex-wife Diane, her friends in Columbus, their daughter and her fiancée, Geoff Scott. On the other side, there were Gary's closest buddies—Terry Arenson, Keith Neff and others—who had surrounded him since his early days at Maryland and accompanied him to the nuptials. By the end of the wedding weekend, the two camps had bonded, due in part to the generous spirit of Williams's former wife Diane, and also because of the coach's nascent relationship with their daughter.

For Williams, it was the first time he had been back in the house where he lived with Diane since their divorce and his move to Maryland in 1989. Though Williams had been waiting in the wings to have some kind of relationship with his daughter, she had remained angry at her father until, with the passage of time, she was able to follow her mother's advice not to shut her father out of her life. During her senior year of college in 1992, Williams bought her a new Honda Accord so she could navigate the rural roads of Ohio while she worked as a student-teacher. And for the next three summers after graduating from Miami of Ohio with a teaching degree, Kristin worked at her dad's basketball camp in College Park, living with him, sharing meals and spending time together. Now, he was footing the bill for her wedding, a personal touchstone of her own that also enabled her to reach out to him and his friends more comfortably.

"At some point, I just had to decide whether I was going to spend the rest of my life being angry at him for divorcing my mom or have a relationship with my father," Kristin said. "It wasn't like we were estranged. I was angry, and he was kind of waiting for me to stop being angry. I had a choice of being mad or letting things go."

After the wedding, Diane Williams had a brunch at her house, invited all of Gary's friends and was a gracious hostess. "My dad's friends will say to me, when he is not around, 'I can't believe he divorced her. She is a great lady,'" Kristin said.

Kristin also said she and her mom had some fun planning the wedding after Gary missed a flight to Columbus for a food tasting after promising he would be there. He had been on a pay phone in the airport talking to a potential recruit. "My parents, while planning the wedding, were really cordial with each other and there was no stress there," Kristin said. "Dad was a big part of the wedding. Dad was supposed to fly in and go to the tasting with my fiancée and me and Mom, and he missed the flight. He called and said, 'Once again, I lose the father of the year award.' My mother and I were giggling that he was not here to say 'No,' so we ordered whatever food we wanted, without worrying about the price."

Both Terry Arenson and Keith Neff said the wedding experience was memorable because they felt so warmly embraced by Diane as they saw, for the first time, the life Gary had left behind in Columbus. They watched him interact with old friends and family, revisit familiar places in the house, and then proceeded to give him a hard time about how he could have walked away from so much. "There was a rocking chair he had been given at one of his coaching stops that meant something to him. He said, 'I've got to sit in it.' I'd known Gary for maybe five to six years and now saw the sentimental side. I'd never seen it before," Arenson said.

"There was a side to him dear to his heart, and I almost wondered if he was thinking about whether he could have retraced his steps. His former wife is beautiful, a sweetheart and she went out of her way to be nice. She is a great mother, hard-working and everybody likes her. She probably did everything she could to keep things together."

About a year and a half after his daughter's wedding, Gary Williams was visiting Kristin and her husband Geoff in Columbus for Christmas. As they sat in the car together outside the airport hotel where he was staying, Kristin and her father had a brief but important conversation. She had come to realize that both of her parents were content in their lives, and now that she was happily married, it was time for her to reach out to her father. Kristin apologized to Gary for shutting him out of her life for years and remaining so mad for so long. "For both of us," Kristin said, "it was a relief. There had been this third party in our visits, this unresolved tension." Williams also apologized to his daughter, saying, "I wasn't good to you, and wasn't in a good place in my life, but all we have is the future."

Four years later, the future brought something more: a healthy baby boy born on November 15, 1999, to Kristin and Geoff. "Dad called me a few weeks before I was due. He said, 'I want you to call me the minute you go into labor.'" After getting the call, an eager and nervous Williams flew to Columbus where his former wife and her new husband met him at the airport. The trio had dinner that Sunday evening and then headed to the hospital for the duration of Kristin's 12 hours of labor. David, named for Diane's late father, was born at 8:10 the next morning.

Gary Williams was so choked up he couldn't speak. "Geoff went out to tell them that it was a boy," Kristin said. "My dad immediately started to cry. And then they wheeled David out, and my dad took a whole roll of pictures. My dad couldn't even talk to me. Mom said, 'Can Dad walk in? He has to go the airport.' He walked in my room, choked up, patted me on the head, and walked out. And then my mom's husband drove him to the airport."

Explaining his abrupt departure, Williams said, "I have to go back for practice. I don't want them to think I am soft now that I am a grandfather."

Back in College Park, with the exodus of Steve Francis to the NBA and the loss of other talent, Williams needed somebody to step up and take the leadership role in the 1999-2000 season. Traditionally, Williams looked to his seniors, but the centerpieces of the team were underclassmen. Leadership could have easily come from Morris, now a junior, the All-ACC standout who had bypassed the NBA in favor of polishing his game for another year. But Morris was a quiet personality, almost reticent, not one to grab the reins of a team and say, "Follow me."

Juan Dixon recognized the leadership void as he entered his third year on the team. And as he changed his number from 5 to his brother Phil's number 3, he also changed his demeanor, expressing more of a take-charge attitude both on and off the court. As Maryland's starting guard, Dixon struggled in a preseason NIT loss to Kentucky, shooting a miserable 3 for 17 from the field. But he showed a confidence in his game that impressed Williams. No matter how many shots he missed, he never stopped believing he would make the next one. That confidence paid off just ten days later in a 69-67 win over Illinois, as Dixon shot 8 for 16, including a midrange, pull-up jumper along the baseline with less than 10 seconds left to win the game. "I've been working on that shot all summer and all preseason," Dixon said after the game. "It's been falling for me right now."

Williams knew how hard Dixon had been working for just that moment and hinted that a new leader was emerging on the team. "Sometimes sports is tough because you don't get rewarded, but Juan worked hard enough—he earned the right to make that shot," Williams said. "Juan is one of the players on the court for us who wants to shoot the ball in pressure situations."

Juan probably had that competitive thing going as well as anybody I've ever coached. In a lot of big games, he would come off the court and say, 'We are going to find a way to win and we can do it,' and we didn't know what that was, but that is how you have to feel.

If basketball games are on TV, I watch them. I watch a lot of games and see things as a coach that I'd like to try with my team. As a player, I would see a good move or I would like the way someone did something, and I'd try to do that myself. A lot of players today don't even watch basketball. They have their GameBoys hooked up to the TV. I'd say half our guys really like to watch basketball and half won't make any special effort. You miss out on development as a player when you don't become a student of the game. Juan watched games, and he would call me at my house and say, 'Coach, did you see that?' If a guy made a certain move, he would say, 'I would like to try that move.' I would say, 'You can do that' and he would work on it. He would call up and say, 'Coach, we can beat these guys'—whoever he was watching. He was right. It wasn't false confidence or him trying to be tough.

If the Terps were truly a team to be reckoned with in the ACC, they were not showing it with their early-season play in the 1999-2000 campaign. Most disturbingly, Terrence Morris did not seem to be progressing in his junior year. An All-ACC choice averaging 15.3 points per game in his sophomore year, Morris struggled to match his previous production and did not look aggressive on the floor. The Terps were upset by George Washington University, and after five straight wins to go into the conference schedule, they struggled, dropping their first three ACC games, including one to conference favorite Duke at Cole Field House.

Dixon and another young player, Lonny Baxter, attempted to step up when the upperclassmen faltered. Like Dixon, Baxter was another Williams recruit whom many within college basketball circles doubted could play in the ACC. They looked at his 6'8" wide-body frame and said he was too short and too fat to be an effective post player. But Williams had seen the same kind of determination in Baxter that he saw in Dixon, and when the big man got to campus, Williams challenged him to get in better shape. Baxter spent countless hours in the weight room, put himself on a diet, and by his sophomore year was doing serious damage to ACC opponents on the inside. Along with Dixon and Baxter, Williams could call on sophomore forward and former McDonald's All-American Danny Miller and highly touted freshman point guard Steve Blake, from Miami Lakes, Florida, who had attended basketball powerhouse Oak Hill Academy. Blake immediately came in and took the reins of the team, starting at the point guard position as a freshman.

With several young players leading the way, Maryland turned its season around, going 11-2 over the rest of the conference schedule, including a 98-87 win over the Blue Devils on their home court in Durham. The Terps finished second in the conference standings to Duke and then made it all the way to the ACC Tournament finals before losing to Duke 81-68 in Charlotte. Their run at the end of season earned Maryland a No. 3 seed in the NCAA's Midwest Region, being played at the Metrodome in Minneapolis. By this time, virtually every Maryland fan knew about the team's problem getting past the Round of 16, and there was considerable finger-crossing that this would be the year that Gary Williams and his Terps would break through. But after defeating Iona in the first round, they didn't get far enough to find out.

In the second round, the Terps faced a bigger, quicker and hungrier UCLA squad and got demolished, 105-70. It was a rout from the start; the Bruins jumped out to a 14-2 lead and never looked back. The 35-point defeat was the worst tournament loss in Gary Williams's tenure at Maryland. "I have a lot of pride, and you never want to get kicked. We got our butts kicked tonight. I hate it," the coach said. Earlier in the year, before they began their winning streak, UCLA coach Steve Lavin had dubbed his struggling team "the Bruins in Ruins." But Lavin's crew had peaked at just the right moment, capping an eight-game winning streak with their blowout of Maryland. Williams credited the sixth-seeded Bruins for playing a great game, but he was disappointed in his team's performance, which he described as sluggish.

Maryland trailed 49-33 at the half before a 16-2 Bruin blitz to start the second half slammed the door on any comeback hopes and left the Terps trailing by 30 points, 65-35. During that stretch, UCLA nailed four straight three-pointers and a number of alley-oop dunks. Williams tried to cool off the Bruins, calling three timeouts in under two minutes, but it was to no avail, as the Terps were torched by their opponents' stunning 72.4 percent shooting.

Juan Dixon, who averaged 18 points and nearly four assists and three steals per game, and Lonny Baxter, both surprise first-team All-ACC players as sophomores, were overpowered by UCLA, as was junior Terrence Morris. "I don't think this feeling will ever wear off," a despondent Baxter said after the loss. But Dixon, who hit four of eight shots, including a pair of three-pointers, was more upbeat. "We had a great season," he said.

"We had a young team and a lot of people counted us out early. But we worked extremely hard all year long, and we knew we could be a good team. We won 25 games; that's three short of the school record. We had a heck of a season."

In a sense, Dixon was right. The Terps had achieved exceptional results during the regular season, beating Kentucky for the first time in 43 years, defeating Duke for just the second time in 11 tries under Gary Williams, and making it to the ACC Tournament final for the first time in 16 years. But their tournament run had ended with a thud. Williams ripped out the page from the game program with a photo of the Bruins as motivation for next season.

In the immediate aftermath of the game, Williams did not sulk. That was typical, according to reporters, columnists, basketball analysts, announcers and assistant coaches. They say that after victories and defeats alike where Williams appears totally wired during the game, he is at ease after the buzzer. "Thirty seconds later, he is a calm voice talking to you in the locker room," Wilbon said. "I have been with him after Duke losses, ACC Tournament losses, and NCAA losses. He brings himself down so quickly. When you vent, I guess maybe there is nothing left. I have heard him crack jokes after tough losses. Go to dinner with him off the job, and he is as rational as it gets."

Johnny Holliday, the voice of the Maryland Terrapins, agrees. "As soon as the game is over, he can let go of it," said Holliday. "A lot of people read him the wrong way. They think what they see on sidelines is what he is like 24 hours a day. Just when you think he is going to explode after a devastating loss, he will say, 'We can't expect to win a game when we shoot like that, and we have to learn to protect the basketball and not come down and take the first shot we get.' He is great now. Years ago, after a bad loss, it would have been short and sweet, and 'Let's get to it,' and 'We gotta go.' Now, he spends as much time with us as I want him to spend."

Despite the season-ending loss to UCLA, Williams looked ahead with optimism, sensing that the team's prospects for next season were very promising. Morris would be back for his senior year, and hopefully he would be able to get himself back on track and become the dominant force that he promised to be in his early days. Dixon and Baxter would also be back, with one more year under their belts. So would Blake, the reliable point guard who had been given the keys to the Terps' offense. Maryland also had a transfer from Tulane, Byron Mouton, who would be eligible to play next year. Mouton was a highly recruited talent out of Louisiana who had been the Green Wave's leading scorer as a freshman and sophomore, but he told Gary Williams he was coming to Maryland because he wanted to win a national championship. And the Terps also would be welcoming a new recruiting class that included a 6'10" forward named Chris Wilcox, plucked from the small town of Whiteville, North Carolina.

The Terps had finished second in the ACC to Duke. With North Carolina receding and Maryland rising, the Terps had established themselves as the top challenger to the Blue Devils' crown. With a win in Cameron Indoor, the Terrapins had gotten the message across in Durham. Fans on both sides looked to next season with championship aspirations, and they looked at each other as a primary obstacle. A new rivalry had begun, though no one could have predicted just how far their battle would take them.

13

NO LEAD IS SAFE

One minute.

That's how long it took for a game, and nearly an entire season, to fall apart. On the evening of January 27, 2001, Maryland fans were treated to triumphant basketball over the Duke Blue Devils, a performance so magnificent that commentators declared the Terps the finest squad in the land as the game wound down. "They are playing outstanding on both ends of the floor, playing with such a purpose," said Brad Daugherty, covering the game for ESPN.

With 1:51 to go and Maryland up by 11 points, Steve Blake fouled out, diminishing the team's ball-handling ability immensely. Blake, who had nine assists for the night, was named the New York Life Player of the Game, the award given to the outstanding player on the winning squad. "When Steve fouled out, you could feel a sense of panic," guard Earl Badu said. "He's our floor leader. When he's not out there, the team's not the same." Despite that feeling, however, few in the building believed that enough time remained for Duke to make a run. Sensing the magnitude of the moment for the Terrapins, ESPN analyst Mike Patrick projected the impact of

Maryland's domination of No. 2 Duke. "Talk about the psychological boost this is going to give Maryland for the rest of the year," he said.

With a minute left, Maryland led by 10 points. "O-ver-rat-ed, O-ver-rat-ed," the students began chanting at the Blue Devils. Security guards on the College Park campus began moving toward Byrd football stadium to prevent students from tearing down the goalposts, just as they had done one year earlier when the Terps beat Duke at home. A stream of Maryland faithful left the arena with an extra bounce in their step, headed for their cars, and turned on their radios to catch the postgame show, hosted by Johnny Holliday. He always did a postgame analysis with Gary Williams after the final buzzer, and this was one they surely didn't want to miss.

What happened next was surreal. "The thing at Cole was one of those crazy times," said Duke coach Mike Krzyzewski. "After reviewing the game, it was clear to me we really did lose to Maryland. They outplayed us for 39 minutes. Realistically, when you are down by 10 points with a minute to go, you don't think you are going to win." Though implausible, the implications of that one minute were far-reaching for Terrapins fans and players alike. And its lasting influence exacts a toll on Maryland basketball that can be summed up succinctly: No lead is safe.

"That's the worst loss I've ever been associated with," said Maryland senior Mike Mardesich. Gary Williams wondered what to tell his squad in the locker room. "I know all of the clichés. I want to tell them, 'This is just one game.' But deep down, I knew it was more than one game. To lose that game at the end was a tremendous blow to us psychologically."

The morning after the shocking two-point overtime loss to Duke, Gary Williams went to the Super Bowl in Tampa to root for the Baltimore Ravens and support his friend, Ravens co-owner Steve

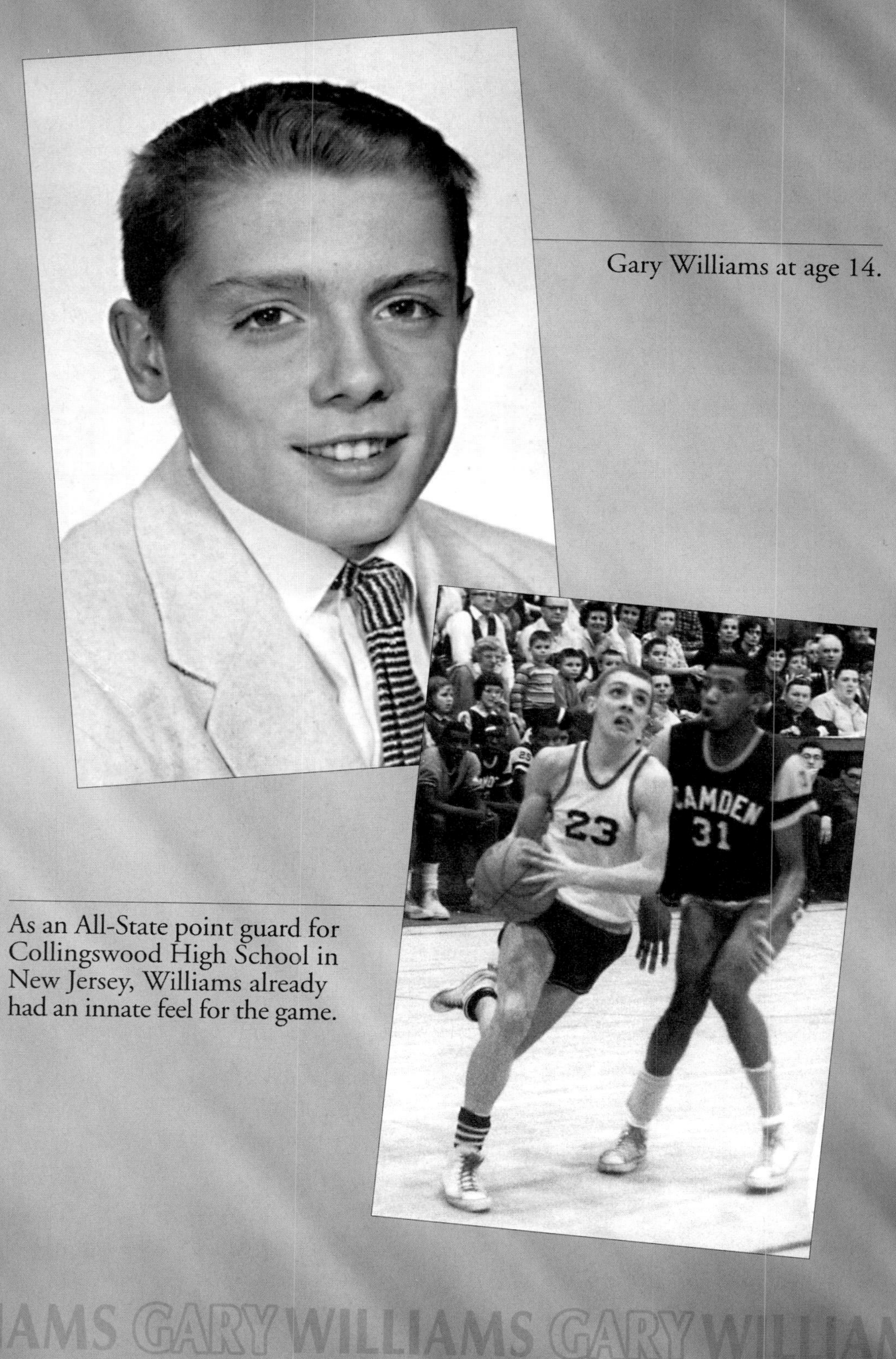

Gary Williams at age 14.

As an All-State point guard for Collingswood High School in New Jersey, Williams already had an innate feel for the game.

Williams was the Terps' starting point guard for three years. His schooling under coach Bud Millikan gave Williams a solid foundation in coaching defense.

Williams, his former wife Diane, and their daughter Kristin.

At Boston College (top), American University (middle), and Ohio State (right), Gary Williams took his teams to new heights.

Len Bias was Maryland's brightest basketball star, but two days after being drafted by the Boston Celtics, he died from a cocaine overdose. When Williams took over as the Terps' head coach three years later, the program and the university were still reeling.

Coach Gary Williams proves he still has the moves at the 1991 Maryland alumni game.

Williams's efforts to mend fences in Baltimore netted the coach his most important recruit in his early years at Maryland — Keith Booth.

Joe Smith (top) and Johnny Rhodes (right), who came to College Park in 1993, were part of Gary Williams's first stellar recruiting class at the University of Maryland.

Kristin's wedding in 1995 brought Williams closer to his daughter and rekindled a friendship between him and his former wife, Diane.

When superstar Steve Francis (23) finished his career at Maryland and entered the NBA draft, he left a leadership void that Juan Dixon (bottom, with Gary Williams) quickly stepped in to fill.

Former Maryland coach and current Georgia State coach Charles “Lefty” Driesell and Gary Williams greet one another prior to their game in the second round of the 2001 NCAA Tournament. Maryland beat Georgia State, 79-60.

Coach Williams addresses his bench en route to a win over Georgia State, 79-60, in the second round of the 2001 NCAA Tournament.

Williams greets Coach Mike Krzyzewski (top left) and gives his trademark fist-pump to the Terps' student section (top right) before the 97-73 victory over Duke on Feb. 17, 2002.

Maryland forward Chris Wilcox (54) puts the pressure on Duke forward Mike Dunleavy during the Feb. 17 game at Cole. Wilcox turned in a star-making performance that day and developed a reputation for elevating his play in big games.

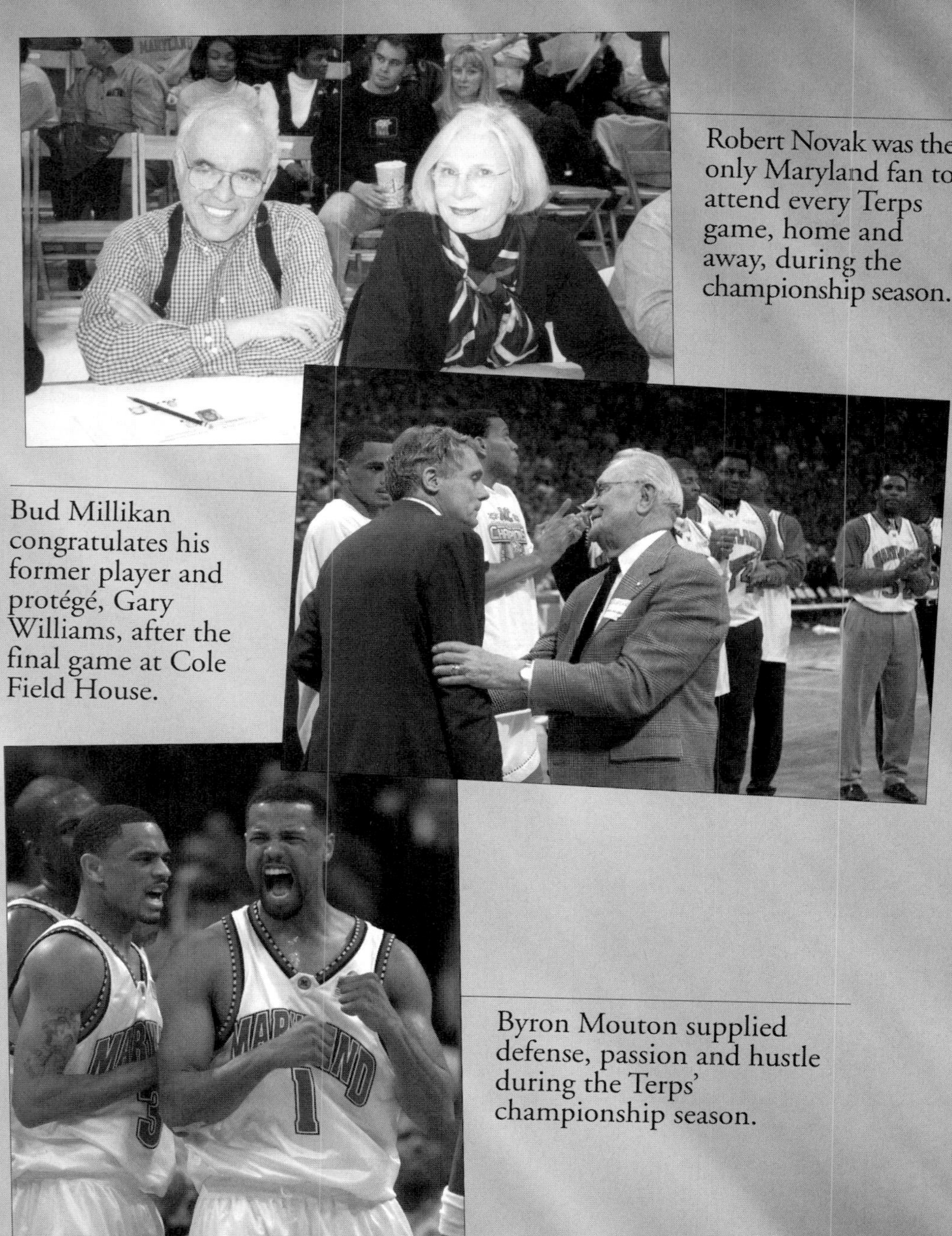

Robert Novak was the only Maryland fan to attend every Terps game, home and away, during the championship season.

Bud Millikan congratulates his former player and protégé, Gary Williams, after the final game at Cole Field House.

Byron Mouton supplied defense, passion and hustle during the Terps' championship season.

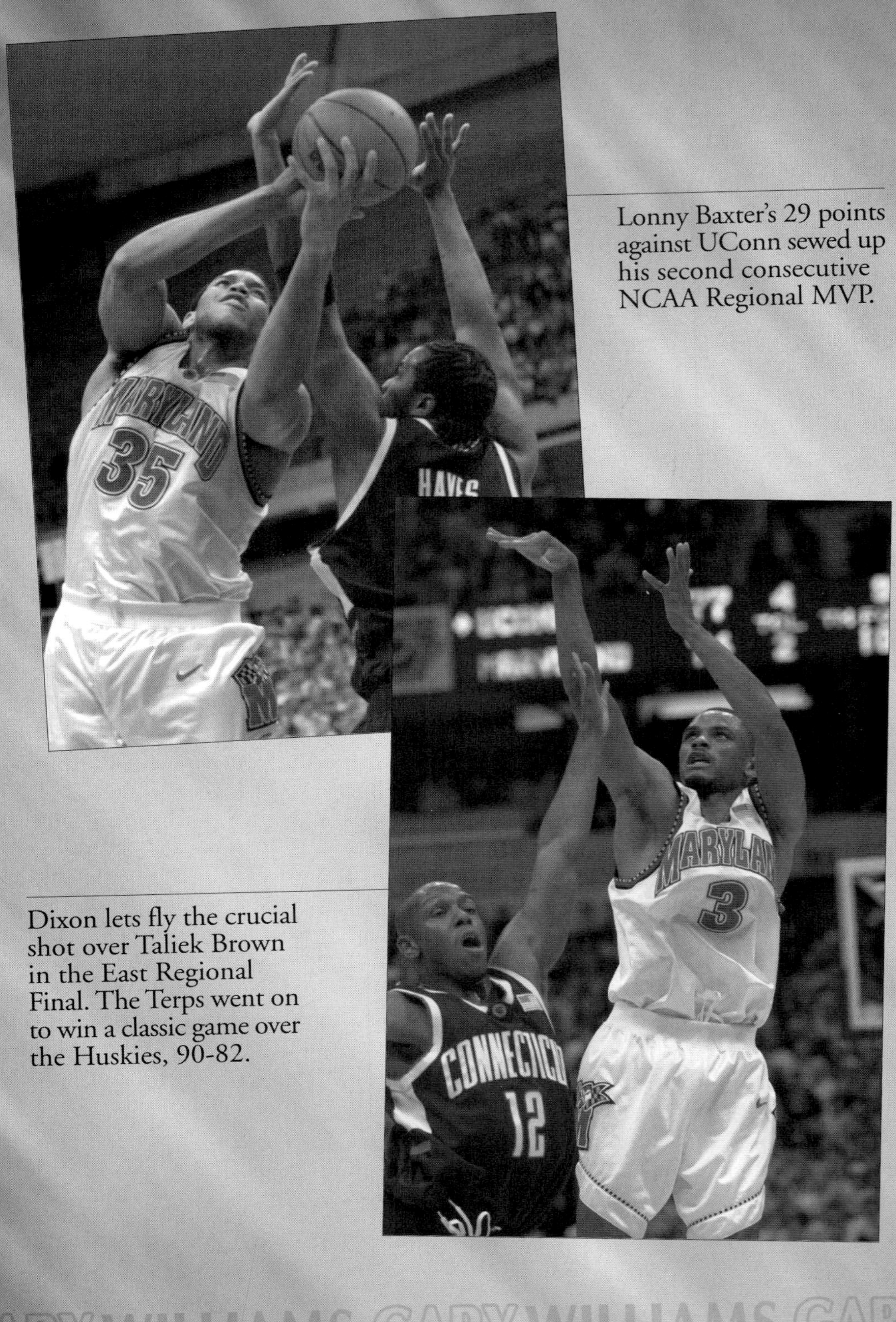

Lonny Baxter's 29 points against UConn sewed up his second consecutive NCAA Regional MVP.

Dixon lets fly the crucial shot over Taliek Brown in the East Regional Final. The Terps went on to win a classic game over the Huskies, 90-82.

As part of the Terps' postpractice ritual, Juan Dixon and his teammates launch shots from half-court. Coach Williams continued the ritual even during practices before the NCAA tournament games to keep the players relaxed.

Chris Wilcox blocked several early Jayhawks shots. "We were intimidated," Kansas coach Roy Williams said.

Steve Blake, the starting point guard since his freshman year, led the nation in assists in the 2001-2002 season.

Dixon and Baxter fall onto the court in celebration moments after winning the NCAA championship.

Grandson David, daughter Kristin and Williams (top) are all smiles after the Terps beat Indiana. Below, Williams and his players accept the national championship trophy.

President George W. Bush sizes up Lonny Baxter as Baxter and Juan Dixon give him a team jersey during a ceremony on the South Lawn of the White House.

Gary Williams, standing with the trophies from the Maryland Terrapins' first national championship.

Bisciotti. He had looked forward to going to his first Super Bowl and hoped his attendance would signal his squad that they had to move on. But it wasn't that simple. Not long after his arrival in Tampa, a stunned Williams, amid a crowd of 80,000, heard a familiar voice, instantly recognizable to sports fans across the nation. "Gary! Gary baby—how could you lose that game, baby?"

He had run into basketball maven Dick Vitale, who was also attending the Ravens pregame party. Vitale told his wife he was shocked to see Williams after what had happened the night before. "I would have told anybody, 'He is a basket case, he hasn't been to sleep, and he is going to jump off the nearest bridge,'" Vitale said. "This is less than 24 hours from the most devastating loss in his career. That told me a lot about him, about his ability to handle defeat. I saw a man I would not have seen 20 years ago. He would have been in the corner sulking. Sure, he was disappointed in the loss. But it was, 'Hey, man, I gotta pick it up and get ready for the next one.'"

Williams found that, unlike Vitale, who is never at a loss for words, others at the Super Bowl didn't quite know what to say to him. It was like there had been a scandal or a death. "After the game, people were so happy for the Ravens. They'd congratulate Steve. Then they'd see me, and there would be an awkward pause, that silence."

After the devastating Duke defeat and the Ravens' Super Bowl victory, the Terps went into a nosedive. It would take more than a trip by the coach to Tampa for the Terrapins to recover, and things would get worse before they got better. After the 98-96 overtime loss to Duke, the tale of the tape told the story, as the Terrapins lost five of their next six games. Virginia 99, Maryland 87; Maryland 69, Clemson 54; Georgia Tech 72, Maryland 62; North Carolina 96, Maryland 82; Florida State 74, Maryland 71. There was no love lost on Valentine's Day, when the Terps, after a 15-4 run to open the game, were booed at Cole Field House as they struggled and lost to the lowly Florida State Seminoles. "The whole team kind of just collapsed," Blake said.

Johnny Holliday vividly remembers how upset Williams was after the Florida State loss, in part due to the outcome and in part due to the home crowd's behavior.

"That was the most hurt I've seen him," Holliday said. "That Duke loss was devastating, but I think the Florida State loss was tough too."

Williams, knowing just how much he needed to restore the Terps' confidence and drive, was angered by the booing in Cole Field House. "I've got a vision of Gary Williams I will never forget," Holliday continued. "As soon as he came over to us and put his headset on after the Florida State game, he really got after the crowd on the air. He was really upset. I let him go early. As he was walking toward the tunnel, they start playing the Alma Mater, and he turns and stands at attention, just looking up at the crowd. I don't ever recall him standing there like that." Holliday nudged fellow broadcaster Chris Knoche and urged him to look at Williams glaring at the students and others in the stands. He was, Holliday said, sending an unmistakable message: "I don't like it, and I want all of you to know I don't like it."

Juan Dixon didn't stay out on the court. Instead, he went straight to the team's weight room, and stood, silently and alone, staring at his reflection in a mirror. He could not understand how such a talented team could see its season turning to ash. The man who understood and relished his role as team leader could not face the notebooks and microphones waiting for him in the locker room. Nor did he want to see his family, who had come to watch the game; he sent them away, saying he needed time to figure things out. "I was embarrassed, man. That was tough. I was shook at the time. I didn't want to talk to anyone," Dixon said.

After the loss to Florida State, Williams couldn't sleep. By 5:00 a.m. the next morning, he was watching game film and trying to figure out what to do to reignite the Terps. "I didn't know if we were going to win another game," Williams said.

Mike Mardesich said the coach figured out exactly what to do. "The best job he has ever done coaching is the day after we lost to Florida State," Mardesich said. "He changed and realized that we are people as well as basketball players. He came into practice, and he didn't preach to us. He was as loose as he could be for a man like him, and he just told us to concentrate on Wake Forest, which was the next day. We went out and had a tremendous practice. Without him raising his voice once, we had the most intense practice. That turned our season around. At our lowest moment, he had a cool head. That is the mark of a great coach.

"In his heart, he had to be just dying and ready to spit fire."

Mardesich and the other seniors spoke to the team, telling them they could suck it up and win or hang it up for the season. But Dixon had already taken the message to heart, in the emptiness of the team weight room after that bitter loss. With gritty determination, the star guard took responsibility. Night after night, long after practice had ended, teammates had gone and darkness had come, Dixon returned to Cole Field House. Sometimes he got the key to the gym from his suitemate, team manager Brian Cavanaugh. Sometimes he brought along his girlfriend, Robyn, to feed him the ball. But all the time, he practiced—shot after shot after shot. "He'd be in there at 11 o'clock at night, working on his shot, because he felt responsible, as all great players do, and Juan took that as a challenge," Williams said. The tattoo on his arm spoke volumes: "Only the Strong Survive." And the image of his deceased mother, emblazoned on his heart, which he touched before every free throw, added deeper meaning and passion to his pursuit of excellence.

Ironically, the boo birds in Cole Field House did the Terps a favor; they gave Williams the evidence he needed to convince his team that nobody else could be relied upon to turn things around. It was up to them. The fans' behavior made it clear the team was truly on its own, with its back to the wall and responsibility on its shoulders. "We kept waiting for something to happen to change things and there was nothing," Williams said. "It had to be from us, ourselves. In the locker room, we talked about not feeling sorry for ourselves. The booing at halftime got the message to the players: nobody will feel sorry for us. If our own students boo us, who do we have on our side? We have us, the team. Maybe we had to get to that point."

Dixon told his teammates that the only way he could rid himself of the "demons" left behind by the shocking loss to Duke and the downward spiral in the aftermath was to go to Durham and beat the Blue Devils at Cameron Indoor Stadium. And he did it.

In a season ultimately defined by four fierce games against Duke, there was, among the nine wins in a row that the Terps then reeled off, a huge victory in Durham that spoiled Senior Night for the Blue Devils and left some of Duke's upperclassmen in tears. Led by Dixon's 28 points and five steals, including a big pair of back-to-back baskets and a crucial steal with just five minutes to play, the Terps whipped Duke 91-80. Dixon's anticipation and quickness on defense even prompted Duke's head coach, who described the Maryland star's performance as "sensational," to alter his offense and instruct his players to avoid Dixon when driving to the hoop. "Maryland played a great game, matched our intensity, outworked us," said Duke defensive ace Nate James. "It's unbelievable there would be a game where we were out-hustled."

Dixon, who seemed like he was everywhere all the time, played 39 minutes of determined, impassioned basketball, gaining further respect from coaches, teammates and opponents. "I don't think I've ever admired an opposing player more than Juan," said Duke's Coach Krzyzewski. "I love Juan Dixon. He is a hard worker, classy and one of the greatest players in the history of the ACC. The personal tragedies that he's had to overcome make you respect him before you ever meet him. Then when you watch his work ethic out on the court and his competitiveness, you really stand in awe of just how good this kid is."

Still, Dixon might not have realized his potential playing just anywhere or for any coach. "Give Gary Williams a lot of credit for putting Juan in a position to use his talents," the Duke coach said. "You need the right system and coach to do those things, and Gary put him and the team in a position to succeed."

In beating nine teams in a row including Duke, Maryland regained its confidence and became more relaxed. Williams also made one important strategic change, encouraging fifth-year seniors Mike Mardesich and LaRon Cephas to play more of a leadership role. Despite limited playing time, the pair, Williams said, had the respect of their teammates and saved Maryland's season.

Maryland and Duke would tangle two more times before the 2000-2001 campaign was over. The Terps brought a nine-game winning streak into the finals of the ACC Tournament against Duke, which was played in Atlanta, at the request of Williams and a few other coaches, rather than its traditional North Carolina home. Duke, which trailed 45-42 at halftime, won the contest with 1.3 seconds left when Nate James tipped in a missed shot by Jason Williams. But neither Williams nor the Terps hung their heads in defeat. They had turned things around, and their real goal was the one Williams had written on the board in the locker room at the beginning of the season: Minneapolis.

The competitive game against Duke only served to reinforce that both teams, perhaps, belonged in the Final Four. "A great game," Williams said. "The intensity level out there was tremendous." As much as he hated losing, especially to Duke, Dixon, too, had a good feeling after the game ended and as the new NCAA Tournament season began. "We bring out the best in each other," Dixon said.

Going into the NCAA Tournament, Williams was pleased with his team's overall performance and its effort against Duke. He truly felt the Terps were playing up to the level of any team in the country. Juan Dixon had established himself as the team's leader on the court, even as Steve Blake continued to run the plays and control the ball at point guard. Williams and the Terps had regained confidence fully at the right moment because, fortunately, it was time for March Madness.

Up and down and then, eventually, up again. This Terrapin team had come a long way, endured plenty, but still had plenty of fire in its belly. "We didn't waver," Williams said of the ACC final against Duke. "To a man, we knew we could get back if we could just do a couple of things. We did get back and put ourselves in position to win the game. I'm really proud of our team, and I told them, "Let's go play next week and see what happens.'"

In the first round of the NCAA Tournament, Maryland's roller-coaster season almost came to a sudden, embarrassing halt. Playing in Boise, Idaho against George Mason University in the first round of the NCAA Tournament, the Terps narrowly escaped an upset, winning 83-80 after Steve Blake hit a clutch three-pointer and forced a turnover in the last minute. Juan Dixon and Byron Mouton led the scoring with 22 points each, but the Patriots shot a sizzling 55 percent, controlled the flow and nearly sent Maryland packing in a game that featured four lead changes in the last two minutes. "I'm not sure we could have won this game a month ago," Coach Gary Williams conceded. "But I thought we were going to win the game in the end, no matter what. We didn't play well, but don't ever question our character or whether our guys played hard. We dug down deep in the second half and struggled. We found a way to win, which this team has developed this year."

Next up for the Terps was No. 11-seeded Georgia State and legendary coach Lefty Driesell, who had built the Maryland program into a national powerhouse and steered the team for nearly two decades. The Atlanta-based school was the second unheralded basketball program Lefty had taken to new heights since departing from College Park in the aftermath of the Len Bias tragedy. But all the Lefthander's magic couldn't save his team from Maryland's power inside as the Terps pounded the much smaller Georgia State squad, 79-60. "We stayed with them for 25 or 30 minutes, but their talent took over. They just kicked our butt," Driesell said.

The Maryland victory over Georgia State set up a showdown the following week in the Sweet Sixteen against the Georgetown Hoyas. The two teams, recruiting rivals for talent in the Baltimore-Washington region, had not met since November 26, 1993. In that game, Maryland defeated the Hoyas in an overtime thriller on national television that Gary Williams considered his most important victory since returning to College Park. Now here Williams was again, in Anaheim, California, thousands of miles from Washington, facing Georgetown in a game that could take him further in the NCAA Tournament that he had ever journeyed before.

The game also pitted Juan Dixon against his childhood pal, Georgetown's Kevin Braswell. The two grew up together in Baltimore, and Dixon, as a youngster, lived with Braswell's family for a time in the early 1990s. "The way Coach Williams has us playing right now, "we're playing as well as anybody in the country," a confident Dixon said.

Byron Mouton summed up the state of the team well. "People say Coach is known for putting on added pressure as you get later in the season, but he's done a great job controlling his temper and staying positive. The whole thing about Maryland has been that during the course of the year it would be good, but when the conference tournament and NCAAs came along, they would go downhill. This time we struggled throughout the year. But the last couple of games, we've gone uphill."

By now, many basketball analysts who had pronounced Maryland dead after their midseason slide and the "Miracle Minute," as the Dukies called it, were now predicting the Terps would make it to Minneapolis. And Williams did nothing to quell the enthusiasm. "I'd like to win a national championship," he said, heading into the Georgetown game.

Maryland moved one step closer to that goal, beating the Hoyas 76-66 on March 23, 2001. Though Maryland was in control down the stretch, Williams wouldn't ease up, or come out of his trademark crouch, until the final buzzer sounded and victory was assured. "You never know after Duke," the coach said.

Led by Lonny Baxter, who scored 26 points and grabbed 14 rebounds, Maryland out-muscled and outplayed the physical Hoya squad in the second half. After the game, Williams and his assistants immediately turned their attention to all that stood between them and the Terrapins' first ever trip to the Final Four: the Stanford Cardinal.

Two days later, Stanford (31-2), a No. 1 seed, was history, falling to Maryland 87-73. It was a decisive win by a team that knew where it was heading. Lonny Baxter, whom many said was too small to play center and too slow to play forward, controlled the paint and led the way with 24 points. Never mind that the game was played in California or that Stanford may have been the oddsmakers' choice to go further in the tournament. The win propelled Coach Gary Williams and his Terrapins into the Final Four for the first time in school history and the first time in his coaching career.

As the players and coaches cut down the nets, a jubilant Williams snipped the last piece and swung it like a lasso. They were, after all, on the frontier, and they had come through a season that felt as wild as anything the West had to offer. And they had been on a remarkable journey, from the depths of defeat to the attainment of that singular lofty goal of "Minneapolis" that Williams had written on a sign hanging in the locker room since the fall. And they had stepped up, shooting 58.2 percent from the field and nailing nine of 13 three-pointers to beat a talented Stanford squad. "That's great to play the best you can in the game that means the most," said a smiling Gary Williams.

The talented tandem of Lonny Baxter, selected Most Valuable Player in the West Regional, and Juan Dixon had put the doubters in their place. Dixon had 17 points against Stanford, hitting seven of 10 from the field. Steve Blake continued dishing out assists left and right. And no matter what happened next, Gary Williams had climbed the next rung on the ladder, entering that select cadre of coaches whose teams made it to the Final Four. For Williams, the harrowing journey, and the opportunity to take his alma mater to new heights, made it that much sweeter. His players had bought into his program and approach. "We wanted to get Coach there for the first time," Baxter said. "But I'm not satisfied. We still want to go on and win the national championship."

Next, the Terps would face a team they knew all too well, one they had taken on three times already during the season. The national semifinal game in Minneapolis would pit Maryland against Duke, the fourth time these two ACC teams would be joined in battle. For the Blue Devils and Terrapins, it would be a memorable matchup that shattered Final Four records and reinforced a Maryland maxim.

No lead is safe.

14
MAYHEM IN MINNEAPOLIS

One of the things Gary Williams enjoyed most about Maryland's first trip to the Final Four was how it galvanized fans, alumni, university officials and the team itself, as they joyously headed to Minneapolis sky-high after achieving their season's goal. The coach had brought the team a long way since his arrival in 1989, but he had not always felt that those outside the team and its core fans recognized just how good the program had become. "We had respect nationally before we had respect right here in this area," Williams said. Eight NCAA Tournament appearances in a row and repeat trips to the Sweet Sixteen had not been enough. It would take something more for the Terrapins, toiling in the shadow of Duke and North Carolina, to overcome that hurdle. It took a trip to the Final Four.

There were many new things to deal with—unusual workout schedules, a deluge of media attention and the adulation that goes with being in the national spotlight. But while the stakes were different and much larger, the adversary was the same. The rivalry that had consumed college basketball fans along the Atlantic Coast was ready to take over the national stage. For the fourth time in one season, the Maryland Terrapins and the Duke Blue Devils prepared to do battle—this time around for a chance at a national championship.

It is great to be in the Final Four. The whole sports world is focused on you, your team and your university. All the attention is great for the University of Maryland. You can't buy that kind of exposure. You wouldn't believe the number of letters I got from alumni around the country who feel so proud of the way Juan Dixon spoke or Steve Blake handled himself. That is the X factor you can't measure in recruiting.

Making it to the Final Four for the first time was a big moment for Maryland. For our older fans who had been following Maryland for years and had never been to the Final Four, it was really special. You've got guys who have been going to Maryland games since Cole opened, and I know how much it meant to them. They had watched other ACC teams make it almost every year and then all of a sudden, it is Maryland. That to me was one of the best things about going to the Final Four. It gave satisfaction to those people and fans who cared the most and supported the program.

I told the players to make sure they enjoyed themselves. I also told them we were going to work really hard to get ready to play. I said when people want autographs, take the time to enjoy it. When you do interviews, be yourself and have fun with it. And they did. We didn't get tight at all.

Like it or not, the Final Four is the way your program is judged. If you are a Final Four program, it sets you apart from the schools that aren't. We have allowed the media to make the Final Four bigger than the regular season. I have always tried to keep that in perspective. I didn't get carried away with our making it to Minneapolis. I was very happy and it was great for Maryland because it changes the respect people have for us. Nationally we didn't need it, but right here, we needed it.

Given their previous three games that season, it seemed likely that Maryland-Duke would be a close contest decided in the final seconds. But Duke's stars struggled to get on track, and Maryland surprised everyone by racing out to an early 23-10 lead. Playing with the same confidence and composure they had displayed against Stanford, the Terps nailed shot after shot, made sharp passes, played aggressive defense and moved up and down the floor with ease. Duke shot poorly, hitting only four of its first 16 shots. The Terps, on the other hand, canned five out of six three-point attempts early. Maryland could not have been hotter; Duke could not have been flatter.

After Steve Blake sank a three-pointer with just over 12 minutes to go in the first half, Coach Mike Krzyzewski called the earliest timeout he had taken all year. A frustrated Shane Battier, Duke's star forward who had missed a number of shots, hurled a cup of water to the floor. The Duke coach didn't like calling time out when his team hit an early rough patch, but with Maryland building such a big lead, he felt he had no choice. "We're losing by 20 points," he said to his team. "What are you afraid of—that we'll lose by 40?" Krzyzewski abandoned all set plays on offense. "Look, fellas, we're playing as bad as we can, and they are playing as well as they can. This is not going to last the full 40 minutes. Just go out and play ball." After the timeout, Maryland extended its lead to 39-17, a 22-point margin, over the flabbergasted Blue Devils with about five minutes left in the first half. "I thought Dixon not only mentally dominated us, he dominated the first half," Krzyzewski said of the sharp-shooting guard, who scored 16 points in the opening 20 minutes.

But before long, Duke began to get into the flow of the game, hitting three-pointers and playing better on both ends of the court. The Terps froze, as if they had not been prepared for the Blue Devils to mount a serious run. On the offensive end, Maryland grew tentative. "You can't do that in a Final Four," said Dixon. "We could have easily pushed the lead to 30. We've got to develop a killer instinct."

By halftime, Maryland led by 11 points, but the momentum had shifted to Duke as the Blue Devils cut the 22-point margin in half. "We played great to get up 22. But nobody is 22 points better than Duke," Gary Williams said. "I knew they'd make a run."

But inside the Hubert H. Humphrey Metrodome in Minneapolis, Terps fans hung their heads. Memories of Duke's comeback in Cole were still fresh in their minds, and they could see it happening all over again. Two Maryland players, Terrence Morris and Tahj Holden, were in foul trouble, with three apiece. Though their team had a double-digit lead, for Terrapins fans, a Duke comeback and victory seemed inevitable; the only question left was how long it would take the Blue Devils to get the lead for good.

I told them at halftime I was proud of the way we came out. Duke has more Final Four experience than any team. We came out with confidence and made shots, and I told them that we were up 11 and most people would have settled for an 11-point lead against Duke. I tried to get the idea through to them that even though we lost some of the lead, we played well. But we allowed Duke to get close, and with the number of threes they take, they could bring it back. Duke got their confidence back by halftime. It was too early for us to start getting so cautious in the first half. We just stopped making plays.

In the second half, Duke scored the first four times it had the ball. Having come back against Maryland earlier in the year, the Blue Devils had the confidence they could do it again. During halftime, the Duke locker room was a cauldron of emotion; the loud appeals to team pride were heard from outside the door. But the team still had to try something new on defense to stop Maryland's hot hand, Juan Dixon. Duke's Nate James volunteered to take on the challenge. "I had to dig down and deny Dixon the ball or get a hand in his face when he did shoot," James said. "When he had the ball, I concentrated on his left hand, because it usually tipped off whether he was going to shoot, pass or drive. I also felt I could take advantage of my three-inch height difference over him."

Meanwhile, the Blue Devils continued chipping away at the Maryland lead and gaining confidence by hitting threes, jump shots and free throws. Maryland was finding it difficult to play with a shrinking lead and a determined Duke nipping at its heels. The Blue Devils finally took the lead with just under seven minutes left, 73-72, on a three-pointer by Player of the Year Shane Battier. The Terrapins did not give up. Twice, Maryland moved back out in front on baskets by Terrence Morris, but with just under five minutes to play, Carlos Boozer hit two free throws to put Duke out in front to stay, 78-77.

With players in foul trouble and several questionable calls going against the Terps, Williams became visibly upset with the officiating, and that ire seemed to grow as the game wore on. A fifth foul called on Baxter, who didn't score from the field in the second half, appeared to be a non-call or a foul on Duke's Carlos Boozer, who said afterward he thought the foul was on him. The Blue Devils would never trail again, as the Terps went four minutes without hitting a field goal. The extraordinary game ended in defeat for the Terps, 95-84. Nate James held Dixon to a single three-pointer in the second half. For the fourth time that season, the team trailing at halftime had prevailed when these two squads met. And three of those four times, Duke had come out on top.

"We were right there in a lot of situations this year," Williams said. "Hopefully, we'll have a shot to be a very good team next year. I don't expect this loss to go away any time soon. But since no team from Maryland had gotten to the Final Four, this is the team that broke the ceiling." Added Dixon, "We'll know what to do next year if we get in this situation. Now that we know what this feeling is like, guys will want to get better. I'm going to want to be stronger. I'm going to want to put the ball on the floor better. I'm going to work so hard in the off- season, it's going to be ridiculous."

Despite the Terps' resolve to build upon their impressive 2000-2001 season, their pain over losing again to their archrival was immense. Gary Williams had finally accomplished his lifelong goal of reaching the Final Four, but as he returned to his hotel, all he could think about was the loss. Williams's daughter Kristin said, "We just kept David up and the two of them played with toys on the floor and not a word was said about the game. I said to my husband later, 'At least we were able to take his mind off of it for a while.'"

In the second half, we played okay. There were key moments in the second half that went against us. For instance, it was a very big play when Lonny Baxter fouled out. That foul could have been called on Lonny or Carlos Boozer from Duke. It probably would have been best for the referees not to call anything in that situation.

Looking ahead, I was concerned that we lost three seniors off that team that gave us good leadership. Mike Mardesich was valuable as a 7-foot backup center, and LaRon Cephas was a good player and one of those guys with a great attitude who kept everybody honest, including guys that played more than he did. Terrence Morris was criticized a lot, but if you look at his numbers career-wise, he is in the school's top 10 in four or five categories. We lost one starter, our backup center and we lost a spiritual guy.

But after our loss to Duke in the semifinals of the NCAA championship, you could see the resolve in our players. They didn't take a lot of time off. They started lifting weights and playing basketball again. They were not satisfied just getting to the Final Four, even though that had not been done before in the history of the school. The fact that we had quite a few players returning helped. They wanted the ultimate shot.

While the spirits of Terrapins fans sunk after the loss to Duke, Maryland's players went to work. Assistant coaches Dave Dickerson and Jimmy Patsos saw an unusual level of determination from their returning players and sensed the next season held the potential for greatness. "We were very hungry coming off of that loss," Patsos said. "We felt we should have beaten them. We wanted to win it all. We were out to prove to people we should have been champs, and we were going to win it."

Players came in on their own to shoot, lift weights and work on their fundamentals that spring. The two assistants watched the Maryland players, instead of going into a funk, shift into overdrive, led by Juan Dixon. And having reached Minneapolis, the new goal of winning the national championship next season was clear, at least to the players and coaches.

While the loss to Duke hurt, it was a great motivator that vaulted the Terps forward.

"It was disappointing, but I think the thing that came out of that experience was we were going to win the national championship," Dickerson said. "We were going to be committed to winning the national championship. Not winning the BB&T, not winning Coaches vs. Cancer, or the ACC tournament. We were going to win the national championship. To me, that was the beginning."

But something happened before basketball practice formally began in October 2001 that shook the nation and its citizens. On September 11, members of the al-Qaeda terrorist network killed thousands of Americans by hijacking and crashing planes into the World Trade Center and the Pentagon. Another plane, headed for the White House, crashed in Pennsylvania after passengers overpowered the terrorists. Along with other Americans, Gary Williams was stunned, outraged and upset as he watched the events unfold.

On the morning of September 11, I was right here in my office at Cole Field House watching it all on television. The buzz went around here in a hurry. I didn't see the first plane crash into the World Trade Center. I turned the TV on, and I was watching the fire in that first building and I was wondering, 'How could a plane make that mistake?' Everybody thought it was an accident. Then I saw that second plane fly in there, and I knew this wasn't an accident.

I just couldn't believe what I was watching. I had a feeling that this couldn't be happening, but I knew that it was happening. I didn't know what else was coming. I wondered, 'Are they going to hit the West Coast now or Chicago?' I didn't know what was going on or if somebody had a nuclear bomb.

September 11 was right at the start of the recruiting period, and we were focusing on who we had to see next and who was going to come visit. All that stopped in a hurry. A couple of our players came into my office. I could see the disbelief on their faces.

After the Pentagon had been hit, I immediately called my daughter, Kristin. She was teaching school in Columbus, Ohio, and I left a message. I said, 'Everything is fine here on campus. We are okay.'

I felt a great deal of anger. They violated us. You can't do that. It is like my team. Somebody makes a run at us, I feel like, 'You can't do that to us, we are too good.' Our country is too good.

Maryland coaches talked to their shaken players about September 11. Some of the players from the New York area had special concerns about family and friends. At the same time, the coaches sought to keep the players focused, without ignoring the magnitude or consequences of what had occurred.

Just as it had helped Gary Williams and Juan Dixon through rough childhoods, the game of basketball helped the Maryland Terrapins cope with a national tragedy. Across the nation, nerves were frayed. Inside Cole Field House, basketballs were bouncing. "I went home on September 11," Patsos said. "We worked out the next three days, just to keep the kids' minds off of it."

15 MIDNIGHT MADNESS

Just over a month after September 11, Maryland basketball coach Gary Williams stood on the floor of Cole Field House with the Terrapins players before a standing-room-only crowd of students and loyal fans at the annual Midnight Madness season kickoff, October 13, 2001. "Last year, we really wanted to get to the Final Four," Williams declared. "This year, we want to win the national championship,"

The fans roared as the coach asked for their help and support. It was the kind of public statement that many coaches would have avoided due to fear of the pressure or failing to meet expectations. He hadn't thought of making such a strong statement before the words came rolling off his tongue, but after he had done it, Williams was pleased. "You have to have the balls to put it out there, and the players have to have the balls to go out and win."

Now it was no longer just private locker room talk or a silent target for Terrapins players and coaches. Last year, Williams had written "Minneapolis" in the locker room for his players, and the Terps had punched that ticket by making it to the Final Four. For the new season, Williams had set the highest possible goal. By his public statement, the coach brought the fans under the tent, making them feel an integral part of the Terrapins' drive to win it all, while simultaneously reinforcing the message to his players that anything less was unacceptable.

"I was stunned to hear Gary make that declaration. Coaches don't do that," said political columnist Robert Novak, the only Terrapins fan to attend every home and away game during the 2001-2002 season. "It was a very bold thing to do. I think it set the tone for the whole year."

If the Terps felt any added pressure from their coach's brash statement, they didn't show it. Dixon, in particular, had comfortably settled into his role as senior leader and as a confidant to Williams. And for his part, Williams was relishing the opportunity to coach this group that he genuinely liked so much, especially Dixon, who had taken to calling him "G-Dub." People could see the pair's close relationship during one preseason practice. "Gary was looking toward one end of the court," said his friend Don McCartney. "and Juan went by and gave him a huge smack in the ass. Gary was startled, and then just smiled. Juan had earned his way to the point where he could do that."

With four returning starters—Dixon, Baxter, Blake and Byron Mouton—and 10 returning players, the Terps were a seasoned group with Final Four experience, and they decided early on that success in the upcoming season would be defined by a national title. "The biggest challenge is to win it all," Baxter said. "We know we have the potential. We know we have the right players."

As far as what I said to the students at Midnight Madness about winning the national championship, it was time to put it out there. We were always walking on eggshells around here, afraid to say the wrong thing. The players really felt we had a chance to win the national championship.

It is kind of a gamble to put too much emphasis on the Final Four, because you can work that hard again and the way the tournament is set up, there is no guarantee whatsoever. All you have to do is play poorly for 20 minutes of a game and you lose. There are no second chances, no best out of seven. It is a tremendous risk to put all your time and energy into that goal of winning the national championship. But we felt we could get it done.

On the way to the Terps first game, a Madison Square Garden contest against Arizona in the Coaches vs. Cancer Classic on November 8, the team's bus broke down. They remained stranded on the New Jersey Turnpike for hours before a second bus arrived. Later, after reaching New York, the players and coaches solemnly rode past the World Trade Center rubble in lower Manhattan, a moment the team absorbed in silence. "The drive down was a little eerie," Patsos recalled. "There was a weird feeling."

The day before the opening ballgame against Arizona, Coach Dickerson's father died after a painful bout with cancer. Dickerson, nevertheless, was on the Terps bench for games at the Garden, before leaving to join his family at the funeral.

In the season opener, Maryland suffered a disappointing 71-67 loss to Arizona, sending Williams into a rage about his team's uneven performance. After the game, the coaching staff gathered in Williams's hotel room, where he expressed anger about players not competing hard enough, shooting too quickly before working the ball inside, and missing free throws. "Some players just assume things, that things will continue from the year before, but that isn't so," the coach said.

Attention immediately turned to the game the next day against Temple, and Williams sought to drill the importance of focus and maximum effort into his players. He sensed his team was not listening well before the Arizona game, and he made certain that wouldn't happen again. Instead of a relaxed game day shoot-around before playing Temple, the team went to Madison Square Garden for a full-throttle practice. Williams also imparted specifics about how to beat Temple's swarming zone defense. The coach emphasized the need to make Temple's zone shift position and then make the extra pass to find the open man. "Do it, you win. Don't do it, you lose," Williams said starkly. "If you are not going to listen, and pass the ball, and stop your guy, and do what we say, then obviously we don't want to win and don't want to be that good of a team."

Williams had transformed the loss to Arizona into a motivating force. By the time Maryland took the court against John Chaney's Temple Owls, the intensity, focus and will to win that had been missing in the season opener was back. Dixon led the Terps to an 82-74 victory over the No. 16-ranked Owls with 25 points, including five three-pointers. Point guard Steve Blake tossed in a career-high 20 points as well as four assists. After shooting only 7-27 from three-point range in the opener against Arizona, the Terps' long-range shooting improved to 12 for 19. And Maryland shot a perfect 10-10 from the free-throw line in the final minute after hitting a paltry 4-12 from the charity stripe against Arizona. "I'm very proud of my team, not just with the win but for the way they came back from a very tough night," Williams said. "That was a tough loss, and when you're ranked No. 2 right away, the questions were, 'What's the problem?' We don't have a problem."

The victory over Temple allowed Maryland fans to breathe a sigh of relief. The back-to-back performances made it clear that the team had determination. After a lackluster game against Arizona, a second loss to open the season would have been hugely disappointing to a team with such high hopes. Instead, the Terrapins showed a fighting spirit and proved that they could bounce back from a tough loss. The increased intensity from the Terps was no mistake, according to Novak. "I was told Gary and Juan got on everybody to stop reading their clippings and play basketball."

We had a target on our backs, being ranked high in the preseason. We played the Arizona game with the pressure of being ranked like that for the first time. You had to play the game to understand how teams would come after us. So we went up to New York and lost that first game to Arizona. We shot 4-12 from the line. If we had normal free-throw shooting, we would have won. There were so many people, after that game, ready to jump ship.

It showed our players that we were going to have to do it ourselves. I circled the wagons. First, there were all the people saying nice things about us, and those same people suddenly were saying that we were overrated and not that good. I used that as a motivator and to keep the team really close. We beat a Temple team that was playing with confidence at that time. That was an important win for us. We didn't waver.

After opening the season against two strong opponents, Maryland rolled through its next two games at home, easily defeating American University 83-53 and Delaware State 77-53. The highlight of the game against AU was the unfurling of last season's Final Four banner in Cole Field House just before the opening tip.

Two days before Thanksgiving, the team faced a tougher foe when second-ranked Illinois came to Cole to play Maryland in the ACC-Big Ten Challenge. Led by Juan Dixon and Chris Wilcox, Maryland buried the Illini 76-63 before a rowdy crowd at Cole, handing Illinois its first defeat of the year and putting to rest any lingering questions about Maryland's ability to beat the best. While Dixon poured in 25, Wilcox took charge inside, scoring 19 points and benefiting from the deft passing of the irrepressible Steve Blake, who had nine assists to go along with his 10 points. Maryland, at one point, had a 20-point lead, before Illinois whittled away at the unexpectedly large margin. "The hardest thing to do in basketball is play with a lead," Gary Williams said. "But I thought we did a good job of that in the late part of the game. You try and stay aggressive, and you try to run some clock."

It was a physical game that saw Maryland big men Lonny Baxter and Tahj Holden both foul out. But as they would throughout the season, Maryland benefited immensely from its bench strength. Illinois couldn't stop the 6'10," 220-pound Wilcox, the Terps' sixth man. Said Illinois coach Bill Self, "Wilcox just owned us inside."

Illinois was a key game. They were ranked very high, and we came out and played great. It was really the first game that people nationwide got to see us play, and they saw us play well. Illinois had beaten us the previous year. The win established that we were a good team this year.

This time around, we looked quicker. Juan Dixon and Steve Blake played well. People said Illinois had the top backcourt in the country, and our backcourt played better than theirs. We were able to rebound with them, and they were big. The game was never really close. I got a pretty good feeling that we were probably as good as anybody. At the top of our game, nobody was going to put us away easily.

Maryland next played in the BB&T Classic, held in nearby Washington, D.C. at the MCI Center. The immediate challenge were the always-vexing Princeton Tigers, who played a patient, low-scoring brand of basketball that contrasted sharply with the Terps' up-tempo style. Princeton had a history of giving good teams fits, with their ball-control offense and back-door cuts. In the first half, the Tigers did just that, executing their game plan to perfection and taking a 36-23 halftime lead over the Terps into the locker room. Maryland played poorly, prompting a smattering of boos from its fans.

Behind closed doors, Coach Gary Williams ripped into his players, telling them in a locker-banging rage that they were playing like a bunch of pussies. There was no reason for the Terps not to dominate Princeton. All they had to do for the next 20 minutes was play their high-pressure, trapping defense instead of letting the Tigers lull them to sleep and eat up the clock.

Thanks in part to the fire Williams lit under his Terps, Maryland looked like a different team in the second half. They came back, tying the game at 46 after a 14-2 run and taking the lead with about five minutes left to play. Dixon, who had hit only one bucket in the first half, suddenly seemed omnipresent on defense, anticipating passes, knocking balls loose off the dribble, and wreaking havoc all over the court. "That's what pressure does," Williams said. "It doesn't always get you steals, but the mental and physical part of pressure is the wearing-down process." Meanwhile, Princeton had no one to contain Baxter inside, and he led Maryland with 19 points and 12 rebounds. Maryland survived its biggest scare of the young season, a valuable 61-53 gut-check win that Williams believed would help the Terps immeasurably as the team moved through its schedule.

We were in a fog in the first half. Sometimes you try to find something that shakes them up so they can snap out of it. The players might not like you at the time because of what you say, but that's okay, you have to say whatever it takes to win. Sometimes you have to get angry and say things to motivate the players. Positive motivation is what you try to do. You can't get really, really angry too often, but there comes a time when you have to let everything go, and let everything come out, and not worry about it.

I said a lot of negative things at halftime, but I try to leave them with something positive by the time they leave the locker room, by saying if we play hard and we will, we can win. They have to know I believe they can win.

In the long run, it is good, once you do come back in a situation like that, because you know you can do it. You can't duplicate that in practice, and you use it as a positive.

The next day, Maryland geared up to play the Connecticut Huskies in the finals of the BB&T Classic. Lonny Baxter, playing before the hometown crowd, led the Terps to a high-powered 77-65 victory and won tournament MVP by scoring 24 points and snaring 10 rebounds. After jumping out to a big lead early, Maryland's edge was just two points at halftime, 36-34. At the start of the second half, the Terps went on a powerful 16-4 run that put them up 52-38. UConn, led by Caron Butler's 20 points, never cut the lead to less than seven points after Maryland's second-half run. "That's obviously one of the best teams in the country," Connecticut coach Jim Calhoun said of Maryland. "I was most impressed by the way they played so well with each other. Maryland gave our kids a good lesson on how to play team basketball."

Connecticut had a young team in December, and we had more experience. Their quickness impressed me. They were as quick as we were, and we had a quick team. That was a good basketball team, two to three weeks away from hitting their stride.

We played like a veteran team in that game. It is hard to play with a lead sometimes. You get a 10-point lead, and you don't want to change the way you are playing or take bad shots. But sometimes players get too cautious and stop taking the shots that got you the 10 point lead. There is a fine line between playing smart and playing too cautious. We did a good job that night.

Before the game against the Huskies, assistant coaches Dave Dickerson and Jimmy Patsos were informed of tragic news—Kevin Mouton, brother of the Terps' senior forward Byron Mouton and the reputed comedian of the family, was shot and killed by a stray bullet while standing on a sidewalk in Houston, TX. Mouton's other brother Clyde, who lives in Maryland, asked the coaches not to tell Byron of Kevin's death, saying he would talk to him after the game. "We drove on the Beltway for a while, and I didn't know how to tell him," Clyde said. "So finally I just let it out and said, 'Something bad happened. Our brother just got, you know, shot, got killed.'"

"I just said, 'No, stop clowning. It's not true,'" Byron said. "And then he just started crying, and, you know, just a moment of silence, and then I just started crying, too. I just couldn't believe it."

Mouton, shocked by his brother's death, returned to Louisiana for the funeral but came back in time to be in uniform for the Terps' next game and score 13 points off the bench in a 79-54 win over the University of Detroit. And he found, among his Terrapins teammates and coaches and a brother who lived nearby, immense emotional support. With the support of his roommate Calvin McCall and the benefit of Juan Dixon's experience dealing with the loss of both of his parents in high school, Byron Mouton, remarkably, coped with his brother's death without going into an emotional tailspin, losing his touch on the court, or diminishing his drive to win the national championship.

"Juan was very, very good for Byron, and I think that experience gave Byron a second wind and a renewed focus," said assistant coach Dave Dickerson. "You learn through experience. Byron was helped by having guys on the team who have endured some hardship, like Juan, calling and talking to him about that and then reiterating those things when he came back on campus."

On Dec. 11, Williams clinched his 250th win at Maryland with a runaway 91-55 victory over Monmouth, the Terps' eighth in a row as the team headed into first semester exams. After that 10-day hiatus, Maryland went back on the road to play Oklahoma on December 21. Local newspapers in Norman described the matchup as the Sooners' biggest non-conference game in 10 years. And while the game was close at halftime, the Terps folded in the second half, shooting only 38 percent of their shots from the field, three for 19 from three-point range and losing to a strong squad. With Maryland shooting poorly from the outside, Oklahoma's defense collapsed on Baxter and allowed him just five shots in the Sooners' 72-56 win. "They got their ass whipped," said Novak, who joined Williams and the Terps on the charter flight to Oklahoma and back. "It was a long plane ride back from Oklahoma City, and it was quiet."

We just didn't have the sharpness coming out of exams. We hung in there in the first half, but Oklahoma was playing better than we were. And we ran out of gas. I told the team, 'Look, this is not us. We will see how good we are the rest of the season.' I know what happened. We were not tough enough mentally or in good enough shape. We can get it back.' Oklahoma was too good, and they were really focused. They had something to prove. And they did.

What could we have done differently? Not much. When we got into exams, we didn't have all of the players together for six or seven days. We practice, but one guy has a test, and he comes late, and another guy leaves early due to a study session. The players get out of their normal routine and go to sleep later. All of a sudden, they don't eat as well and they eat at funny hours. People think because guys are basketball players, they don't act like other college students. They do.

16

REVENGE

Maryland kicked off its ACC regular season play on the road, taking on the Wolfpack of North Carolina State on December 30. Coach Gary Williams made one major change to begin the ACC campaign: he inserted sophomore Chris Wilcox into the starting lineup at forward, making Tahj Holden a reserve. Though he did not always work hard in practice and failed to play up to his potential against lesser opponents, Wilcox had an intimidating presence on both ends of the floor. His thunderous dunks and blocked shots had a way of shifting the momentum and getting his teammates pumped. In addition, Wilcox had proven his mettle in big games, where his flashes of brilliance against Maryland's toughest opponents revealed his emerging potential.

Given the extraordinarily competitive nature of the ACC and the extreme difficulty of winning games away from the friendly confines of Cole Field House, every contest posed its own challenge. Despite all the talented players the Terps had under coaches Lefty Driesell, Bob Wade and Gary Williams, Maryland had not won the

ACC regular season title since 1980. Along with the ultimate goal of the national championship, the ACC crown was one that Williams and his team hoped to claim as their own. As a believer that one game during the regular season didn't define a team, winning the conference title appealed to Williams's sense that success revolved around consistency, hard work, focus and perseverance. The Terps and their opponents competed on a level playing field during the regular season, unlike the single-elimination ACC Tournament played most years in North Carolina.

In the opener against N.C. State, Juan Dixon and Steve Blake led the Terps down the stretch to a 72-65 win, even though Maryland hit just three for 16 from the field in the second half. A bruiser from the start, the game included 57 fouls, 81 free throws and an abundance of cold shooting. In the clutch, the Terps made their final 15 free throws, with Dixon hitting eight straight and going 12-14 for the game. In less than a minute, Blake nailed a jump shot from the baseline and a three-pointer to propel the Terps to victory after N.C. State had cut the lead to three points with under four minutes to play. Ultimately, what mattered most to Williams in ACC road games was not the score, but which team came out on top. Here was victory, in the ACC opener, even though Maryland went nearly nine minutes in the second half without scoring a basket. "We had to struggle in the second half to keep our composure, which we did," Williams said. "We weren't pretty, but the game could have been lost very easily."

Later, some Maryland sports fans questioned whether Maryland was overrated since the team had only beaten the Wolfpack by seven points. When Williams heard about that, "he was frosted," Novak recalled.

I was very concerned about getting that first win on the road and thought that was a big step for us. N.C. State was a good team. Our offense wasn't great, but from the first day of practice, I sell the notion that there will be games that we don't shoot or handle the ball as well as we would like but that the defense will always be there. After the game, I told our players this was a typical road game in the ACC. They are not always pretty, but good teams win these kinds of games.

In the final game in Cole Field House against a non-conference team, Maryland whipped Norfolk State 92-69. Maryland increased its string of consecutive non-conference home victories to 84, the longest such streak in the nation. The Terrapins hadn't lost to a non-conference team at Cole since December 1989 during Williams's first season as head coach in College Park.

On January 9, a traditional ACC juggernaut, the North Carolina Tar Heels, paid a visit to Cole Field House. With one of the finest college basketball programs in the nation, North Carolina had struggled throughout the season. Over the years, some of the most exciting games in Cole had pitted the Terps against the Tar Heels. This game proved to be exciting before a sellout crowd too, but for a different reason: the contest turned into the most lopsided Maryland victory over North Carolina ever, 112-79. Maryland's explosive offensive potential was too much for the Heels, who trailed by 20 at halftime.

From Juan Dixon's 29 points and eight steals to Steve Blake's career-high 14 assists, Maryland seemed overpowering. It was the most points ever scored by any team against the Tar Heels. "You don't expect to win a game like that against North Carolina. It doesn't matter what their record is. It is still Carolina," Williams said. However, not everyone was so sure. Author John Feinstein told a friend during the game, "I came here to see North Carolina, and this is not North Carolina playing. It must be impostors."

Four days after their blowout of the Tar Heels, Maryland, ranked fourth in the nation, took on Georgia Tech in Atlanta. In a game that went down to the wire, the Terps would stretch their lead only to let their opponents back in the game. With 30 seconds left, the Yellow Jackets had the ball and were down by two. As Tech brought the ball up, Dixon stalked the ball-handler in the frontcourt. Suddenly, Dixon snuck up from behind and swiped the ball off the dribble, then turned and found Chris Wilcox streaking to the hoop for an alley-oop dunk to close the contest, 92-87.

Dixon finished with 26 points, hitting five three-pointers for the game, and the spindly guard even grabbed a team-high 10 rebounds. But it was his performance in the clutch that meant the difference between victory and defeat for Maryland. "Juan was huge," said Baxter, who added 23 points of his own.

"Our effort was certainly worthy of winning, but we got beat by a great player who makes great plays in a lot of different ways. If Dixon's not making a three, he's making a great pass. At the end, he made that steal," said Yellow Jackets coach Paul Hewitt.

Juan Dixon is as tough as any kid I've ever had. He refuses to lose. That steal he made was an incredible play. He gets on the foul line and I just think he's going to make them. I don't think any player has had a greater impact over the last four years on any team.

When you win a game, no matter what happened during the game, the players are happy. And then you walk in the locker room and say, 'This isn't good enough.' It is easier to get on the team after we win than after we lose, because after we lose, I worry about their confidence. I can be pretty tough on our team after a win and say, 'If you think that is a good enough effort, we are going to lose some games like this.' When I do that, I try to get specific by saying something like, 'If that is how well we handle the ball, something is wrong.' If we win, they know they did something right. After a win, the players sometimes need to be deflated. After a loss, I might turn it around and say, 'Even though we lost, we played good defense.'

In a battle for first place in the ACC on January 17, third-ranked Maryland traveled to Durham, North Carolina and Cameron

Indoor Stadium to take on the nation's No. 1 team, the Duke Blue Devils. The first half raced along, with 25 lead changes and Maryland up 49-48 at the break. With 10 minutes to play, the game remained close, with the Terps trailing by three. But they scored only eight points the rest of the way, and Duke, led by Jason Williams's 34 points, put on a sizzling offensive display to post a 99-78 victory. The Blue Devils put the clamps on Dixon, holding him to just nine shots and 10 points, his lowest total for the season. Before fouling out, Baxter carried his team with 24 points and 14 rebounds.

"There is nothing worse than flying back with a losing team. It is very quiet. It is like being at a funeral. The coach is the only person on the plane talking at all, and he is talking very quietly," Novak said. "They take these losses very, very seriously."

The Terps had been soundly defeated by Oklahoma in Norman, struggled at N.C. State, and survived a close game at Georgia Tech before losing by 21 in Cameron Indoor. Quietly, Maryland fans began to question whether their team was strong enough to win on the road against the top teams in the nation.

After the Duke game, I told our players, 'Don't worry about the score. You either win or lose. We didn't play well enough to win this game down here against a great team. That doesn't mean we can't win these types of games in the future. We can.'

It is quiet after a loss. I don't want anybody feeling happy after a loss. Good teams always hurt when they lose. It gives players the will to come back to practice the next day with the willingness to work hard. When we lose, I am still wired. There is an urgency to review the game and get right to the next opponent. After a loss, I never feel comfortable until we walk out on the court again. I just want to put that game behind us, and that next game can't come quickly enough.

The first half down there was as good an offensive half as any in college basketball. The thing about Duke is they have such great confidence. Mike Krzyzewski obviously does a great job with offense because they play with such confidence. They think every shot they take is going in. At halftime, I told our guys we were playing great but had to play better defense. We tried to cut off the threes in the second half, and we opened up inside, and they took it to the basket.

We learned that night that if we were going to be good throughout the year and into the NCAA Tournament, our defense was going to have to improve. We were still ranked high nationally, but we had players that bought into the idea that we could get better. A mature team like the one we had never feels it can't get better as a team, even at the last weekend of the NCAA tournament.

The Terps rebounded with a 99-90 win over the Clemson Tigers at Cole. Dixon scored 23 points, while Wilcox posted a double-double, scoring 17 points and grabbing 14 rebounds. Blake played the point with distinction, posting 13 assists, while Mouton hit double figures with 14 points.

Maryland appeared to break open a close game with a 10-3 run at the beginning of the second half. But their defense allowed Clemson to regain the lead with five minutes left, 81-80, by way of its 15 three-pointers. The Terps scored the next time down the floor and never trailed again, riding seven straight points down the stretch from Drew Nicholas and clutch scoring by Dixon. "It's all about winning," Dixon said. "It doesn't matter how you get it."

But Williams was unappeased. He was very concerned that by the middle of January, they were still not playing consistently solid defense. If his team had any hopes of achieving its goals for the season, the defense would have to improve—and quickly.

There is a tendency to assume we lost at Duke but now we are going to win against Clemson, versus actually going out and earning that win like we should. I didn't think we played well against Clemson. They shot well, and we gave up a lot of open shots and 90 points. I was very concerned with that.

I was upset, and after the Clemson game, I got on them. The defense was not acceptable. I told the players, 'If we want to be a good team this year, we have to work on both ends of the court.' I didn't go in there with any preset thing other than what emotion I wanted to convey. This was a time where I could get upset. If the coach got on me and I thought I was busting my ass, that would piss me off. But they knew I was right when I got on them. I try to get a sense of how they feel and what they are thinking, and then go from there.

The players were confident, they won, they felt good about themselves. But I can't let them off with just winning in that situation. They have to know that is not going to be good enough against some other teams we play.

Maryland won its next two games, against Wake Forest in Winston-Salem and against Florida State at Cole, by virtually identical scores: 85-63 and 84-63. Wake Forest had won nine in a row at home prior to being defeated by the Terps. It was the bench that stepped up and led the way, with Tahj Holden scoring 11 points and Nicholas adding 10 as big men Baxter and Wilcox, both in foul trouble, watched most of the first half from the bench. Dixon and Blake led the scoring with 19 points each. Against Florida State, Coach Williams reverted to a tactic he seldom used: a slogan. After being humiliated at home by Florida State the previous year, Williams made sure his Terps were focused. Dixon got the message, scoring 25 points, grabbing a team-high 11 rebounds, and making eight steals. Mouton tossed in 18 points in addition to staking his claim on defense, as he did often during the season.

B*efore the Florida State game, I wrote the word REVENGE on the board in the locker room. I didn't like having our fans booing us last year when we lost at home. This was a reminder that it was up to us, and us alone.*

17

THE COMEBACK

On January 31, Maryland traveled to Charlottesville to take on the eighth-ranked Virginia Cavaliers in a regular season game between two top 10 teams. Down 46-44 at halftime, Maryland faced what appeared to be certain defeat down the stretch as the Virginia squad, backed by a rowdy crowd, widened its lead to nine points with just over three minutes left to play. For Juan Dixon, however, the game wasn't over. For most of the game, he had heard the cruel jeers of Cavalier fans behind one of the baskets, chanting "crack-head parents." He was further enraged when, after Williams called a timeout, two of Virginia's players on their way to the bench said something to the Maryland coach suggesting that he might as well pack up the bus then and there. "They thought they had the win, so I guess they wanted to show off a little bit," Dixon said. "We wanted to protect our coach, and we allowed that to motivate us." Faced with long odds in a hostile environment, the Terps didn't panic, and the next three minutes marked a turning point in their march to a championship.

With the team down by nine at 83-74, Juan Dixon hit two free throws and Chris Wilcox followed that by stealing a pass and slamming it home. Then, Drew Nicholas, who had been inserted for Steve Blake down the stretch for his outside shooting, stepped up and nailed two clutch three-pointers. Finally, Dixon capped a remarkable comeback, hitting from the baseline to put the Terps ahead 88-87 with 30 seconds left. Maryland benefited from its nearly perfect free-throw shooting, hitting 25-26 for the game, including four of five as the clock ticked down. The stunned Cavaliers could not put a single point on the board in the final minute as Maryland walked off the floor with a 91-87 victory. "We've got a lot of heart," Williams said after the game. "We knew how to act down the stretch."

The Terps' astounding come-from-behind victory against UVA was a turning point for the team in many ways. Nicholas's performance was that of a seasoned veteran, rather than that of a player who at times the previous year had looked lost on the court. "The first year," said senior guard Earl Badu, "Drew was trying to play the point guard position the way Steve [Blake] does. Steve is an old-school point guard. Drew is a scorer first. This year, you could see the change—he was offensive-minded, even at the point guard position. Against Virginia, he stepped up and made some big shots." More importantly, Nicholas's game, along with strong showings from Tahj Holden and Ryan Randle, also showed the team that if the Terps needed it, their bench could come through in crunch time.

The game also marked a change for Gary Williams. Despite his success, a common criticism of the coach was that when the bombs were going off, he was never the calmest one in the foxhole. His intensity, many said, seemed more like browbeating when his team was behind. But against the Cavaliers, Williams and the Terps stared down a nine-point deficit in enemy territory and never blinked. "In the past, a weakness of his teams at every school is they have not been able to come from behind to win," Williams's daughter Kristin said. "I think it's because it is difficult for him to relax and calm the team down. He just gets wound up tighter and tighter and tighter."

Novak, who drove down to Charlottesville rather than traveling with the team, described the victory as the most important win of the season. "This was the defining moment. Maryland was never the same," he said. "They knew that no matter what, they could always come back." After the game, he went looking for Williams to congratulate him. "He was smiling," Novak said. "It was jubilation and almost disbelief."

A lot of times there is a game during the season that makes your team better, where you come from behind and win, and it gives you confidence. You have to get a little lucky in those situations, but the biggest thing is to believe you can win. We were a good enough team to win that game, down nine, with three minutes left. The one thing about our team was we played 40 minutes, regardless of the score. I knew once we won that it would be a big win for us and help us the rest of the way.

Virginia was playing well, and it didn't look good with three minutes left. But we talked about the game not being over, that there was enough time left for us to win. It is one thing to talk about it and another to believe it. We believed it. It wasn't that Virginia quit playing defense. We made some great shots.

I told them after the game that I was really proud of them. I said I knew we weren't going to quit. I told them a lot of teams would not have won that game on the road. As much as it helped our confidence, that three minutes hurt Virginia's confidence. That is why one game sometimes is so important in the middle of a college basketball season.

After its dramatic come-from-behind victory over the Cavaliers, Maryland won its next three ACC games handily, defeating N.C. State at home 89-73, dominating the Tar Heels in Chapel Hill 92-77, and beating Georgia Tech at home 85-65.

By the time Maryland played North Carolina on February 10, the Tar Heels were already well into a nightmare of a season. Williams worried that the Terps' week off before the game, as well as the possibility of his team's overconfidence against a struggling Carolina squad, could make them ripe for an upset in Chapel Hill. "He told us North Carolina was ranked No. 1 in the country last year and they had a week off and they went to Clemson and lost," Byron Mouton said. "He wanted us to be mentally tough and not get into the same situation." Maryland jumped out to a 47-30 half-time lead before Dixon repelled a brief Tar Heel run in the second half, putting down a pair of three-pointers. And with nine points and nine assists, Steve Blake continued his steady performance at point guard.

I am not used to going into the Dean Dome worrying about our players being overconfident. But North Carolina was struggling and we were playing well, and we walked in there and got up by over 10 points pretty quickly. Every time we put a little run on, and it looked like we would put them away, they came back. That whole game, I never felt comfortable that we had it put away. The crowd reacts to the scoreboard. But as a coach, I also get my own feel for the game, and I felt we were not grinding it out as hard as we needed to. In the crowd's mind halfway through the second half, the game was over. I'm there trying to keep the players focused. They think I am nuts because I'm yelling and everything. But you don't have to relax much to let a team like North Carolina get back in the game. I told the players after the game, though, that we had to do more than just show up. We were not tough enough in that game. We had to go out and earn it. That was the theme all year.

Before their long-awaited rematch against Duke, coaches reviewed how to defend the Blue Devils' Mike Dunleavy, whose range, scoring ability, and 6'9" frame made him a matchup problem in nearly every game he played. Dixon maintained that Wilcox could do the job, but others weren't sure. "Juan was upset we were not going to have Chris play Dunleavy," Jimmy Patsos said. Dixon and

Patsos discussed the strategy after a practice, and Patsos suggested that they talk to Williams about it.

"Wilcox wants to cover Dunleavy, and Juan thinks [he] should," Patsos told Williams. "Whatever you think. It's your deal."

Williams asked Dixon, "You think Chris should cover Dunleavy?"

"Yes, Chris wants to shut him down."

"Let's do it," Williams said.

Duke marched into Cole Field House on February 17 for a Sunday afternoon national TV game, tied with Maryland atop the ACC and ranked No. 1 in the nation. The Blue Devils left College Park humbled after falling victim, 87-73, to a Maryland team that looked bigger, stronger, smarter, quicker and sharper, as it stretched its lead to 25 points in the second half. Williams put Wilcox on Dunleavy, and the Terps' athletic big man turned in his most impressive game of the year, shutting down the Duke forward throughout the key stretches of the game and finishing with 23 points and 11 rebounds. Dixon added 17 points and Blake controlled the flow, threading the Duke defense for 13 assists and just one turnover while putting the shackles on Jason Williams. "Maryland did a great job of always knowing where I was as soon as I caught the ball," Duke's All-American guard said.

The decisive triumph could not have been sweeter for Maryland fans. It was the last time the Terps would play Duke in Cole Field House, and the resounding victory catapulted Maryland into sole possession of first place in the ACC. And there was a magic moment in the game too, a big play that left Maryland fans ecstatic.

Just before halftime, while Jason Williams dribbled out the clock to play for one shot, he turned to listen to instructions from Coach Mike Krzyzewski. An alert Blake came dashing forward, stripped the Duke star of the ball, and took it down for a layup. Blake's defensive maneuver fueled the Terps' momentum, giving them a 38-29 edge at halftime. "That was one of the great moments in 32 years of watching this team. I can't tell you how high people were going into the second half," Novak said. "I still think about that moment sometimes."

For the Blue Devils, it was their biggest margin of defeat and worst beating in years. Duke was unable to get any penetration against the staunch Terps' defense, nor could they kick the ball out for open shots on the outside. Demolishing Duke added to the Terps' confidence and left Maryland fans, who streamed onto the floor of Cole Field House after the victory, euphoric.

The rattled Duke squad missed half their free throws and hit just 36 percent from the field, their worst shooting performance of the season. "We weren't that good, but Maryland had a lot to do with it," said Duke coach Mike Krzyzewski. "We got flustered. They played like a veteran team. Gary had his team well prepared. The team that should have won, won, and they won in convincing fashion."

After blowing a 10-point lead against Duke at home the previous season with less than a minute remaining, and losing to Duke in the Final Four in Minneapolis after leading by 22 points, the Maryland victory, the first over Duke at Cole since 1997, gave the Terps an extra measure of satisfaction. Also, since Duke had two conference losses, the win positioned Maryland, 11-1 in ACC play, to win the conference championship. But they would have to stay on guard to do so.

We were a very confident team going into that game. We really controlled the game and tempo throughout. It was one of those games where everything seemed to work. They had 99 points against us down there, and we held them to just 73 points up here. We played as smart defensively as any game all year.

The biggest play occurred just before halftime when Steve Blake stole the ball from Jason Williams and scored. He was dribbling out front for Duke, holding the ball for the last shot. We usually stay back on defense and don't extend in that situation. That means typically there would be plenty of time for Williams to look back over his shoulder at his coach to find out what play to run.

When Jason Williams looked back the first time, nothing happened because there still was too much time on the clock to run a play. Steve got a little closer to Williams. When Williams looked back a second time after letting some time run off, Steve stole the ball. He timed it perfectly. The way you steal the ball when someone is dribbling is that you have to get it just as it leaves his hand to go back down to the floor. Everybody remembers the steal, but Steve also made a great play on the offensive end. Jason Williams came after Steve to challenge him. He made Steve go up high and put the ball up very high off the glass on the layup. It was a very tough shot since Jason Williams can leap a foot above the rim. The steal and layup broke the little momentum they had gotten, and instead, we went into halftime with the momentum. It was a great defensive play to steal it and a great offensive play to finish.

Defensively, we were able to get out on their shooters without giving up dribble penetration. We stayed in front of them and didn't let them penetrate. Steve did good job on Jason Williams and Chris Wilcox did a good job on Dunleavy. People said Steve had Jason Williams's number that game.

After the Duke game, I told them we could beat anybody if we played that well.

In the locker room after the Duke victory, Gary Williams also told his team that his 85-year-old father, William, had died and that he would be traveling to New Jersey to attend the funeral. Though Williams had known about his father's passing, he had kept it to himself rather than risk distracting his players before the Duke game. As with assistant coach Dave Dickerson and forward Byron Mouton, death once again had visited the team during a season marked by great accomplishments and personal adversity. Maintaining focus would be the big challenge. "It has been a tough week for us, after the emotional win and the stuff with Coach," said Terps guard Juan Dixon. "Coach Williams is like family. For him to see his dad die, and see the emotion on his face, you feel like crying."

My older brother Douglas called me at 2 a.m. on Saturday morning to say that my dad died. The phone doesn't usually ring at two in the morning, so I knew it was not good news. From talking to the doctors and my brother, I kind of expected it. There was a sense that this might be it. He was 85 years old, and the great thing for my dad was that he had been sick for only a month. That was it. He got a blood infection that attacked his heart. It happened pretty quickly from there. He had 84 years and 11 months of pretty good health. If you get your choice, maybe that is not a bad way to go.

When somebody dies at 85, it is the natural progression of things. I tried to focus as much as I could on the game. I kept everything inside, and so once the Duke game ended, I allowed myself to think about my father dying.

I wasn't as close to my father as a lot of people are to their dads, but he was still my father, and I thought about a lot of situations that I had not thought about for 30 years. I went through some natural feelings. I wish I was closer, I wish I was this, I wish I was that. That is just the way it goes. He lived a good life and was able to live and take care of himself until he went into the hospital in Camden.

His funeral was Orthodox Presbyterian. It wasn't an uplifting service, but I was ready for it. You think, 'Let's celebrate his life.' Not this church. There are no laughs and no guitar playing. The church really believes that you are passing through this life to get to the hereafter. That is the service my dad would have liked. For me, I try to live the best I can now.

Several days later, the Terps played Clemson in South Carolina. Maryland had trailed 35-31 at halftime, and in the first half, the team didn't resemble the squad that had dominated Duke. The Terps, undoubtedly, suffered a letdown after defeating Duke, and they were also affected by the death of their coach's dad. "It was tough for them to concentrate," Williams said. "I wasn't at practice—that's not normal. They missed me yelling at them." But the struggling Clemson Tigers, dead last in the ACC, could not capitalize, and Maryland held onto the top spot in the conference after a stronger second-half performance propelled them to an 84-68 win. Dixon, once again, led the scoring with 21 points, Baxter had a dozen rebounds, and Blake notched nine assists, becoming Maryland's all-time assist leader.

On February 24, before the start of the Terps' game against Wake Forest, Dixon and Baxter officially entered the pantheon of Maryland basketball greats, as their jerseys were retired and hung from the rafters of Cole Field House. The two seniors' day, however, was nearly spoiled, and the game went down to the final seconds with the outcome still in doubt. "I just told the players we were going to figure out a way to win," Williams said. "Of course, I hadn't figured out a way yet, but it sounds good to the players to say that." In the end, the Terps won in the unlikeliest of ways. With 1.3 seconds left and the score tied at 89, Demon Deacons forward Josh Howard grabbed a rebound and then called a timeout his team did not have. The resulting technical foul put Juan Dixon on the free-throw line, and Dixon hit the winning free throw, squeezing by the Deacons 90-89 and hanging onto first place in the ACC. Blake, on his way to leading the nation in assists, dished out another 13 against Wake Forest, while Baxter and Dixon tossed in 25 points and 20 points, respectively.

"That's a great win for us," Williams said afterward. "A lot of teams wouldn't win that game, but we found a way to win it. I don't care if it's pretty. We won the game." Added Blake, "A little luck never hurts."

Three days later, Maryland went down to Tallahassee to take on Florida State in its next ACC duel, a game the Terps took quite seriously after escaping with that one-point win over Wake Forest. (Meanwhile, assistant coach Jimmy Patsos had lost one of his grandparents. But fearful that the team had endured all the deaths it could stand, Patsos told no one and did not attend the funeral.) Florida State, while not having a great season, had beaten Duke and Virginia on its home court. But this time out, the Maryland squad dominated, racing out to a mammoth 48-29 halftime advantage and winning going away, 96-63. The 33-point win marked Maryland's biggest margin of victory on the road against an ACC team since 1953, the very first year of conference play. But the satisfaction of the victory was tempered for Williams by his knowledge that it most likely eliminated any hope of Seminoles coach Steve Robinson saving his job after the season. After the game, Robinson said of the Terps, "They're as good as advertised. They sure convinced me they're playing as good as anybody in the country."

The win clinched Maryland at least a share of the ACC regular season title. All that stood between the Terps and the outright conference championship was winning one more time. That opportunity, fittingly, would come before the largest crowd ever at Cole Field House in the last game the Terps would play in the storied arena.

18

CROWNING COLE

On the evening of Sunday, March 3, Maryland played Virginia, the same university it had beaten in the very first game at Cole Field House in 1955. To commemorate the final game in a gym that had given the Terps a tremendous home-court advantage for nearly 50 years, Maryland invited its All-ACC players from over the years to participate in a special ceremony. Star alumni on hand included Jack Flynn, Bob Kessler, Len Elmore, Tom McMillen, Buck Williams and Keith Booth. In addition to the players, Bud Millikan, Williams's coach in the 1960s, also attended the game.

The old arena was packed with emotion, which worried the coach, who felt even more pressure going into this pivotal contest. Not only would a win secure Maryland's first ACC regular season championship since 1980 and an undefeated record at home, Williams did not want to be remembered as the coach who lost the last game at Cole. As a youth in South Jersey, Williams couldn't imagine a better place to watch a college game than the Palestra in Philadelphia. But by reviving the dormant Terps basketball program, he had reignited Cole and turned it into a high-energy, overheated gym that felt like the Palestra on steroids. This was the grand finale, for the arena and for a celebrated senior class of Dixon, Baxter, Mouton and Earl Badu, who were all playing their last home game.

"It felt like it was both a wedding and a wake," Elmore said. "We had a reception and all the guys from years past were able to get together, but then afterward when you realized it's the last game played in Cole Field House, and you were looking around at the rafters and fans and nooks and crannies you knew so well, it was kind of like a funeral and saying goodbye. It was a special night and one I am not likely to forget."

Those in attendance will remember the way Maryland played for years to come. In a high-powered offensive performance, Maryland put the finishing touches on its ACC championship run, beating the Cavaliers 112-92. Six Terps hit double figures, and every senior scored, ranging from Dixon's 23 to a bucket in the waning moments by walk-on Badu that brought the fans to their feet.

The Terps finished their last season at Cole Field House a perfect 15-0, and as the team cut down the nets, Williams turned to the crowd and pumped his right fist into the air one more time. "We might as well leave in the right way," he said. "For everybody that has been a part of Cole Field House, we want this to be a great year. It's incredible how Cole has been a big part of people's lives over the past 50 years. We wanted to go out on a high note."

In a moment that symbolized their close relationship, Dixon cut the last net cord, saw that Williams had not had a chance to climb the ladder, and tied the cord back onto the rim so his coach could have the last snip. After Dixon handed the game ball to Millikan, the first Maryland coach in Cole, Bud didn't keep it. Instead, Millikan turned the game ball over to Williams, his star protégé.

"It is sweet redemption," said Elmore, a 10-year NBA veteran, Harvard Law School graduate and entrepreneur. "This basketball program has gone from tragedy to irrelevance to a long climb to national prominence. The fact that Gary was a former Maryland player had something to do with it. If it was an outsider as coach, I'm not sure the same effort would have gone into rebuilding and launching the program. Give Gary credit for maintaining that passion and drive. It is redemption, too, for those of us who toiled in the program and had that progress stopped by tragedy. It got kick-started again. What an amazing feeling."

Although official attendance at the game was listed at the standard 14,500 sellout, some estimated that as many as 20,000 people may actually have crammed into Cole to bid farewell that Sunday evening. "It was like something out of fiction," Novak said. "I'll never forget the last shot. I thought Gary had given the signal to do what the pros do and dribble out the clock. Instead, the little point guard off the bench, Andre Collins, hit a three, the last basket in Cole Field House. Everybody stayed. Nobody wanted to leave."

We came out flying. There was a lot of pressure with all the former players back. It was a nostalgic crowd. And it was senior day. I made it clear to the players in the locker room that I was completely focused on the game. I had to put what was going on inside me aside and coach the game.

Afterward, during the ceremony, I realized I was getting pretty old. I looked around, and I was one of the older players there. I saw guys like McMillen and Elmore. Those guys are younger than me, and people look at them as older Maryland players.

When you coach, you are with young people and basketball all the time and you don't realize time goes by. Somewhere in there you go from being a hot young coach to a veteran coach and you don't know when that is. But when a building is being closed that I played in 35 years ago, I realize time has gone by.

Finished with the regular season, the Terps began to prepare for one of their coach's least favorite events: the ACC Tournament. Typically played in North Carolina, Williams always felt that the tournament was stacked in favor of the schools from the area whose fans lived nearby. And this season, particularly, the Maryland coach had made it clear that his team's goal was the NCAA championship in Atlanta, not the conference championship in Charlotte.

In their first game, the Terps struggled against lowly Florida State. Despite being up by a dozen points at halftime, the Terps were sluggish, and the Seminoles came out firing in the first five minutes of the second half, going on a 13-2 run. The two timeouts Williams called early in the second half didn't do much to stem the tide as Florida State cut the Maryland lead to a single point.

Finally, during a TV timeout, Williams became so angry and frustrated that he left the team's huddle and sat by himself at the end of the bench. "I had nothing good to say, so I got out of there," he said. "I had made my point the previous timeout."

When Williams left the huddle, Byron Mouton spoke up. "I wanted to get them mad and frustrated," Mouton said, "I wanted them to go out there and be aggressive. I wanted them to take it out on Florida State." The ploy worked, as Maryland scored the next 21 points and went on to a comfortable 85-59 win. Dixon led the slumping Terps, scoring roughly half of his 20 points after his coach's silent reproach. When it was over, Williams described the first several minutes of the second half as a "nightmare," and said that despite its lead, Maryland played lousy in the first half. Chris Wilcox, continuing his consistently poor performances against weak opponents, scored only four points.

Maryland's opponent in the semifinal game was N.C. State, an upstart squad that had exceeded all expectations for the year. While the Terps had beaten the Wolfpack twice during the regular season, Maryland's 13-game winning streak had made the team complacent. "I didn't think we had a good practice prior to the N.C. State game," Earl Badu said. "Our concentration level wasn't very high." The Terps trailed by two at halftime before things fell apart for Williams and his team. The Wolfpack opened a 13-point lead in the second half before Maryland staged a valiant comeback to make it a one-possession game with just over a minute to play. But Julius Hodge hit an awkward, arc-less shot to give the Wolfpack a six-point lead and a stranglehold on the game. "I don't mind a guy taking a nice-looking shot," Williams quipped, "but that was unbelievable." The Wolfpack held on to beat Maryland 86-82 after the Terps saw, of all things, Dixon missing a three-pointer in the final seconds that would have tied the game. "It was a good look," he said. "Next time, I'll hit it."

In the locker room after the game, a calm Gary Williams made it clear that he wanted everyone to pack up their things, get out of North Carolina and head back to College Park on the double. No reason to replay this one in our minds, he said. And without raising his voice, he boosted his team's confidence and morale heading into the NCAA Tournament.

"It was a great postgame speech," Patsos recalled. "Gary said, 'Let's get out of this state. We want more than this. We are about the NCAA. We are not about the ACC. We can be so much better than that. They hit a lucky shot. Let's get on a plane and go home. No sad faces. We are 28-4. Let's go win the NCAA Tournament. That is what really matters. Let's play well for the next three weeks and see how far we go.'"

Sitting with his friend Keith Neff after the game, Williams, uncharacteristically, didn't appear distressed about the defeat. If there was such a thing as a good loss, this was probably it. The sooner they got out of North Carolina, the better. Instead of running the risk of peaking too soon by getting emotionally up for the ACC finals, the Terps would focus solely on the Big Dance. The extra rest before the NCAA tournament would make his players stronger. And at the appropriate time, he could use the loss to motivate his squad as it prepared for its first NCAA Tournament game.

Losing, said Earl Badu, actually seemed a "good thing" because it allowed the team to "refocus." The only risk was that the

NCAA Tournament Committee might give Maryland a lower seed or send them to play out West, as they had in so many previous years. Thanks to newly adopted NCAA rules, the Terps knew that as one of the top-ranked teams, they would spend at least the first weekend of the tournament close to home, in the friendly confines of the MCI Center in Washington, D.C. But since the Terps had won the regular season ACC title, Williams believed they still deserved to be a No. 1 seed and play in their home region throughout.

In the immediate aftermath of the loss to NC State, Dixon took a similar philosophical view to Williams. "Maybe this is good for us. This brings us down off that high," he said.

But other members of the Dixon family, especially his brother Phil, did not see it that way. All they saw was an unfocused floor leader of an unfocused team. They didn't care where the game was played. What they cared about was performance, and Juan's performance—six for 16 shooting, two rebounds and no steals—was unacceptable.

For the Dixon family, the loss—any loss—was a bitter pill. After the game, Mark Smith drove with Phil Dixon to meet Juan in the team hotel. In the car, Smith already knew the one question he wanted to ask his nephew: Was he really prepared to play this game? But Smith never got a chance to say a word. In the car ride over, "Phil was sitting next to me, and I could see that he was kind of simmering," he said, "and we got into Juan's room and Phil jumped at Juan with two feet, with two barrels."

"Don't you know," Phil asked, "Uncle Mark and I, we get tired of driving—how many hours we got to drive, Uncle Mark?"

"Eight hours," Smith said.

"Eight hours! To see you play bad! Don't you know we're tired of that? You weren't ready for this game. We don't mind you losing if you play good, but we didn't come down here to see you play bad.

"I'm sick and tired of this," Phil continued. "I don't want to see this anymore. I don't want to come this far and see you lose because you played bad."

Juan sat silently on the bed and listened to his brother, who had come out of the stands one more time to punch him in the chest and tell him to get tough. He sat, and listened, and thought about the upcoming NCAA Tournament.

"That really changed Juan," Smith said. "He was more focused, he cut out the distractions altogether. He practiced more, shot more in the gym, worked out more, stayed focused. All he did was study and get ready for basketball."

19

FLYING HIGH AT MCI

In a lounge adjacent to the Terps' locker room, Gary Williams gathered with eager Maryland players and coaches to watch the televised NCAA Tournament Selection Show on Sunday, March 10. There were five legitimate candidates for No. 1 seeds and only four top slots to place them; one team was bound to be given a No. 2 seed and sent out to the West bracket. The Terps, along with Duke and Kansas, had been one of the three top-ranked teams in college basketball for most of the regular season. But the team's loss to N.C. State in the ACC Tournament semifinals a few days earlier injected some uncertainty into the draw. The other two contenders for the final No. 1 seed had made strong cases for themselves at the end of the year. Cincinnati was the only team of the five to have won more than 30 games to that point, and Oklahoma had just knocked off top-ranked Kansas in the finals of the Big 12 Tournament, handing the Jayhawks their first loss of the year to a conference opponent.

For the Terps, who in NCAA Tournaments over the years felt they had spent more time in the West than Lewis and Clark, the prospect of regional games in San Jose was not appealing. And for Williams, the selection committee's choice was clear: "You work hard all year to get a No. 1 seed," he said. "One game shouldn't change the way the selection committee feels."

In the end, Williams and Maryland got what they longed for. Maryland was named the No. 1 seed in the East Region, and both Cincinnati and Oklahoma were shipped out west. The sounds of jubilant applause rang through Cole Field House as the Terps learned that they also would have a home-court advantage of sorts. Their first-round games would be played less than 10 miles away from College Park at the MCI Center in Washington, D.C.

Two days later, Maryland learned it would play Siena in the first round, which won a playoff game to qualify for the final spot in the field of 64. The brackets were set, and March Madness, which CBS commentator Lesley Visser joked must have been named for Gary Williams, was ready to begin.

For the Terps, the road to the championship began on uneasy footing as Williams brought his team together for practice in Cole Field House on Wednesday, two days before the game against Siena. Williams was fired up, but he saw that the lackadaisical effort that characterized the Terps' performance in the ACC Tournament had carried over. Incensed, Williams declared the practice over and ordered his players off the court. "What you have to understand is that this is a whole new season, and your play is not reflecting that," he said angrily.

Players stood frozen, looking at each other and down at the floor and wondering what to do next. Juan Dixon immediately stepped forward and shouted at his teammates, imploring them to step it up, and then pleaded with Williams to let them stay and finish practice. After a minute or two, Williams agreed to give the team one more chance, and the rest of practice went smoothly. "I just kind of got the feeling that coach wanted the seniors to understand it was our job to take control, so I did," Dixon said.

Before Siena, the team and coaches moved into the Renaissance Hotel downtown near the MCI Center, even though they could have stayed at home. The goal was complete and total focus. If they wanted to go all the way, they would have to do more than just suit up. They would have to earn it.

The partisan Terrapin crowd eagerly anticipated the beginning of Maryland's march, knowing that this was the Terps' best opportunity to win the NCAA Championship. "Everything is out there for us," Drew Nicholas said. "I'm not saying we're putting pressure on ourselves, but this is the Big Dance. I think everybody in this room understands we're after one thing, and that's a national championship."

In the opening game against Siena at the MCI Center, the atmosphere was celebratory, as much Midnight Madness as March Madness. A No. 1 seed had never fallen to a No. 16 in the history of the NCAA Tournament. Terrapin fans expected a lot of points, some rim-rattling dunks, and no worries. Most importantly, they expected to watch the Terps on Sunday in the second round against Wisconsin. "What do say if you lose a game like that, as the number-one seed: 'I'm going to Mexico?'" Maryland coach Gary Williams asked. "You don't say, 'I'm going to Disneyworld.' I know that."

Siena, on the other hand, had won five games in a row and was looking to make history. And for much of the first half, they hung in with the Terps, keeping the game tied for the first six minutes and then staying as close as 21-19. But Nicholas responded with a three-pointer, and Baxter banged inside for a layup to extend the lead to 26-21. Then Dixon took over, going six-for-eight from the field for 20 points in the first half and propelling Maryland to a 52-38 lead. Siena never made a serious challenge in the second half, but the Terps didn't finish them off, either, instead cruising to an 85-70 win behind a season-high 29 points from Dixon.

Though Maryland was never seriously challenged in advancing to the second round, Williams was not happy with his team's performance. The Terps' streak of uninspired play had now reached nearly two weeks. They may have been able to slide by Siena, he told them, but if they didn't pick up their intensity the rest of the way, some team was going to send them home.

Every number-one seed is tight, but once you are into the tournament, you remember how that feels from the year before, and it loosens you up. But now we had to get up to play Wisconsin, and they are a really good team in a very good conference, the Big Ten.

After Siena, I said to the team, 'Get off your feet. Get as much rest as possible.' The coaches took care of getting everything ready so we could meet the next day and practice at MCI. During the week, I really concentrated on Siena, and the assistants each took one of the other teams we might play. Dave Dickerson had scouted Wisconsin, and Jimmy and Matt had St. John's. I had tapes ready to watch in my hotel room after Siena, and so we met that night and began looking at Wisconsin quickly. I stayed up until I got tired and couldn't watch anymore. During tournament time, I slept three or four hours a night.

I had a feel for Wisconsin and how they played. But the key was making sure our team played well. I could have the best scouting in the world, but it wouldn't matter if we didn't play well. So the most important thing for us was making sure we were ready for practice the next day, because there were a couple of things we had to go over before the game.

With its players resting for the Sunday game, the Maryland coaching staff gathered in Williams's hotel room to prepare for No. 8-seeded Wisconsin. The Badgers posed a formidable challenge for the Terps, especially for a second-round opponent. The co-champions of the Big Ten in the regular season, Wisconsin had defeated the Terps 78-75 the year before in the ACC-Big Ten Challenge. They were led onto the floor by Big Ten Coach of the Year Bo Ryan, who though in his first year in Madison was no stranger to big games and national championships. Ryan made his name at the University of Wisconsin-Platteville, turning around that program and winning four Division III national titles in a decade. After a two-year stint at the University of Wisconsin-Milwaukee, he brought his ball-control "swing offense," built of multiple screens and cuts, to a Badger team just one year removed from a Final Four appearance, and he produced immediate results.

Ryan was in many ways like Gary Williams, a self-described gym rat whose childhood memories included watching triple-headers at the Palestra. After an 80-70 first round win over St. John's, Ryan feigned ignorance of the Terps. "I can't even name the starters for you right now," he said after his team's Friday night win. "I'm going to find out as soon as I leave here." But the coach of the Badgers was very aware that an upset of Maryland on Sunday would cement Wisconsin's place on the national scene in college basketball. Led by sharp-shooting junior Kirk Penney, the team's strength was a balanced scoring attack. The Badgers were 14-0 when at least four players scored in double figures. "They'll try to slow the game down," Nicholas said. "Anytime they get a chance they'll try to hold the ball and get a good shot. It's just a matter of how hard we play on defense."

The MCI Center was awash in red on Sunday, though the Badger fans in their red and white colors were largely drowned out by the Maryland faithful who had returned to see their team try for its fourth Sweet Sixteen appearance in five years. They also came to see Maryland's favorite son, Juan Dixon, who was on the verge of breaking the school's all-time scoring record. "I can't believe I'm just seven points from breaking Len Bias's record," Dixon said before the game. "To do it just 40 miles from home makes it just that much more fun."

But Wisconsin controlled the game early. The Badgers stymied Maryland's efforts to quicken the pace, and their defense kept the Terps from scoring second-chance points. To make matters worse,

Dixon was struggling early, hitting only one basket in the first 15 minutes. For all of this, neither team was able to get out to a substantial lead. With 6:39 left in the first half, the Badgers led 23-19. And then, the Terps woke up and began to play their kind of basketball. The Maryland run began with a Baxter catch and layup, and the Terps scored two more when Wilcox finished a fast break. After three-pointers from Nicholas and Blake, Maryland had scored 10 points in 90 seconds and taken a 29-23 lead. The Terps did not let up. Then, with 4:01 left in the opening period, Dixon made Maryland history, hitting his first three-pointer of the game to break the university's all-time scoring record and send the MCI Center crowd into a frenzy.

After extending the lead to 38-30 at halftime, Williams challenged his team in the locker room to put the game away early. "I was really on them about that," he said. "We have to have a killer instinct." Following his halftime talk, the Terps came out and squashed the Badgers and any hopes of a comeback with a 17-3 run in six and a half minutes to start the second half. Dixon broke out from a relatively quiet first half to account for 13 of those 17 points despite cramps in his left leg.

The Terps led 55-33 with 13:39 to play, and the Badgers could only hope to withstand the storm and keep the final outcome respectable. Their top scorer, Penney, was completely shackled by the Maryland defense, going 3 for 14 from the field and scoreless from beyond the arc. With just nine points, he was held under double figures for the first time in two months. With their 87-57 win, the Terps had given the hometown fans the dominant performance they had been hoping for and sent a powerful message to the remaining teams in the East region. "When we play like that, we don't think a lot of teams can play with us," Nicholas said. "And the few that can will have a hard time withstanding our punch. We're not trying to be cocky, but that's the way we feel."

Against Wisconsin, Dixon again matched his season high of 29 points, hitting four of seven three-pointers and continuing his ace free-throw shooting by hitting five of six from the line. Maryland's big men also played well, with Wilcox adding 18 points and Baxter scoring 16. Told by a local television reporter after the game to "forget Len Bias, you're the scoring champion," Dixon, who now had 2,172 career points, recoiled. "We can't forget Len Bias," he said. "He was a great player and a great person. Even though I didn't know him personally, I've heard a lot about him from coach Dave Dickerson, who was one of his teammates." Shortly afterward, Dickerson approached Dixon and offered his own congratulations. "You're a very special player," he said, "because you've broken the record of a great player."

Wisconsin was a game we thought we could win. We thought we were the better team. The players had confidence they could win that game. Being a veteran team, they wanted to play better than the game before. We have a certain pride in that. We want to win, but we want to look the part of a number-one seed, and we did in the second half of the Wisconsin game.

We felt if we kept the tempo up, we would win the game. We pressed as much as possible and had an edge with our bench. We thought we could wear them down, and Wisconsin got tired.

They couldn't stay with us in the second half. That was probably the best half we played since the game against Virginia at Cole Field House. A lot of things worked in our favor. We had started to play again as I knew we could play. We didn't play particularly well against Siena, but now we were back. That gave me a very good feeling. I told the guys, 'That is us. The way we played in the second half is how we should be playing the rest of the way.'

20

TANGLING WITH TUBBY

One day after the scrappy Indiana Hoosiers upset Duke by overcoming an 18-point deficit, Gary Williams led the University of Maryland onto the floor of the Carrier Dome in snowy Syracuse. While the team enjoyed playing in front of the home crowd for the first two rounds, Williams was happy to be in upstate New York and away from the distractions on campus. Waiting for the Terps in the Round of 16 were the University of Kentucky Wildcats. With 13 Final Four appearances and seven national championships, Kentucky was one of the nation's most heralded and successful basketball programs. The team had played erratically during the regular season, but the 'Cats, coached by Tubby Smith, were tournament tough and playing well of late.

The March 22 match-up generated plenty of excitement, given Maryland's superb team play and Kentucky star Tayshaun Prince's explosive brand of offense. The 6'9" senior had scored 41 points in the Wildcats' tournament win over Tulsa, and containing him with tough, smart defense was one of the Terps' top priorities. "They're very athletic and they're big enough to give us problems," Williams said.

One thing Gary Williams had learned about the NCAA tournament was the importance of keeping his team loose. There was enough external pressure on the players that if he kept them focused but relaxed, they would play better. As he had done during the regular season, Williams had his players shoot from half-court at the end of each practice. Everybody enjoyed it. Big men, small guards, forwards and even coaches participated in what had rapidly become a favorite Maryland ritual. Hook shots, two-handed set shots, jumpers and baseball-style lobs alike came flying as the team's managers raced to retrieve the basketballs so the shooting spree could continue unabated. There were no rules, but the first one to sink it from half-court made sure everyone else knew about it and then headed to the showers first.

CBS analyst Billy Packer said before the game, "I've never seen a No. 1 seed looser than Maryland was." Williams, too, carried a quiet confidence into the Carrier Dome. "People are so used to saying 'Duke, Carolina, Kentucky.' You never hear Maryland in the same breath," he said. "I think with what we've done in the last few years, we deserve to be mentioned in the same breath. We've earned the right to know we're a good team without being cocky. If somebody beats us, they'll beat a good team."

Kentucky is one of the few teams that has as much basketball tradition as a Duke or North Carolina. We knew they could handle tournament situations. They had won the national championship a few years ago, and they were playing their best basketball coming into this game. The season that Steve Francis was here, we played them in Puerto Rico, and in Juan Dixon's sophomore year, we played them in the preseason NIT. The players knew each other. We knew we couldn't intimidate Kentucky due to our seeding.

Prince had hurt us before. He is a little different. He's 6'9" and can play like a guard. And then they had some big people. With Lonny Baxter, Tahj Holden, Chris Wilcox and Ryan Randle, we knew we were not going to get outmanned inside or killed on the glass. We had a good backcourt in Juan Dixon and Steve Blake, but it was not as physical as their backcourt. Byron always plays well against physical teams. We knew we were not going to get pushed around by Kentucky.

A capacity crowd packed the largest basketball arena in the country to see the Maryland-Kentucky game. Tubby Smith understood that if his squad wanted to avoid Wisconsin's fate, it would have to do a better job against Maryland's team speed. "You see they've got it, but you really don't know how fast they really are," Smith said. "They don't look like they're that fast, but Steve Blake, he pushes the ball. ...That's all we talked about to our players—'Get back! Get back! And don't be back-pedaling, either, because they'll be laying it up. You better run back.'"

But from the opening tip, it was Kentucky's athletes, particularly junior guard Keith Bogans, who made a strong first impression, hitting a pair of three-pointers in the opening minutes. Bogans grew up in the Washington area and had been recruited heavily by Gary Williams and the University of Maryland. Before Kentucky could open up an early lead, the Terps got the ball into the hands of their senior leader, and Dixon was able to get clear of Kentucky defenders on the perimeter and nail two straight three-pointers, pulling the Terps even at 10 apiece. Smith marveled at the abilities of the Terps senior leader. "Dixon, man, he can fly. You can't get to him because he's so fast. Then you add quickness to speed, and he's deadly," Smith said. "He's got speed in the open court and quickness in half-court sets. And when you've got that, you become very hard to defend."

After Kentucky held a three-point lead, 19-16, with about 12 minutes left in the first half, the Wildcats held the Terps without a field goal for seven straight possessions before Dixon scored to end the drought. From there, Maryland went on a run, one of very few in the game by either team. As they had so often this year, the Terrapins owed the spurt to their defense, which held Kentucky to just three points over the next five minutes. With 7:27 left in the first half, the players went to their respective benches for a timeout with Maryland leading 24-22.

Straight out of the timeout, Dixon, left alone in the corner, canned a three to give the Terps some breathing room. Later, Mouton raced down the court ahead of the Kentucky defense, made a tricky catch of a full-court pass from Nicholas, and hit the bucket, plus a free throw. The Maryland run stood at 15-3, with their lead now up to seven points, 29-22. The streak could have continued. After Kentucky's Jules Camara got behind the Terps' defense in transition, Dixon ran down the seven-footer and stripped him clean as Camara was going up for the basket. Replays showed that Dixon had made a tremendous defensive play, but the trail referee, beaten down the court, did not have the proper angle and called a foul. Williams became incensed on the sideline, but he calmed down just as quickly. Still, a great play was lost, and the Terps' momentum was, for the moment anyway, stemmed.

The 'Cats came roaring back. Throughout the first half, Kentucky's big men had done an excellent job keeping the ball out of the post on the defensive end. Tubby Smith said of his interior players, "My guys may not be as big and strong, but they've got long arms," and it became increasingly clear that the long arms of the 7'0" Camara and 6'9" Marques Estill, and the Wildcats' athleticism, were frustrating the Terps, who could find only three shots for Baxter in the first half.

With Baxter on the bench for a breather, Kentucky made its move, cutting the Terps' lead to three points with three and a half minutes to go in the first half. Though Maryland was able to build the lead back up to six, 39-33, before going into the locker room at halftime, the Wildcats had forced Maryland out of its usual inside game. Meanwhile, point guard Steve Blake was struggling offensively, putting up hasty shots and going 0-3 from beyond the arc. Coming off the floor, Williams said, "We weren't patient enough, really. When we were patient and got to go inside, I thought we were okay. But we were really quick shooting the ball tonight," adding that in the second half, he wanted the Terrapins to "really grind it inside."

The only way for us to get open shots from the perimeter is to make them adjust to us going inside. We came out with the idea we definitely wanted to go inside. The great thing is if people tried to really stop Lonny, Juan would be open or Byron would be open or Steve would get some looks. We always went inside out. When you play against a great defensive team, it's like in baseball—good pitching will beat good hitting every time. The only way for us to get open shots was to drive it in or throw it in to Lonny. Our players bought into that.

Lonny knew he could play against big guys. The thing people don't know about him is that he is very quick. They see his size and don't understand his quickness. He made some really good plays, and it wasn't a fluke. It was something he could do because of quickness.

Chris Wilcox's key role was to get it in to Lonny. When Chris was open, we would get it in to him too. It was a pretty good combination to have two guys like that who could score inside for you. Chris's methods were to jump over you. Lonny was craftier than Chris had to be.

Williams sent the Terps out in the second half with one directive—pound the ball into the post. Do it early. Do it often. While Baxter had only three shots in the first half, his teammates found him several times in the opening possessions of the second half, forcing Kentucky to double-team him.

The offensive strategy did not pay immediate dividends, as Kentucky clamped down on defense and inched its way back from the halftime deficit. With four minutes gone in the second half, Prince hit a three-pointer to tie the game at 45. But midway through the second half, the Wildcats began to wither. Williams's strategy of repeatedly going inside to his big men, and Maryland's depth in the interior, were wearing down the 'Cats. Shots that had been contested earlier in the game found their way into the net easily, and the Terps began dominating rebounding on the offensive end. To try to turn things around, Tubby Smith inserted 237-pound freshman Chuck Hayes to help against the Maryland big men. But no one for Kentucky could stop Baxter, who with 3:30 left had already scored 14 second-half points in leading the Terps to match their biggest lead of the game, 70-63.

From there, the Maryland defense closed out the game. Beforehand, Dixon noted that "when we play defense, we win by big margins," and though they had not succeeded in putting the game away early, the Terps were playing excellent defense, especially against Prince, Kentucky's go-to guy and the Southeastern Conference Player of the Year. Inspired play from defensive stopper Byron Mouton, who at 6'6" gave up three inches to the Wildcats star, held Prince to 17 points on 6-16 shooting from the field. "Tayshaun is one of those guys, he's hard to guard by anyone," Smith said. "I thought Byron did a good job on him. A guy like Byron can get up under him, and he's quick enough to not let him get by."

Despite playing well enough to tie the game in the second half, the Wildcats could not regain the lead, and the experienced Maryland squad never seemed rattled by anything Kentucky threw at them. When Kentucky needed a run to close the gap at crunch time, the Terps instead stopped their opponents from scoring a field goal for four minutes. Meanwhile, Maryland's dead-eye foul shooting, going 21 for 24 from the line, cut off any opportunity for a last-minute Wildcat rally. "Everybody made their free throws," Tubby Smith said. "I mean *everybody.* I couldn't believe it."

In the final seconds, after being fouled to stop the clock, Dixon clapped his hands as he walked down the court. Along with the rest of the Terps, Dixon knew that victory was just moments away. But after the buzzer sounded on a 78-68 victory, there were no celebrations from the Maryland players, just handshakes and a quiet walk off the court. They departed the floor as confidently as they had entered—"a veteran team," Williams said. "We are not surprised when we win."

After the Kentucky game, Tubby Smith came up to me and said, 'You guys are good enough to win it.' That meant a lot, coming from him. I thought we had played a strong game. I worried about what it took out of us physically. Everybody was sore. It was a gut check for us to see how physical they were, and they have heart. A lot of times in a game like that, it comes down to a battle of wills. We had to hang tough.

Maryland's 78-68 victory was not overpowering, but all that counted at this time of year was finding a way, any way, to win. Blake had played an uncharacteristically poor game. Dixon was held to his lowest output of the tournament, 18 points. Michael Wilbon expressed one view from the Maryland side in *The Washington Post*, saying that perhaps one day soon it might be possible to "look at the box scores and videotapes from Friday night's game, which wasn't its best, wince and laugh." But the Terps had also shown tenacity against a rugged team. And they were moving on to the Elite Eight, without fellow No. 1 seeds Cincinnati and Duke, which had both been sent packing.

The Kentucky Wildcats, the basketball juggernaut refashioned as an underdog, had given Maryland all it could handle. And yet, the Terps had survived, won and advanced. While they were but one win away from a return to the Final Four, they were about to be put to their greatest test.

21 THE MOST DANGEROUS GAME

Standing between Gary Williams, his Terrapins and their second straight trip to the Final Four was one of the hottest and most explosive teams in the country, the University of Connecticut. The Huskies were led by co-Big East Player of the Year Caron Butler, a dynamic player averaging nearly 25 points per game in the tournament. Like Juan Dixon, Butler could take charge of a game and single-handedly determine its outcome. Under the leadership of Coach Jim Calhoun, UConn had won a dozen games in a row, including the Big East Championship, knocking off top 10 teams along the way. After a slow start, its young squad gained valuable experience and the Huskies ended the regular season brimming with confidence, sporting a 24-6 record and improving with every game they played.

With only one senior in a key role, the Huskies had grown dramatically since losing to Maryland 77-65 early in the season. In that game, Connecticut came back from an early 21-6 deficit to tie the game at halftime, but ultimately, the experience of the Terps proved the difference in a 77-65 win. One player who got a particularly rough lesson was freshman center Emeka Okafor. Maryland's wide-bodies pushed around the 6'9" 240-pound Okafor and got him into foul trouble early. While the freshman finished in double figures in rebounds, neither he nor the rest of the Huskies could stop Lonny Baxter, who scored a game-high 24 points and snared 10 rebounds. Okafor noted that the battle was only the fourth game of the Huskies' season and of his college career. "I was basically still a high school ballplayer back then. Now I'm a much smarter player," he said.

Okafor had gone on to break Patrick Ewing's freshman record for blocked shots and acquire the moniker "Emeka the Rejecta." So, too, did the Huskies' young backcourt tandem of freshman Ed Gordon and sophomore Taliek Brown develop throughout the year into bona fide perimeter threats that helped take defensive pressure off their go-to guy, Butler. The Huskies had become battle-tested by a tough Big East conference schedule and a run through their conference tournament, and once UConn reached the Elite Eight, Gary Williams knew that his Terps squad would have a difficult game ahead of them. During the tournament, "We shadowed each other, and he saw us handle that tough game against Hampton and we got by that, and then got by a very good N.C. State team," Calhoun said. "He watched us coming."

In the locker room, Connecticut's coach reminded his team of that December game and how far they had come. "We are as good a team as them," he said. "Maybe we couldn't beat them then, but we can now."

I think Connecticut might have been the best team we played. The teams get seeded based on how they played during the regular season. Connecticut was on a roll the last half of the year right into the NCAA tournament. They were very confident when they played us.

In terms of their recent basketball history, Jim Calhoun coached and won a lot of games at Connecticut, including a national champi-

onship. Connecticut had no weaknesses. I knew I had to coach a good game and our players had to play a good game in order for us to have any chance to win. People assumed we were going to get back to the Final Four. Well, we were the only team from last year's Final Four that even made it to the Elite Eight. That shows you how tough it is in college basketball.

Gary Williams's squad had grown in the months since December, too. In addition to the increasingly talented duo of Dixon and Baxter, the most notable change was the emergence of Chris Wilcox, who entered the starting lineup in the middle of the season and whose raw physical skills made him one of the most feared interior players in the ACC on both ends of the court. His emergence also deepened the Terps' unusually strong bench, with experienced big men Tajh Holden and Ryan Randle able to step in without diminishing the team's inside game.

After Gary Williams and the Terps walked off the court with their 78-68 win over Kentucky, the whispers of redemption among the Maryland fans had grown louder. They could taste another chance to get to the Final Four and a shot at the national championship that eluded them last year. Media outlets focused their eyes on the hard-driving Terrapins coach who, so went the popular line, was mellowing with age and success. But Williams was having none of it. When one reporter asked him whether the world was beginning to see his softer side, he replied, "Thank you," but said that while he might be more serene around his grandson, David, he was still the same intense coach on the sidelines. That intensity would be on full display against UConn.

The stage was set, and fans once again packed the Carrier Dome in Syracuse for the final game of the East Regionals on March 24. Their attendance was rewarded with an instant classic, a game with non-stop lead changes and ties that showcased the finest of NCAA tournament play. Both teams came out sizzling from the opening whistle. Wilcox tipped the ball back to Dixon and Maryland was off and running. Baxter hustled behind the UConn defense, caught a Dixon lob in mid-air and threw it down for the team's first two points.

The battle was quickly joined, as the Huskies came down on their first possession and took the lead on Taliek Brown's three-pointer from the top of the key. UConn and Maryland battled back and forth through the opening minutes of the first half, the Terps having success finding open looks for their shooters coming off of curl moves, while the Huskies controlled the pace, creating an up-and-down running game that muted the ability of Maryland's big men to bang away on the inside. UConn also sent a message that while they were a smaller team, they would cede no corner of the basketball court to the Terps, especially on the offensive glass. This statement was made emphatically before the first TV timeout when a succession of offensive rebounds led to a three-pointer from Connecticut's Tony Robertson to tie the game at 10.

The two teams traded baskets throughout the first half, neither one extending a lead beyond one or two possessions. From a 10-10 deadlock at the first timeout, they moved in tandem to a tie at 18 after the 12- minute mark, and then again at 24 slightly more than halfway through the first half. The game was not only closely contested but also was being played at an extremely high level. Both teams were hitting over 50 percent from the field. Each possession mattered and became infused with tension. The fans sensed they were witnessing a struggle that was bound to go down to the wire.

While the game was a seesaw affair, Maryland was doing an excellent job of containing the Huskies' best offensive and defensive threats, Butler and Okafor. Foul trouble helped. With under 10 minutes to play in the first half, the Terps found Wilcox open on the baseline. He received the pass just as Okafor slid over to defend the basket. The two 19-year- olds, one of the nation's premier dunkers and one of the nation's best shot blockers, went up together. Wilcox's legs brought him high above the rim where Okafor strained for the ball but could reach only the wrist. When the pair descended to earth and the referee blew his whistle, Okafor had picked up his second early foul and walked back to the bench with a look of thinly veiled disgust and a degree of disbelief.

Butler, too, picked up his second foul, sending him to the bench with only six points in the first half. Maryland's defensive stopper Byron Mouton had stymied Butler, denying him the ball in positions to score and forcing him to rely on second-chance opportunities and offensive rebounds to get his points. With its star on the bench, the UConn offense stalled, missing on five straight possessions and going without a field goal for four minutes. But the Huskies' reserves stayed tough on the defensive end, and the Terps could muster no greater than a four-point lead going into their final possession of the first 20 minutes. As the seconds ticked away, Maryland's set play broke down amidst the fierce UConn defense. Blake picked up his dribble out beyond the three-point line and looked frantically for a teammate. Finally, he passed to 6'10" Tajh Holden, who was standing far beyond the top of the key. Holden turned and fired a dead-on three-pointer before the buzzer, giving Maryland its largest lead of the game, 44-37, going into halftime.

Looking at their largest deficit of the tournament, the Huskies and their rejuvenated leader Butler came out firing in the second half, opening the scoring with a three-pointer that cut the Terps' lead to four. But they still could not find a way to stop Baxter inside. The Terps continued to feed the ball in to the post, and the Maryland senior gave the young UConn team an education in hard-nosed inside play. Okafor, who preferred defending with separation between himself and his man, was having problems with Baxter's close-quarters game, and he picked up a third foul early and again was relegated to the bench. A few minutes into the half, Baxter already had 18 points.

In response, Calhoun once again tried to push the tempo and rotated several big men in and out of the game, hoping that the increased pace and fresh bodies would eventually empty Baxter's tank. Meanwhile, Butler was beginning to heat up and take charge, getting to the free-throw line and finding his stroke from the field. After Butler hit a medium-range jumper over Holden, Gary Williams called a quick timeout, a bid to break Butler's flow. But after Maryland's next three possessions resulted in two turnovers and an offensive foul, suddenly the Terps had gone without a field goal for four minutes. And Calhoun's strategy of multiple substitutions and pushing the pace began taking its toll on Baxter, who was breathing heavily when he finally came to the bench to recharge his battery.

Meanwhile, Butler, determined to will his team to victory, hit another three-pointer that gave the lead back to Connecticut 56-54. Playing in a realm of his own, Butler was controlling the game, and there appeared to be little Maryland could do about it. Suddenly, the Terps' dream of returning to the Final Four was threatened by one man who was hitting from everywhere on the floor. In less than eight minutes, Butler torched the Terps' defense for 15 points. "We couldn't stop him," Gary Williams said.

The Terps' best offset to Butler was Juan Dixon, and the game pitting two talented teams against one another soon evolved into a singular battle between two of the finest players in college basketball. Refusing to cede anything, Maryland scratched back to a tie at 58, and coming out of a timeout, Dixon and Butler traded buckets on consecutive possessions. The Husky continued to grab offensive rebounds and get to the line against frazzled Terps defenders, but each time Dixon had an answer at the other end of the court.

Back and forth they dueled. With just over twelve minutes gone in the second half, Dixon took a pass from Blake and nailed a three from the left side to regain the lead, 70-69, the 20th lead change of the game. Later, with UConn running a four-on-two fast break off an Okafor blocked shot, Butler took a pass from Taliek Brown and hung in the air for what seemed an eternity to finish a double-pump reverse layup that put Connecticut on top by one.

With the Carrier Dome abuzz, Maryland trailed 75-72 with five minutes left to decide its fate. Understanding the importance of the next possession, Gary Williams called a timeout, and in the huddle, the Terps' on-court leader told his teammates one thing:

"Give me the ball, and I'll take you to Atlanta."

After trading free throws on their next possessions, Dixon took the ball at the top of the key, surveying his man and the moment. Having elevated his play so often in the clutch, Juan Dixon readied to lift his team again. Eyeing his defender, Taliek Brown, Dixon feigned as if he would not shoot, and then at the 3:49 mark with no dribble, he pulled the trigger on a three-pointer that ripped through the net and the hearts of the Connecticut faithful. With the game tied, Calhoun called a quick timeout. Normally all business on the court, Dixon headed back to the Maryland bench swinging his arms like a windmill, pumping his fists and shouting at his teammates:

"We are NOT losing this fucking game!"

"I never showed that much emotion in my life," Dixon later said. "There was no way this was going to be our last game."

That was a big shot. It was really big because of the consequences of what would have happened if he missed. If Juan had missed, we would have gone down five or six with not much time left. Any time a game like that winds down and gets in the last five minutes, we know we have to score, because we were having trouble stopping Butler, and they were going to score. If we don't score, we lose. What made Juan such a great player is that a lot of guys think about the consequences. He thinks about winning.

Now the pressure was on Connecticut to put the ball in the hoop. That game was tied versus us being down five or six. All of a sudden, Connecticut questioned whether they could stop us, and we had renewed energy to stop them. The shot when we were trailing was the toughest shot. It was a great shot by a great player.

Even after Dixon's big three-pointer gave Maryland the momentum, the game was still up for grabs. Fans at the Carrier Dome and on television had long since recognized that they were witnessing an exceptional game, with 25 lead changes and 21 ties. With the seconds ticking down in the final minute of play and Maryland up by three, Connecticut swarmed Dixon and the Terps called time out.

In the Maryland huddle, Williams outlined a play to get the ball to Dixon for a shot. But Blake, who had not scored in the game, realized that UConn would probably try to double-team the Terps' shooters, and if they were going to leave anyone alone on the play, it would be him. Blake turned to his coach and coolly said, "I'm going to take the shot if I'm open."

"Go ahead," said Williams.

The in-bounds pass came in to Blake. With 25.4 second left and Maryland leading 83-80, Blake dribbled up to a point just beyond the arc on the right side and found himself open, as the Huskies sought to deny Dixon the pass and prevent Maryland from getting the ball inside. Sure enough, Connecticut was leaving Blake alone at the three-point line.

Blake gave Okafor a shoulder fake to keep him honest on the inside, and then stopped, pump-faked and swished a three-pointer that drove the final nail into the UConn coffin. "That shot," Blake said. "was the biggest one I could hit for this team."

In that timeout, we ran the shot clock down to 14. We set up a play we usually run and are confident in, with Drew Nicholas and Juan in there, two good perimeter shooters. The other team knows we want Juan to shoot. And we have Lonny inside and they have to worry about him. And we put Tahj Holden up there setting a screen so that if Blake got double-teamed, he could hit Tahj.

Steve got the open look for a brief instant. He had not had a good offensive game, but he shoots better at the end of the game than he does at the beginning. Whether Steve has played poorly or not you want him on court in the clutch. It didn't surprise me when he took that shot. All good players think they can make the big one.

Steve never scored a lot of points for us. It was not unusual for him to have five points. With the shot clock running down, they took away the first option. We got a good look, we took a shot, and we had done it before. In that situation, we were not going to get a wide-open layup.

To get to the Final Four, we almost had to win this way. Those shots by Juan and Steve were as big as any in Maryland basketball history.

Dixon finished with 27 points, continuing his torrid NCAA scoring spree that was well above his season average. Baxter turned in a sterling performance of 29 points, including 7-12 shooting from the field and 15 for 18 from the free-throw line. He also added a game-high nine rebounds and hit the hook shot that put Maryland up for good at 81-79. For his outstanding play, Baxter was awarded his second consecutive NCAA Regional Tournament MVP award.

After the final buzzer sounded on a 90-82 Maryland win, Baxter, who had given his all for 40 minutes, was a picture of exhaustion, his body a spent frame. Meanwhile, Dixon sat on the scorer's table, his cheeks glistening with sweat and tears running from his eyes. He greeted Butler, the man who had scored 26 second-half points and single-handedly pushed the Terrapins to the brink of defeat. "You don't have to wait," Dixon told the sophomore, who, with his season ended, had to decide about a possible future in the NBA. "You're ready."

Dixon, too, had given it his all. "I probably have never experienced a game like this before," he said. "I've played in a lot of great games, but not with this much on the line."

Novak said Caron Butler played so well he was "scary," Dixon performed brilliantly, and Baxter seemed awesome. "The Connecticut game was one of the greatest basketball games I've ever seen," he said.

Back in the locker room after cutting down the nets, the elated and exhausted team that had prided itself on its businesslike run through the tournament cornered Williams and showered him with a bucket of ice water. The coach ended up so drenched that he attended the postgame press conference wearing reserve guard Andre Collins's warmup suit. And for a moment, as buckets and bottles were emptied onto the heads of players and coaches, Gary Williams looked like the same south Jersey kid who came to Maryland more than 30 years earlier to joke and compete and win with his guys.

22
JAMMING THE JAYHAWKS

Gary Williams sat beside his fellow Final Four coaches on the stage of the famed Fox Theatre in Atlanta. It was two nights before Maryland was scheduled to square off against the Kansas Jayhawks in one of two semifinal games, and the nation's college basketball coaches had gathered to honor them. Williams felt at home as he looked out at the sea of familiar faces. At the helm of the only team to return to the Final Four for the second straight year, Williams was enormously proud of his Maryland program. Yet he also knew that their job was not done and that it would take two more all-out efforts for the Terps to attain their goal of winning the NCAA Championship.

Serving as emcee for the evening, CBS sports anchor Jim Nantz asked the Maryland coach to project ahead. If you win the national championship on Monday, he asked, "who will come to mind, who will share that moment in your mind with you?"

Williams thought about the question and then answered in a quivering voice. "My daughter," he said. Before he could answer further, Williams got choked up. With tears in his eyes, Williams spoke of sharing the moment with Kristin and his grandson, David.

Players have breakthrough games and teams have breakthrough seasons. For Gary Williams, this was his breakthrough moment with the college coaching fraternity. "They had seen a hardened, intense guy in the past, and they had not seen a softer side to him before. Boy, they saw it that night," Nantz said. "I had people come up and tell me they never thought they would see that side of Gary Williams. People were pleased to see Gary up there emotional about it. People were pleased to see this had struck a chord with him. Everyone was touched by his comments about how much it meant to him to have his daughter and grandson at the Final Four. They walked out of the theater with their hearts and rooting interest committed to seeing Gary Williams finish off his quest for the title."

The night provided some levity too. Nantz noted that he had discovered a statistical quirk. If Maryland ultimately prevailed, the Terps would win the 2002 NCAA Championship in the school's 2002nd game. Kansas Coach Roy Williams, who had said that he wanted win the championship "about as badly as I want to breathe," threw up his hands and cried in mock exasperation, "We might as well not show up on Saturday!"

With a high-powered offense that was tops in the nation and a superb transition game, the Kansas Jayhawks deserved to be one of the tournament's No. 1 seeds. Averaging 91 points a game, Kansas had become the first team ever to go undefeated during the season in the Big 12. The team's starting lineup included one senior and three juniors, giving the Jayhawks an experienced crew to go up against the veteran Terps. Guards Kirk Hinrich, Jeff Boschee and Aaron Miles shot well from three-point range and ran the swiftest fast break in the nation. And with juniors Nick Collison and All-American Drew Gooden underneath, Kansas had one of the most formidable front lines in college basketball, a duo that could run the floor, rebound the basketball and put it in the hoop.

Gooden made headlines leading up to the game, saying he believed that he and Collison were the finest frontcourt in the country. The Maryland big men took that statement as a personal challenge and used it as further motivation for the game. "I wouldn't have said that," Wilcox warned.

For his part, Williams paid little attention to the pregame chatter reported in the media. Instead, he gave his team one day off at the beginning of the week to rest up after the Connecticut victory. Then he held a series of practices to prepare for the Jayhawks. When the Terps didn't seem focused or determined enough that week, Juan Dixon spoke up, and his teammates responded. Williams told CBS commentator Bonnie Bernstein that "Juan lost his shit during practice, and you could just see this week his higher level of confidence and that he believes we are destined to win it all."

Williams also sought to ensure that his team remained loose enough amid the heightened pressure that came with being in the Final Four spotlight. While in years past that would not have come naturally to him, it was an essential part of making a successful championship run. "Gary was joking around a lot with the players and more jovial than usual," said Bernstein. "It was a different approach. Gary is intense by nature, and for him to have the wherewithal to see all the pressure was a testament to how far he had come as a coach."

I really tried to keep things loose. We had the media circus first in College Park. I got asked the same question a couple hundred times, and the last player gets almost as much media as the first. Earl Badu did a lot of interviews that week. Our top eight guys except for Ryan Randle, who was at Allegheny Junior College last year, had all been there before. They knew the circus that Final Four week is.

I wanted the players to get enjoyment out of making the Final Four. Everybody on campus was telling them 'Congratulations. Great job.' The great thing about this team is that they were not going to let that get to them.

There's a tendency to think, 'Now that we're in the Final Four, we have to do things differently.' You can't do that. The best thing is to not change what you've done. Stick with whatever works. You prep for the Final Four like you prep for Kentucky in the Sweet Sixteen. Again, I trusted these guys, and that had a lot to do with their maturity level. There's no sense in changing the things you do. A lot of times, that's a sign of weakness to your players. I told them, 'We're good enough to win this game if we execute what we do.'

At practice, we only talked about Kansas. I never mentioned the teams playing the other semifinal game, Indiana and Oklahoma, because they didn't matter at that time. We felt Kansas was equal to us in many ways and thought this was going to be a great game. They were a very good team, and we were a very good team. They have great shooters, and they're capable of running and scoring a lot of points. We expected it to be a high-scoring game.

We knew they were one of the best teams in the country. I saw Kansas play against Oklahoma, and I knew how quick Oklahoma was because we had played them. Kansas looked quick against Oklahoma, so that told me how quick they really were.

Our team had an edge up front because of our depth and our size, so we wanted to go inside against Kansas. But that's our game anyway. We try to go inside in the beginning of every game. It gives Juan some room to operate, and maybe Blake can get some penetration. We didn't want to get into a three-point shooting game with Kansas.

Even though we were happy we'd made it back to the Final Four, there wasn't that same relaxation which was there the year before. We knew what lay ahead. I told our players that our motivation was to win the game. When you get to the national semifinals, you don't need any more motivation than that.

On their way into the Georgia Dome, thousands of fans and the players were greeted by a giant, lighted billboard which read,

"This is Garyland." Most people who packed the arena on the night of March 30 assumed that from this matchup of No. 1 seeds, which had jockeyed around the top of the national polls all year, would come the eventual national champion. The crowd had been properly warmed up, having seen the Indiana Hoosiers continue their Cinderella run through the tournament with an upset of Oklahoma. But that was, in the words of the late Jim Valvano, "the JV game." This was the main event.

On Saturday night, under the bright lights of an 80,000-seat arena, Maryland and Kansas, the two leading teams of the 2001-02 season, finally locked horns. Maryland unleashed the opening salvos, as Wilcox blocked Drew Gooden's first two shots, sending the All-American's second attempt into the row of seats at courtside. Those who had questioned how the 19-year-old would match up against the Jayhawks' best scoring threat got their answer quickly and emphatically. But the rest of the Terps were playing sloppy, and careless passing led to four turnovers in the first two and a half minutes. After an opening bucket from Nick Collison and two three-pointers from Kirk Hinrich, Maryland found itself in an eight- point hole.

A steamed Gary Williams, yelling and screaming at bench players and assistant coaches on the sidelines, called a timeout to settle his troops, and soon after, Mouton scored a transition bucket for the first Maryland points of the game. But the Terps were still playing out of sorts, and three minutes into the game, Dixon had still not even touched the ball. Meanwhile, the Kansas fast break and long-range sharpshooters were playing their game. After a Dixon miss on his first touch of the game, the Jayhawks came out running. Point guard Aaron Miles received a quick outlet from Gooden and found Collison, who was fouled on the shot after beating the Maryland defense down the floor. Shortly after, Jeff Boschee stepped up and hit Kansas's third three-pointer.

As both teams went to their respective benches for a TV timeout, Gary Williams was furious. This was not Maryland basketball he was watching. Instead of looking razor-sharp, his team looked ragged. Just four minutes into the game, Kansas led 13-2. Williams's displeasure was clear and audible. "You guys aren't ready to play!" he shouted. "How can you not be ready to play? This is what you dreamed about. This is why you're here."

The team had to play with aggressiveness, Williams said, before turning to Wilcox and telling the sophomore, "I want you to get every single ball."

Williams calmed himself and his players before the end of the timeout. "We've been here before," he reminded them. "We're used to this. Let's go out and do what we're supposed to do."

In the stands, the Maryland faithful were disconsolate. One year after blowing the biggest lead in Final Four history, their team was looking at the prospect of having its doors blown off within the first five minutes. As the sounds of "Rock, Chalk, Jayhawk!" echoed and rolled through the Georgia Dome, Terps fans began to ask themselves if they could reconcile another near miss, and the prospect of a celebrated senior class leaving without reaching the pinnacle of college basketball.

Over on the Kansas bench, Roy Williams cautioned his team. "This means nothing," he said. Maryland was too good, too experienced, too focused, to fold in the face of an early run.

Nobody was happy being down 13-2. We're better than that. That's not us. We were a little tight, so I tried to shock them by yelling at them a little bit. It looked bad, but there were still 36 minutes left in the game. I reminded our guys that we didn't come here to lose this game. The biggest thing I told the team was, 'All we need to do is play the way we played to get here.'

We always said the first four minutes never decided any game. Our guys had been around, so it was nothing they hadn't seen. We'd been down at Wake Forest at halftime and won. We'd been down by nine at Virginia with three minutes left and won. We knew we were going to come back. We're talking about a team that's been through everything. We were in a situation last February when people thought we weren't going to make the NCAA's. And this year, you look at who we lost to: just Duke, Oklahoma, Arizona and N.C. State—those are four pretty good basketball teams. That's it. Nobody else got us. We weren't going to get down and out in this game.

Both coaches were right. Maryland was unfazed by the Jayhawks' quick start, and coming out of the TV timeout, the Terps took advantage of a defensive breakdown on the in-bounds pass to slip the ball underneath to Wilcox for a quick dunk. Dixon followed up with two buckets of his own, one from beyond the arc. Just as quickly as they had found themselves down, Maryland stormed back with an 8-2 run of its own, needing only four minutes to cut the Kansas lead in half. During this run, Wilcox, spurred on by assistant coach Jimmy Patsos to make an impact by blocking a couple of shots early, turned away a third attempt by Gooden, who was now going up much more tentatively against the Maryland shot-blocker. "He intimidated us for a few minutes," Roy Williams said. "There's no question Chris Wilcox blocking the shots changed our makeup and our focus on the inside play. And we got more hesitant playing than at any time all year. ...It would be coach-speak if I said anything else."

Chris had a couple of blocks on Gooden, and I'm sure Gooden wasn't used to having his shot blocked. Those plays were bigger than the points Kansas didn't score. If somebody blocks Lonny's shot against us, our guys go 'Wow. Not many people can do that.' Chris played well in the NCAA Tournament, and by the time he played Kansas, he was battle-tested. The thing I like about Chris is that he welcomes the added pressure of big games. He's a guy on the court who can make great plays, plays that mean more than that situation. He sent the message that it's going to be hard to score inside. We're always looking for that mental edge, and Chris was great at giving us that energy play. A lot of times people think that's just a dunk, that's a hot dog move. But that's a big play for us. It says, 'Here we come,' and you want to send that message to the other team as early as possible.

Chris was a big-game player. I don't think there was any doubt that he played better in big games. With Chris, I tried to teach him that every game was important. If you're a guy with his ability, you have to play big every time out. Part of a player's development is to do what you do best on a consistent basis.

What did concern Williams was losing Baxter to foul trouble early, as the big senior picked up two fouls in the first three minutes of the game. Williams had enormous confidence in his bench, but Baxter had been the big man in the paint offensively in recent games. "That was scary," Williams said. "Lonny was the constant." Those early fouls forced Baxter to languish on the bench for the rest of the first half.

In Baxter's stead, Williams called on Tahj Holden and Ryan Randle. Throughout the year, the coach had relied on his front-line bench players to wear opponents down on the inside or to put out fires just like this one. Now, in the biggest game of the season, on the biggest stage, the duo of Holden and Randle would be put to its biggest test and respond magnificently.

With rugged play inside, Maryland refused to yield control of the paint to the Jayhawks. And Juan Dixon's 10 quick points, which brought the Terps back from their early deficit, were helped by solid screens set by Holden. With Baxter on the bench, Maryland on one defensive possession blocked or altered three Kansas shots, making it clear that points on the inside would be hard to come by. With just under eight minutes left in the first half, after two free throws by Ryan Randle, the gap was down to two, 25-23.

Our players were really good at playing with whoever they were on the court with. If Ryan was on the court because of someone being in foul trouble, the guys respected Ryan and knew they could win with him. That comes from him working hard in practice. He knew that he didn't have to prove anything to anyone. At the start of the year, no one thought Ryan could play with Collison and Gooden. But he worked hard all year, and by Final Four week, the guys could see how well he was playing.

Coming out of the TV timeout, Dixon took charge. Maryland went into a trapping zone defense, and after Kansas missed a shot, Dixon grabbed the tipped rebound, brought the ball across half-court, and when no one picked him up, stopped and popped a three-pointer from the right side, giving the Terps their first lead of the game, 26-25.

Moments later, Dixon anticipated a reverse dribble from Collison at the foul line and made his second steal of the night, which led to another two points. Receiving a pass for an open look at a three-pointer in the corner, Dixon saw Boschee lunging wildly at him and very slightly altered his shot so that Boschee would hit his elbow for a three-shot foul. It was a delicate move from a supremely intelligent ballplayer. But other parts of his game were about as subtle as a dagger, like the long-range shots Dixon was hitting over the Kansas zone. With two minutes to play in the half, Dixon had already scored 19 points, and Kansas players were left wondering how to stop the Maryland ace.

Buoyed by Dixon, the Terps began shooting better from the field, from the foul line, and from beyond the arc. And despite having Baxter marooned on the bench with zero points and two fouls, Maryland controlled the paint and shut down the Jayhawks' All-American, Gooden. Heading into halftime, Maryland had its biggest lead of the game, 44-37.

We felt we played well enough to have the lead. I told the team we couldn't relax. We had the momentum going our way. Sometimes I hate to see halftime come, because I don't want that break. I emphasized how important it was to get off to a great start in the second half. I said, 'Don't give them that confidence. If we stay consistent and play like we did at the end of the half, we're going to win.'

The Terps came out strong in the second half, as Blake found Wilcox on the baseline for a monster dunk to open the scoring. But the Jayhawks, like Maryland, were a talented, experienced and well-coached group, and with the halftime break, they settled down and went back to the basics of what had gotten them to the Final Four. Using their quickness to stymie the Terps defenders, Roy Williams's crew inched their way back from the nine-point deficit. They took advantage of a Maryland defensive breakdown to lob an in-bounds pass to Hinrich, who tipped it in for an easy score and then fed Boschee, who dialed long distance on a three ball to cut the Terps' lead to 52-48 going into a TV timeout.

During this run, the Jayhawks had been aggressive offensively, and they were rewarded when Baxter and Blake each drew their third foul early in the half. For Blake, who had struggled in the game, it was time to sit and rest. But Baxter had played only a handful of minutes and scored just two points. He had had no time to get himself into the flow of the game. Williams thought, "I might as well gamble a little bit," and rather than protecting Baxter for the stretch run, the coach decided to leave him in the game.

After sloppy play from both teams dominated the next few minutes, the Terps went on a run. It began with Wilcox rising above two Kansas big men to tip in a missed shot from Blake. On the next possession, Blake lobbed a pass over a fronting Collison and in to Baxter for an easy layup and a 60-52 lead. Roy Williams, sensing a momentum shift, called a quick timeout. But out of the timeout, Dixon came off a screen to the foul line and hit an open jumper. Then, on the next possession, Maryland ran a fast break that resulted in Gooden's fourth foul. Shortly thereafter, Hinrich picked up his fourth as well. With just eight minutes left in the game, everything was working for the Terps. Holden was hitting off-balance shots and getting tip-ins, and Mouton, too, began getting in the action, finding easy shots off back-door cuts.

Kansas grew disheartened as Maryland extended its lead with each passing minute. With less than seven minutes left in the game, Blake fed Dixon in the corner for a three-pointer. The Terps' leader nailed the shot and ran back down the court, pointing at his brother Phil in the stands. Against a talented Kansas team, Maryland was up by 20 points, 83-63. The Jayhawks bench was silent, their spirits sunk. Some Kansas fans began heading for the exits.

But for Maryland fans, memories of last year's losses to Duke were too fresh. They knew all too well what it was like to be up by 20 in the biggest game of the year and lose. And so, as Kansas partisans continued heading for the streets of Atlanta, Maryland fans stayed in their seats.

What happened in the last six-plus minutes of the game could have been the most miraculous comeback—or disastrous collapse—in NCAA tournament history. The Terps, up by 20 points and having dominated Kansas for nearly the entire game, began to play sloppy, disorganized, frantic basketball. They shot long three-pointers without running down the shot clock. They committed foul after foul, stopping the clock and sending Kansas to the free-throw line to chip away at the lead. They missed crucial free throws, even though their overall percentage from the line was second best in NCAA Tournament history to that point. Meanwhile, the Jayhawks now seemed to be catching all the breaks they had not been getting for most of the game. At one point during their run, Roy Williams said, "We took one shot and I stood up to scream, 'No!' and it goes in. ...I was dumb enough to feel we were going to win." The Terps had given Kansas, a team that had lost nearly all faith in its ability to win the game, a reason to believe.

From being down by 20, the Jayhawks cut Maryland's lead to eight points with 3:10 left. Some of the Kansas fans who were on their way out turned around and went back to their seats. A little over a minute later, after another three-pointer from Boschee on the left side, the lead was just five, 87-82. Kansas has gone on a 19-4 run, and nervous Terps fans, including those in Dixon's cheering section, began to think back on the previous year's collapse against Duke. As he watched the game unfolding, Mark Smith thought to himself, "If we lose this game to Kansas, I'm going to hide all my Maryland stuff and walk out saying, 'Go Indiana!'" After seeing their Terps in the finals, they were suddenly watching a two-possession game that was far from over. With 1:57 on the clock, a sweating Gary Williams called time out.

We let up. We lost our concentration and we made a couple of stupid plays. We should have known that it was not over, but we let them back in it. Basketball is about ebb and flow. We were down 13-2, and we went from there to go up by 20. But we're not 20 points better than Kansas. From being down 13-2 to going up by 20, we played as well as we had all year. But any time we're playing a good team, and they feel a momentum change, they jump on it.

Kansas was going to keep playing. We helped them by taking quick shots and by fouling, which stopped the clock. We allowed them to score with the clock off. So in that way, we certainly helped Kansas's cause. I was upset because we didn't do that all year. I can't remember playing that poorly with a lead all year. That really bothered me. We were under the gun all year, and then we got to this point and relaxed. We tried to get away with it, and we paid for it.

After the timeout, Maryland tried another quick three-pointer and missed. Now the outcome was really in doubt. If Kansas came down and nailed a three-pointer, it would cut the lead to just two points. But freshman point guard Aaron Miles picked up his dribble, took an extra step, and was called for traveling. For the last five minutes, nearly everything that could have gone right for Kansas did. Finally, it seemed that fortune had turned its back on the Jayhawks. However, the fact remained that Maryland had done very little right in this same period, and they needed someone to step up and make a big play to squash the Jayhawks' hopes once and for all.

Juan Dixon had hit the big shot against Connecticut that made the difference in the clutch. And once again, the Terps turned to their leader. After running some time off the clock, they found Dixon on the left side. He drove hard on the baseline and then quickly pulled up and hit a soft baby jumper, putting Maryland up by eight and making it a three-possession game.

Like a vampire in a horror movie, the Kansas Jayhawks had risen from the dead to give Maryland one last scare. It took the Terps' hero, Dixon, to drive the final stake into the Jayhawks' hearts. Kansas made valiant last-ditch efforts to get back into the game, but Maryland, as it had been all year, was flawless from the free-throw line when it counted. True to form, the Terps didn't miss a free throw in the last minute of the game. By the time Gooden was called for a technical foul for calling a timeout that Kansas did not have, it was all over. Maryland would move on, beating the powerhouse of the Big 12, 97-88.

After scoring 29 points against Connecticut and being chosen as MVP of the East Region, Baxter was a non-factor in the Kansas game, playing only 14 of 40 minutes. But Holden and Randle came off the bench to join Chris Wilcox in dominating the Jayhawks' front line. Once again, Dixon was the king of the court, playing his best basketball in Maryland's biggest game and walking out of the Georgia Dome with a career-high 33 points.

In thirteen years, Gary Williams had taken his alma mater out of the ashes and onto center stage where millions around the world would be watching on Monday night. Asked about the Kansas comeback at the end of the game and his team's seeming inability to play with a big lead, the coach shrugged. "It doesn't matter," he said. "When that buzzer went off, it was a great feeling. That meant we were playing in the championship."

As he walked off the court, Juan Dixon wore a steely glare. There was no celebrating in the Maryland locker room. Whether focused on the next game or exhausted by the last, Dixon and the Terps quietly went about their postgame interviews and headed back to their hotel for a bite to eat and a much needed night of rest. For Gary Williams and the Maryland coaching staff, however, there was work to be done. They had less than 48 hours to get themselves and the Terps ready for the Indiana Hoosiers and the most important game in Maryland basketball history.

23 ONE DAY AWAY

Though Gary Williams was eager to dive into preparations for the Indiana Hoosiers immediately, media interviews delayed his return to the hotel after the Kansas game. "I feel like I've wasted two hours when I've could have been looking at film," he said. Around 1:00 a.m., Williams had dinner with Kristin, sharing a moment's quiet with his daughter amidst a frenetic weekend. Afterward, Williams returned to his room alone to study a tape of Indiana defeating Oklahoma "That game really surprised us," he said, "because we played Oklahoma and we knew how good they were." But Indiana was for real; in getting to the Final Four, they had toppled Duke, and in the first national semifinal game, Oklahoma had become the latest victim of the Hoosiers' hot shooting and stifling defense.

In college basketball, it is not always the two best teams that meet in the NCAA championship game, but the two teams that are playing best in March. By that measure, the Hoosiers took a back seat to no one. With a record of 20-11 going into the tournament, the fifth-seeded Hoosiers had exceeded everyone's expectations. Yet few expected the Hoosiers to continue their run with an upset of the Terps, and before the game, Coach Mike Davis was telling any reporter who would listen that his goal in the championship game was "just not to lose by 30."

The key matchup in the game was Indiana's Dane Fife against Juan Dixon. Fife, the Big Ten defensive player of the year, had shut down Duke's Jason Williams, Kent State's Trevor Huffman, and Oklahoma's Hollis Price. If he could do a similar job against the Terps' hottest player, Maryland could find itself in trouble.

The Hoosiers were led by Big Ten Player of the Year Jared Jeffries, a 6'10" rail-thin sophomore who played well down low, shot from all over the court, hit the boards hard and blocked shots. In addition to Jeffries, Williams believed all the Hoosier big men could handle the ball and shoot like guards. Indiana's floor general, junior Tom Coverdale, continued playing and scoring despite a severely sprained ankle.

Around 3:00 am, I got together with my assistant coaches to talk about Indiana's tendencies. We had to make sure our players understood that Indiana was a good team on a roll. They had confidence that they could beat anybody. We agreed it was important to stop them on the perimeter defensively. We were more physical inside. We felt it was to our advantage to go inside on offense and try to get them into foul trouble. We knew Indiana played well on defense and it wouldn't be easy to score against them.

Indiana was the first surprise team we played. They had upset Duke and we felt it was an upset when they beat Oklahoma. They had shot over 50 percent from three-point range, so we knew we had to take away their three-point shot. They had a great inside player in Jared Jeffries, but we thought even he'd wind up taking a lot of perimeter jump shots. They would dribble-penetrate and then kick it out for the three. We had to stay in front of the dribbler. Unlike most teams, against Indiana, we had to shut them down outside, not inside.

In the Final Four, there is no time to enjoy the game you just won. By the time I was into the interviews about beating Kansas, I was already thinking about what we needed to do to get ready for the cham-

pionship game. My assistants had done a good job getting ready for Indiana, but I felt like I didn't have enough time. There was a sense of desperation there. Normally after a regular season game, I try to get a couple of hours of sleep before coming back into school. But in this situation, I knew I had to go long and hard. The big thing was to have everything ready by the time we practiced on Sunday. It was frantic, but I couldn't let the players know that.

Williams stayed awake most of the night, studying the dossier on Indiana prepared for him by assistant coaches Jimmy Patsos and Matt Kovarik. The team breakfast was scheduled for 10:30 a.m., but Williams awoke from a brief doze around 6:30 a.m. His grandson David was in high spirits that morning, singing his ABCs for anyone who would listen. "He mastered that at an early age," Williams said. After breakfast, Williams gathered his coaches to make final preparations for the Terps' last practice. After the Kansas game, he told the Terps, "We are going to practice for one hour, and I need your brain at practice." They showed the players 20 minutes of tape on Indiana, a collection of highlights illustrating the team's offensive and defensive tendencies. Then, in a near-empty Georgia Dome, Maryland did some light stretching, went through a shootaround, and did a short walk-through of its game plan.

I didn't overanalyze anything. I told our players 'Whatever we did that got us here, we have to do the same thing for one more game.' We were not going to make big changes. After watching the tape, we emphasized to the team that knowing what Indiana does is not as important as executing and playing our best.

I emphasized the need to take away their three-point shooting, take the game inside, and try to run and press them a little bit. We needed to make Jeffries cover us, and hopefully get him into foul trouble, by getting the ball inside to Chris and Lonny. I also talked about making the extra pass to find the open man on the perimeter after their guards collapsed to help out on defense.

After one hour, practice was over and done. Williams was guarding against overburdening his players. The brief practice sent a clear message to his team: No last-minute cramming is necessary. We have earned the right to be here, and we are ready.

Meanwhile, the excitement surrounding the Final Four mounted. There was CBS, the only media outlet allowed inside the Georgia Dome to watch practice, requesting interviews for its hour-long *Final Two Show*. Then there were the national and international media jockeying for time, sportswriters, culture reporters, broadcasters looking for the "human interest" angle, and all the local beat reporters who had followed the Terps since Midnight Madness. Alumni and fans wanted to have a word with the players on the eve of the championship game, too. "The players are like rock stars for the weekend," Williams said.

The coach passed his free time in his hotel room with his daughter Kristin and grandson David. "He liked my room because it faced out over the airport and you could see the runways," Williams said. "I had him standing on my desk to look out the window and watch the planes. You could see them coming in and taking off. It was pretty neat, and he liked it. I also had a marker board set up with pages that flip over to diagram plays. He was drawing airplanes on it." Williams sat with them during dinner and then went back to his room to watch more game film on the Hoosiers.

The Final Four mania was not new to the Terps, who had been to the championship weekend the prior year. But for Indiana, which did not have a player or coach with Final Four experience on its roster, the sheer scale of the NCAA championship was incomprehensible. Even the process of doling out the team's complement of game tickets risked becoming a distraction. "You have friends, and they think you can make up a ticket for them," Indiana coach Mike Davis said, as he struggled to keep up with all the messages on his voicemail. "My mailbox was full, and I'd clear it. The next hour, it's full again. So I'd clear it, and the next hour, full again. Everybody's calling you, calling assistant coaches, players, family members. Everybody wants to see the game."

On Sunday, Williams was overcome with a sense of calm. "I was very relaxed," he said. "I enjoyed Sunday because we didn't play. I enjoyed the way the fans were all fired up about the championship game. I could see the players were happy. It was a good feeling to still be playing. It was the first time I had ever been playing in April. That is where I wanted to be."

I didn't sleep much Sunday night. I woke up, watched a little tape. I had asked my daughter to call me when they were up for breakfast. I had breakfast with them and got a chance to see my grandson. That took up some time, which I was looking to do.

After the team got up and ate, we walked through some reminders with the team around noon. That was just to get them thinking about the game. We didn't go over and shoot that day. Instead, we put down a makeshift free-throw lane in a banquet room and walked through plays. We went over some of Indiana's tendencies one more time. And then, I just read and did things to pass the time.

Williams talked with Bonnie Bernstein on the morning of the game, and the two Maryland alums reflected on his early coaching days at the school, when Williams was sure that he wouldn't last five years in the job. Bernstein was struck by the relative serenity in the high-strung coach. "He gets nervous before games usually, but that morning by his tone of voice on the phone, he felt his time had come and his team's time had come."

He wasn't going to be rushed, either, as game time drew near. Williams, who has a reputation for being punctual, continued playing in the hotel room with his grandson. Kristin couldn't believe it. She knew the team bus was leaving at 6:30 p.m., that her dad typically was ready 15 minutes early, and that it was already 6:29 p.m. "You are going to be late," Kristin told her dad.

"I could not believe this man was at the pinnacle of his career, and he was more relaxed than I had ever seen him. My son asked him to jump on the bed, and he started playing with trains on the floor with him instead."

The Terps and their coach reached the Georgia Dome two hours before game time, went through their final preparations, and adjourned to their locker room. Championship hype and hysteria grew outside, but the mood amongst Maryland players and coaches behind closed doors was quiet and determined. For the last 48 hours, Gary Williams had told his players that they were just playing "the next game." But that was a half-truth, and everyone knew it. The Terps had set the national championship as their goal ever since the team's devastating Final Four loss to Duke the previous year. "It was pretty intense in the locker room," senior guard Earl Badu said. "Juan was really emotional. He was crying. He couldn't even get out clear sentences. The only coherent thing he said was, 'Help me win the game. We've got to find a way to win. Just help me win the game.'"

Across the way, there was little chatter in the Indiana locker room, as the Hoosiers prepared for the game of their lives. Players had gone through their regular game-day routines, many born out of superstitions that had helped them through their improbable run. Tom Coverdale had finished playing Snake, a video game that was programmed onto Dane Fife's cell phone, and was sitting with the trainers, getting last-minute therapy for his injured ankle. Fife and another Hoosier, Donald Perry, traded game shorts, because Perry "likes to wear the shorts past the knees," Fife said, "and I like 'em short and snug."

Fife knew that putting the clamps on Juan Dixon was his responsibility and the key to an Indiana victory. "I was going to give it 100 percent," he said, adding that while he and his teammates had seen Duke as "holy men," they believed they could take the Terps. "We didn't fear Maryland at all," he said. "We gave Maryland respect, but not too much respect. We came out from the get-go to beat Maryland."

Tucked into the Terps' section were well over 20 members of the Dixon family, aunts, uncles, cousins and grandparents all making the trip to Atlanta to see Juan's final college game. They would have been there earlier, but Aunt Janice was so nervous before the game that she told the rest of the family she was going to watch on TV. "She said, 'Well, I'll just stay here and give my ticket up,'" Sheila Dixon recalled. "I said, 'No, you're not! You're going!'"

Nothing could have kept Phil Dixon out of the arena. "This was what we dreamed about," he said. "You have memories of Chris Webber calling timeout in the championship game, Indiana playing against Syracuse, Georgetown losing to Villanova. Just seeing my brother being a part of that history is a great feeling."

With their floor general Coverdale hobbled and still in the trainer's room, the underdog Hoosiers began to feel the pressure of the spotlight. Though the team went into the game with nothing to lose, as individuals, they were losing their composure. Some of the younger Hoosiers, especially, were shaking and looked frightened.

The teams finished warmups, the coaches did their final pregame TV interviews and the players went through the introductions of the starting lineups. Before tipping off, however, the two teams and the Georgia Dome crowd watched in silent reverence as members of the Port Authority Police Department and the Atlanta Police Department carried a torn and tattered American flag onto the court for the national anthem. The flag, which flew over the World Trade Center on September 11 and had been recovered from the wreckage battered but not destroyed, was a stark reminder of the joy and privilege of sport and of the new world in which this game was being played.

Looking at his teammate Kyle Hornsby, who was known to get nervous before games, Fife leaned over during the national anthem and told him the same thing he had said in every tournament game they had played: "There's probably a million people in the Afghan hills that don't give a damn about this game."

It was also true, as Gary Williams liked to say, that competing in this game was the most important thing they were doing right now. The Maryland program had waited 2,002 games for the chance to play for its first national championship. Hoosier fans, who pass down the tradition of Indiana basketball from generation to generation, were no less determined to see their upstart 11 return their team to glory. Players, coaches, students, alumni, universities, states, media—the weight of dreams and expectations pressed down on the combatants, leaving them feeling like a tightly wound spring. The referee brought Chris Wilcox and Jared Jeffries together at center court to begin the game.

Indiana won the tip.

24

MIGHTY MARYLAND

I told them they were the best team and they deserved to win. I told them we worked hard enough all year that we earned the right to win the game. Guys think they should be great players or teams think they should be great. But unless you're willing to work in July when it is hot, you will never be great. Our guys had a consistent spring, summer and fall in terms of their work ethic. Some teams don't earn that right to be a great team. This one did. I told them, 'Just win the game.'

In the opening minutes of the NCAA championship game, both teams played frantically, throwing the ball away, failing to make the extra pass and missing open shots. The Terps, on orders from Williams to push the ball up the floor, committed unforced errors. An ill-advised pass from Steve Blake was picked off by Indiana's Tom Coverdale. The injured Hoosier, in turn, clanked a wide-open shot of his own off the rim. While Maryland's offense struggled to get into a rhythm, the Hoosiers failed to convert on the other end.

Just over two minutes into the game, Coverdale, playing on a bad ankle, stole the ball for the third time and got it to Jarrod Odle, who botched an easy layup. Maryland quickly responded by sending a pass up to Baxter, which slipped straight through the big man's hands. Fans on both sides could only look on with bemusement at their jittery teams, while CBS announcer Jim Nantz summed up what those at the Georgia Dome and on television were witnessing: "Nerves all over the place, fully exposed."

Indiana finally settled down around three minutes into the game, as Coverdale drove inside and kicked the ball out to Fife on the right side for a three-pointer to cut the early Maryland lead to 6-5. But on the next possession, the Terps responded by getting their leader, Juan Dixon, into the game and on the board.

Dixon caught Fife in a screen from Chris Wilcox and found space in the left corner for a three-pointer of his own. The shot sparked a quick run from Dixon that sent Maryland out to a commanding early lead. After another Indiana miss, Blake found Dixon beyond the arc. Maryland's tournament star pump-faked Fife, bringing the All-Conference defender off his feet, and with one dribble, stepped inside the line and nailed a long two-pointer. The decision to take an open two over a contested three was a solid one from the fifth-year senior, and his execution, as it had been throughout the tourney, was flawless. His coast-to-coast bucket off a Baxter block after the first TV timeout sent further notice to the Hoosiers and the crowd that Dixon was not only into the flow of the game, he was ready to dictate that flow.

All the while, Dixon comported himself with the bearing of a trained assassin. "He didn't talk all that much on the court," said Fife. "I tried to strike up a conversation with him on the floor, but he wasn't having it. He was out there to win. More than any other guy out there—certainly on his team—he was out there to win it in the worst way."

Despite Dixon's seven quick points, Maryland was unable to get its offense clicking, scoring only 17 points in the first eight minutes. But Indiana's continuing inability to hit open shots helped

Maryland stay in front early. With 12:03 left in the first half and Maryland leading 17-8, the Hoosiers suffered a serious blow when their star sophomore and leading scorer, Jared Jeffries, was called for his second foul of the game. Davis quickly removed Jeffries, protecting his best player for the second half. Suddenly, Maryland found itself up by nine points to a team that could not seem to put the ball in the basket and now had only one starter, Fife, in the game. This presented an opportunity for the Terps to take charge.

Dixon was the first to launch an attack against the under-manned foe. The Maryland senior, who made ACC history by leading his team in scoring and steals, eyed the passing lanes, readying himself for an opportunity. When A.J. Moye threw a lazy, telegraphed pass, Dixon jumped in, intercepted the ball, and took it to the hoop, giving the Terps their first double-digit lead.

But Indiana, showing the kind of toughness that brought it to the tournament final, refused to quit. The Hoosiers' hobbled court general, Coverdale, nearly single-handedly broke his team out of its offensive slump. Grabbing a rebound tipped out to the arc, he swished a three-pointer from beyond to cut the lead to 19-11. Then, after a baseline jumper from Dixon, Coverdale hit another three-pointer from the left side. With 7:56 left in the first half, some four minutes after Jeffries was taken out of the game, Maryland, unable to add to its lead, was up 25-16.

For most of the first half, sloppy play dominated. Coming out of the next timeout, neither Maryland nor Indiana scored for three minutes. The style played right into the Hoosiers' hands. Davis said, "We wanted to make it as ugly as possible. We knew we couldn't go out and have a clean game against them. It wouldn't have been close." For the Terps, who had gone into the championship game looking to push the tempo, get the ball inside and force their opponent into a high-scoring battle, it created real problems. The longer they allowed the Hoosiers to stay in the game, the more they left themselves vulnerable.

After Indiana's Kyle Hornsby ended his team's scoreless streak with a jumper one step inside the arc, the Terps were forced to call a timeout, because no one stayed back to take the in-bounds pass from Nicholas. Maryland was up by seven but seemed in disarray. Williams lambasted his players for their lackluster play and lack of concentration. Coming out of the timeout, their scoreless streak extended to over six minutes. Baxter was being hounded inside and was forced to take off-balance shots near the basket. Meanwhile, Williams searched for a backcourt combination that would bolster the Terps as Blake struggled and was kept on the bench for much of this stretch.

They kept everybody in the paint on defense and dared us to shoot from outside. But they also got a hand up when we did. They didn't try to do anything spectacular like steal the ball or block shots. They tried to make every shot we took a tough shot. They play great position defense, looking to take charges, giving good help and getting a hand up on the shooter. The great thing about the game is that there are a lot of ways to get it done. For Indiana, that was the best way for them to play, and they executed and maximized the capabilities of each player they had.

While the Hoosiers' defense stymied the Terps, Indiana continued having trouble shooting. During the same stretch when Maryland was shut out completely on the offensive end, Indiana could muster only two points of its own. And so, when Wilcox finally broke his team's 6:10 scoreless streak with just under three minutes left in the half, he also brought the Terps' lead back to nine points, 27-18, where it had been hovering for nearly the last 10 minutes. "We held them to the right amount of points, but we just couldn't score," Indiana's Fife said. "We just couldn't put the ball in the hole."

After cutting the Terps' lead to eight, 31-23, Indiana held the ball for the last shot of the first half. With 10 seconds left, Newton handed off to Coverdale. The Hoosiers' point guard dribbled around the perimeter, past a Newton pick, put the ball behind his back, cut into the lane and after losing his defender Blake, leaned to his right and banked home a shot off the glass just as the buzzer sounded. The bull's-eye was one final blow to a Maryland team that, despite being up 31-25 at halftime, had been thoroughly frustrated by the Hoosiers. Going into the locker room, Williams summed up his team's first half. "We didn't run the offense. We were sloppy with the ball. We're not playing great right now."

I was upset at halftime because they made a run at the end of the first half. That allowed them to make a run in the second half. We had them on the ropes in the first half and let up. They went into halftime thinking they could win. We figured it was going to be tough in the second half, but we thought we would play better offensively.

I was talking to a veteran team at halftime. I said. 'They have confidence now. We have to play great at the start of second half. Maybe we can take that confidence away from them.' I told them to relax. I said, 'Maybe we are trying too hard on offense.' In big games, you can be as intense on defense as you want to be, but on offense, you have to be in the flow, and you have to have a certain relaxation to get that flow.

We always emphasize getting the ball inside to start the second half. It's the same thing we do every game. It was hard to go inside the way Indiana played. They kept everybody packed in there pretty tight. I thought we were going to win the game. I always worry, but I thought we were the best team and thought there would come a time when we would break the game open.

While Maryland stressed the importance of regaining the momentum, the mood in the other locker room was all smiles. The Hoosiers, Davis believed, had played, "the worst we can possibly play," yet they were only down by six points. "I felt really good going into halftime," Davis said. "We talked about trying to make plays offensively, maintain our composure."

Davis was not the only one in the Indiana locker room who felt that the Georgia Dome was about to witness another Hoosier upset. After Dixon opened the game with 11 points in the first 10 minutes, Fife had held Maryland's all-time leading scorer without a single shot for the rest of the half. "I think I had Juan figured out by the time the second half started," Fife said, and at the break, he laid down the following challenge to his teammates:

"I'm taking care of Dixon. You take care of your guys, and we'll beat their ass."

Maryland continued its sloppy play as the second half began. Dixon came out firing, getting himself wide open on the Terps' initial possession and launching his first shot since midway through the first half. It was an air ball. Steve Blake, who struggled during much of the Final Four, threw a lob pass to Byron Mouton that left him too far under the basket to convert. Soon after, Blake had trouble finding an open man on an in-bounds play and threw a weak pass that got picked off. After Baxter blocked an attempt by Jeffries, Blake brought the ball across half-court and launched a wild, errant shot.

Williams immediately pulled Blake out of the game. The coach was in Blake's ear all the way down the bench, and when the point guard finally sat down, Williams knelt in front of him and continued giving him a piece of his mind. But when the coach was finished, the matter was finished, as well. As quickly as Blake sat down, Williams instructed his floor general to go back into the game.

With four minutes gone in the second half, Fife hit a pull-up three-pointer to cut the Maryland lead to five, 35-30. And after Baxter responded with a baby hook off the glass, Fife came down and hit another three-pointer to bring the score to 37-33. All the while, the Terps' sloppy play continued. Despite going with a three-guard offense of Dixon, Nicholas and Blake, Maryland could not control the ball long enough to run its offense and pull away from Indiana. Dixon threw a ball away, Blake telegraphed another pass that was intercepted by the Hoosiers, and the Terps continued their bad habit of running upcourt and abandoning the in-bounds passer. But Indiana was still unable to cut into the lead, as Maryland scored only one point in over three minutes yet extended its lead to 38-33.

Soon thereafter, Hornsby hit a three-pointer from the left corner to cut the Maryland lead to two. Dixon tried to respond, but with Fife's hand in his face, the Maryland star bricked his attempt off the front iron. The Hoosiers grabbed the rebound, brought the ball up and found Hornsby open for another three. Hornsby missed, but no one blocked out Jeff Newton, and the lanky Hoosier swooped in for a tip-in that tied the game at 40.

Williams called a quick timeout. Indiana had kept the Terps off-balance, and now, for the first time since the opening minutes, the score stood even. Hoosier fans at the Georgia Dome, as well as those watching on big screens at Assembly Hall in Bloomington, or in homes and taverns across the hoops-hungry state, smelled an upset in the making.

During the timeout, Williams implored his team to get the ball inside. Back on the court, Dixon took charge, delivering a great feed to Baxter down low, who went up strong, scored and got fouled. Though he missed the free throw, his bucket put the Terps back on top, 42-40. But mimicking Maryland, Indiana came back by going down low to its star, Jeffries. With Wilcox hovering, Jeffries received the feed in the post and went straight up to complete a hard-fought layup, tying the game at 42. On the other end, Jeffries used his 6'10" frame and long arms to block a Baxter attempt in the paint.

With the score tied at 42, and just over 10 minutes left on the clock, Indiana brought the ball down on offense looking for its first lead of the game. The Hoosiers again worked the ball inside to

Jeffries, who went up and scored after Wilcox was called for goaltending. With 9:55 left, for the first time in the NCAA championship game, the Indiana Hoosiers led, 44-42.

I wasn't nervous when they tied it and took the lead. I was upset. I knew this shouldn't be happening. I was trying to figure out how to keep it from happening. At the same time, we had the right to come back because we had won a lot of big games after being behind. We knew we could come back. We didn't panic just because the other team took the lead.

I didn't call time out because sometimes calling a timeout is a sign of weakness. I watch the Lakers play, and teams will make a run at them, and Phil Jackson will just sit there. He is saying, 'That's not good enough to beat us.' You always have psychological things like that going on.

Williams didn't change his hard-edged expression with the lead change. His features remained stoic as he slowly emerged from the crouch that he had held in the coach's box. He was going to let his team play and force the Cinderella Hoosiers to either play with them or crack. After clawing back, Indiana quickly felt the pressure of playing with a lead in the championship game. "We made our push, and we felt the game was in our hands," Fife said. "I wish we would have called timeout, calmed everybody down, and said, 'Let's not panic. Let's play half-court defense and bring it home.'"

Instead, Indiana began to press the Terps guards with their big men. It was a strategy they had not used at all during the tournament and one that they had pretty much scrapped since the beginning of the season after it didn't work. "We panicked defensively, and that was something we never did before," Davis said. "We wanted to win the game at that point, instead of getting into our defense. To this day, I have no idea why we did it."

Though he had struggled all game, Blake stepped up in the single most important moment, breaking the Indiana trap and heading for the hoop. As the defense collapsed on him, the point guard looked to get the ball into the hands of someone who could hit the big shot and lift up the struggling Terps. Out of the corner of his eye, he spotted a teammate open on the right side beyond the three-point line.

He saw Juan Dixon.

Juan showed what a great player he was on that play. He just came down and stuck it to them.

I remember three things about Juan in the NCAA Tournament. What I remember is that against UConn, he hit a shot when we were down three. He hit that shot from 22 feet with a hand in his face. In the Kansas game, we were struggling late, and Juan hit that shot to stop their momentum and lock the game away for us. Against Indiana, in a game for the championship, he hit a big three-pointer for us right after they took the lead for the first time.

I don't remember any guy making bigger shots against three teams in three straight games. He made three big plays, and none of those shots were wide open. He didn't have a good look. That was Juan. It's one thing to make those shots. But he wanted the ball in those situations. Part of being a great player is taking the big shots. Those three plays made it happen.

The Hoosiers' only lead of the game lasted for 13 seconds, snuffed out by a razor-thin shooting guard who carried with him the hopes of so many others from his home state. His shoulders squared to the basket, his form straight and true, Dixon's three-pointer tore through the net.

Up 45-44, the Terps finally had grabbed the momentum. With seven and a half minutes to play, Dixon drove to the right side on

Fife, pulled up, and with his momentum taking him toward the baseline, hit a soft fade-away jumper over the outstretched hand of his defender. "I was with him all the way, and I didn't expect him to shoot it," Fife said. "I missed the ball by an inch. I couldn't believe it went in. That was an amazing shot."

From then on, the Terps' defense took over. Aside from a Hornsby three-pointer with 4:10 left, Maryland held the Hoosiers scoreless until the final seconds. Meanwhile, the Terps came up with virtually every rebound and loose ball and made trip after trip to the foul line, where they were shooting nearly 90 percent for the tournament.

As Maryland grew closer to its first-ever national title, Byron Mouton, the transfer from Tulane and do-it-all Terps swingman, made a play that embodied the Maryland team and its season. After a Blake three-point attempt rattled around and out, Mouton chased the ball down and, while falling out of bounds through rows of photographers under the basket, made a critical save by throwing the ball all the way back out on top to Blake, giving Maryland a fresh 35 seconds on the shot clock. That play "took the wind out of my sails," said Fife. "I thought, 'Damn, they got that?'" With a new clock, Blake got the ball inside to Holden, who in turn made a beautiful touch pass to Nicholas under the basket for an easy lay up. Mouton had told Williams upon visiting Maryland, "I'm transferring because I want to win a national championship," and in his two years at College Park, he had sublimated his scoring role and taken on every tough defensive assignment that Williams asked of him.

As the minutes ticked away, Maryland extended its lead, going on a 15-3 run in seven and a half minutes. Davis pulled back his defense in the final moments. Trailing 64-52, the Hoosiers would not commit a desperation foul to prolong the inevitable. Dixon had possession of the basketball, watching the last minute melt away. But the senior guard was called for a five-second violation on the offensive end for failing to penetrate, and the referee's whistle meant it was Indiana's ball.

From the sidelines, an angry-looking Gary Williams began shouting at the greatest leader he had ever coached, pressing him to explain why he had just committed a turnover. The game was clearly in Maryland's hands, and the players on the bench and the Terps fans in the stands had begun celebrating. But until the game was over, Williams wouldn't back off at all from coaching and teaching. Consumed fully by the moment, he lived the game of basketball too much to do anything else. Dixon was surprised by the whistle, thinking he had not committed a violation, but he was not at all taken aback by his coach's intensity, even though the national championship was in hand.

"He can get caught up in things," Dixon explained. "It shows how competitive he is. He expects the best."

Whatever the reason, the record will show that in the waning moments of the University of Maryland's first-ever NCAA basketball championship, Gary Williams was coaching to the end. When the final buzzer sounded, the ball, once again, was in Juan Dixon's hands, and he hurled it toward the heavens with all the passion and fury that made him and his teammates champions. And lest there be any doubt, a short while later, the most successful coach in Terrapins history told the greatest Maryland player ever exactly how he really felt. "He told me after the game he loved me," Dixon said. "How about that?"

EPILOGUE

Immediately upon winning the NCAA basketball championship, Gary Williams hugged his players and looked for Kristin. "I wanted to see my daughter." It had taken him 13 years to lead the University of Maryland basketball program from the depths of despair to the ultimate prize. And now, Williams had family and friends to share it with. "Yo, Ed, this one is for Pete Wish," Williams shouted at his childhood buddy Ed Pyne, an affirmation of their South Jersey roots and a reference to a consummate gym rat they both knew in high school. "In some respects," Pyne later said, "he will die happy now that he won the Final Four. It was his biggest lifelong dream. It is the ultimate. The night he won it, his feet were not on the ground."

After digging the program out of a deep pit, what pleased Gary Williams most about his success at Maryland, in addition to winning it all, was that his team had reached the NCAA tournament nine straight years and the Final Four twice in a row. To the coach, the university, the Baltimore-Washington corridor, and the sports world, the underlying message was clear: Maryland not only had a super season, it also had a championship caliber basketball program. "We have the opportunity to move into a slot as one of the elite," said Maryland athletics director Deborah Yow.

Gary Williams, Juan Dixon and the Terps had touched the hearts of millions, finally reaching the pinnacle after years of setbacks and adversity. "The kids have done it!" exclaimed radio broadcaster Johnny Holliday. They had won it, too, by beating five universities in a row that all had won national championships before, a feat never before achieved. They had won the 2002 NCAA Championship in Maryland's 2002nd basketball game. And they had bounced back and worked tirelessly to go all the way after what could have been a demoralizing defeat in the Final Four the prior year. "I've covered 23 Final Fours and I've never seen such a partisan press row," said CBS sportscaster Lesley Visser. "Gary Williams gave everyone who loves college basketball a team to root for this season."

So, too, did Juan Dixon, the hardscrabble Baltimore kid whose story of perseverance had been told and retold around the country and made him an inspiration to so many in his hometown and beyond. After the tournament, Sheila Dixon's city council office was inundated with gifts and thank-you cards addressed to her nephew. The basketball court where Juan spent so many hours playing ball—"his sanctuary," Sheila said—was renamed in his honor. Dixon, the child who refused to allow drugs to derail his dreams, became the new face of Maryland basketball, replacing Len Bias, whose own prodigious talents had fallen with him into a pile of cocaine.

On the court after the victory, Kristin and David joined Williams as he stood with Dixon and the team on the hastily erected platform in the Georgia Dome. More than two decades after he started coaching college basketball at American University, the 57-year-old Williams was ready to accept Maryland's first championship trophy. Along with his players, he watched the CBS broadcast of "One Shining Moment," a video montage celebrating March Madness and Maryland's triumph. At long last for Gary Williams, the disparate strands of his life, from basketball to family to friends, had come together as a whole.

"It might have been an ugly game," Williams said of the Maryland-Indiana final, "but it was beautiful taking the championship trophy on that stage."

The great thing about that moment in Atlanta was that there was no next game, at least not until next season. Very few people enjoy the moment, and I'm guilty of that too. I am always worried about the next game. Most seasons end with a loss, unless your team is not good enough to play in the postseason. But this time things were different. We had won the national championship, and this was the best we could do. We went as far as we could go. It was the ultimate.

I wanted to make sure I saw each player. And then I got the trophy, and they played "One Shining Moment," which was neat because usually I am watching that on television. Now, we were it.

Kristin and David got passes to come down on the court and join me. David thought it was cool to jump over the television cables and cords. It was 11:30 at night, and he was incredible, still full of energy.

Only minutes after winning the national championship, something happened that I will never forget. I had to go and do the CBS thing. So I walked over there, and I was getting the microphones hooked up and getting ready to talk to Jim Nantz and Billy Packer. Four rows behind them, there was this guy wearing a "Fear the Turtle" shirt.

"Great win," he said. "How are you going to be next year?"

One celebration led to another after the Terps return to College Park. There was a rally in Cole Field House, a salute from the state legislature in Annapolis and a pep rally in downtown Baltimore. Walk-on Earl Badu got standing ovations when he walked into his political science classes. And there was a letter of congratulations to Williams from former Maryland head basketball coach Lefty Driesell: "You made my prediction of making Maryland the UCLA of the East come true. Keep it rolling."

On May 21, Maryland's players and coaches were honored by President Bush at a South Lawn ceremony on a spring afternoon with a powder-blue sky. Before heading to 1600 Pennsylvania Avenue, the players gathered one final time. As they stood in the locker room at Cole Field House, they joked around like brothers. They posed for team pictures, signed basketballs, and then boarded a bus that took them from College Park to the White House in record time. There was no stopping at red lights, no traffic that blocked their path. This was their day, and a police escort led them.

Juan Dixon and Lonny Baxter presented President Bush with a Maryland jersey. As he accepted the gift, Bush turned and looked straight at Baxter's arm, then slowly tilted his head up higher and higher, until he could look into Lonny's eyes directly. It was the president's way of bringing levity to the White House salute, and it worked.

"You showed some things that I think are important for our country, particularly at this time, that if you serve something greater than yourself, called a team, you can achieve great things," Bush said. It turned out the White House was filled with Maryland basketball fans, and the president knew it. There were a lot of people around here who had some extra bounce in their step on the morning after you won the NCAA Championship, he said. White House security guards brought hats with them for Maryland players to sign. White House staff members who avoided official state ceremonies scrambled to get a good seat and a glimpse of the Terps. After the ceremony, the team and its coaches got a private tour of the White House. "It's great for our team to be here," Williams said. "Working here locally, I know what happens when you win the championship. I was waiting for the call."

With their college careers finished, several Maryland players turned their focus to the next level of competition, the NBA. With several graduating seniors and one underclassman, Chris Wilcox, declaring themselves eligible for the draft, Gary Williams worked the phones and waited to see where his guys would be playing next.

There were questions about whether Juan Dixon could excel in "The League." Some personnel men worried that he was too small to be a shooting guard, not enough of a ball-handler to play the point, or too skinny to withstand the rigors of an 82-game season. For Dixon, the Most Valuable Player in the NCAA Final Four and the ACC Player of the Year, skepticism was a persistent motivator.

But with his performance in the NCAA Tournament and his drive to succeed now well known to all, there were many teams who were ready to bet on the scrappy Terps guard, and one of them played right in his back yard. NBA commissioner David Stern, who had spent most of the night shaking hands with teenagers and trying to pronounce European surnames, wore a wide grin when he stepped to the podium and announced, "With the 17th pick in the 2002 NBA Draft, the Washington Wizards select—Juan Dixon."

"When I heard the man say 'Juan,' tears fell down my face," Dixon said.

It was, for Dixon, a storybook ending and a promising new beginning. The Terps also saw Chris Wilcox drafted with the eighth pick to the Los Angeles Clippers and Lonny Baxter in the second round to the Chicago Bulls. But those choices were overshadowed by the news that Dixon would be staying home to play ball. His selection instantly lit up the region from Richmond to Baltimore as fans reacted with enthusiasm and passion. Though the Wizards took Indiana's Jared Jeffries even higher in the draft, virtually all of the attention and emotion was focused on Dixon, the hometown hero and the competitor who had the kind of fire in his belly the Wizards needed.

With his girlfriend, family and friends nearby, Dixon would have a built-in support network and fan base, given the opportunity to play so close to home at the MCI Center. And with his coach and mentor Gary Williams just a short drive away in College Park, Dixon would be able to attend Maryland games in the new $130 million Comcast Center, while his coach would get the chance to journey downtown and watch Juan play.

Though he could shoot from long range and had great anticipation on defense, the Wizards chose the 6'3" guard Juan Dixon for the same reason Gary Williams was attracted to him initially in a hot Georgia gym: he gave it his all every day and refused to accept defeat. Paying Dixon the ultimate compliment, Wizards head coach Doug Collins compared Juan's drive to that of Michael Jordan.

"People say he's too small, and he won the national championship," Collins said.

"Juan has a Michael Jordan-sized heart. He wants the ball when the game counts. He wants that shot. He's a winner."

With a guaranteed $3.2 million over three years, being chosen by the Wizards presented Dixon with a spectacular opportunity. "Besides winning the national championship," he said, "this is the greatest day of my life."

"I dreamt of this for so long. I had so many doubters on each level. I had to stay focused, stay hungry. It's good to be home. My whole basketball career has been in the Maryland-D.C. area. It's good having people around me. I had a great situation at Maryland and now I have the same with the Wizards, and I'm going to take advantage of it, continue to work hard, and keep the work ethic that got me here."

Williams was elated. "I called him as soon as Juan got drafted by the Wizards," Kristin said. "I was half-laughing and half-crying. Dad was choked up too. Dad was saying, 'Can you believe it? I am going to get to go to the MCI Center and watch Juan play.'"

Amid a whirlwind schedule after winning the national championship, Gary Williams traveled to New York to receive the Wingfoot Coach of the Year Award, to Las Vegas to receive an ESPN coaching prize, and to numerous other cities to recruit and speak. At home, he was celebrated over and over. There were Maryland flags flying from cars, people wearing bright red T-shirts that said "Garyland," and autograph seekers standing in line to meet him at Rehoboth Beach. A group of Maryland students even wrote and recorded "The Gary Williams Song," which got radio air time locally.

Amid all the hoopla, Williams still had a job to do as head coach. Stretched and stressed in new ways, the coach seemed overwhelmed at times by unfamiliar distractions from his work. His loyal executive assistant, the woman adoringly referred to as "Miss Cleo" by all the Maryland players, became concerned about his well-being.

Cleo's concern escalated one day after Williams came back from Columbus, Ohio and enthusiastically began talking to everyone in the Maryland basketball office about how he had gone with his daughter and grandson to the zoo in Columbus. While he was there, Williams said he rode with his grandson David on the merry-go-round. Cleo shook her head. For all the newfound joy Williams had in his family, he often flew in and out of Columbus in a day. Knowing him for years as she did, Cleo found it implausible that this tightly wound "guy's guy" had really let loose, taken a merry-go-round ride and cheerfully participated in a frolic to the zoo. He just wasn't the type.

Fearing that he might have become delusional from the extraordinarily hectic postseason rush, Cleo, unknown to her boss, picked up the phone and called Williams's daughter in Columbus to verify whether he was telling the truth or needed time off. "She called to make sure this was true," Kristin said. "She said, 'Your dad went to the zoo?' I said, 'Yes, but don't worry. He had on dress khakis and loafers if that makes you feel better.'"

People ask me, 'How long are you going to coach?' And I say, 'As long as I have that same interest each year.' I admire Dean Smith. He said, 'Never make a decision on whether you want to coach next year based on how you feel at the end of the season.' I realize after the last game how hard I have been focusing on one thing all the time, and I feel totally spent, win or lose. Then gradually, I get my energy back, start recruiting in July, another season starts in the fall, and I am ready to go.

You don't get much time in coaching between winning and whatever comes next. As a coach, I am almost afraid because I have to get ready for next season, and I don't want all of the celebrating to affect efforts and preparation. I want to be just as intense about winning as I've been every other year. I respect the game too much to change just because we won the NCAA Championship.

SCOREBOARD

Coach Gary Williams and The Maryland Terrapins
A Championship Season

2001-02 Season Results
(32-4)

Date	Opponent	Site	Score
11-8	Arizona	New York, NY	L 71-67
11-9	Temple	New York, NY	W 82-74
11-17	American	College Park, MD	W 83-53
11-24	Delaware State	College Park, MD	W 77-53
11-27	Illinois	College Park, MD	W 76-63
12-2	Princeton	Washington, D.C.	W 61-53
12-3	Connecticut	Washington, D.C.	W 77-65
12-9	Detroit	College Park, MD	W 79-54
12-11	Monmouth	College Park, MD	W 91-55
12-21	Oklahoma	Norman, OK	L 72-56
12-27	William & Mary	College Park, MD	W 103-75
12-30	NC State	Raleigh, NC	W 72-65
1-3	Norfolk State	College Park, MD	W 92-69
1-9	North Carolina	College Park, MD	W 112-79
1-13	Georgia Tech	Atlanta, GA	W 92-87
1-17	Duke	Durham, NC	L 99-78
1-20	Clemson	College Park, MD	W 99-90
1-23	Wake Forest	Winston-Salem, NC	W 85-63
1-26	Florida State	College Park, MD	W 84-63
1-31	Virginia	Charlottesville, VA	W 91-87
2-3	NC State	College Park, MD	W 89-73
2-10	North Carolina	Chapel Hill, NC	W 92-77
2-13	Georgia Tech	College Park, MD	W 85-65
2-17	Duke	College Park, MD	W 87-73
2-20	Clemson	Clemson, SC	W 84-68
2-24	Wake Forest	College Park, MD	W 90-89
2-27	Florida State	Tallahassee, FL	W 96-63
3-3	Virginia	College Park, MD	W 112-92
3-8	Florida State (ACC Tourn.)	Charlotte, NC	W 85-59

Date	Opponent	Site	Score
3-9	NC State (ACC Tourn.)	Charlotte, NC	L 86-82
3-15	Siena (NCAA Tourn.)	Washington, D.C.	W 85-70
3-17	Wisconsin (NCAA Tourn.)	Washington, D.C.	W 87-57
3-22	Kentucky (NCAA Tourn.)	Syracuse, NY	W 78-68
3-24	Connecticut (NCAA Tourn.)	Syracuse, NY	W 90-82
3-30	Kansas (NCAA Semi-Final)	Atlanta, GA	W 97-88
4-1	Indiana (NCAA Final)	Atlanta, GA	W 64-52

Coach Gary Williams and the Maryland Terrapins The Building of a Championship Program

Season	Overall	ACC Conf. Finish	Postseason
1989-90	19-14	T 5	1-1 NIT
1990-91	16-12	7	—
1991-92	14-15	8	—
1992-93	12-16	8	—
1993-94	18-12	T 4	2-1 NCAA
1994-95	26-8	T 1	2-1 NCAA
1995-96	17-13	T 4	0-1 NCAA
1996-97	21-11	T 4	0-1 NCAA
1997-98	21-11	3	2-1 NCAA
1998-99	28-6	2	2-1 NCAA
1999-00	25-10	2	1-1 NCAA
2000-01	25-11	3	4-1 NCAA
2001-02	32-4	1	6-0 NCAA

Gary Williams: A Winner Everywhere He Has Coached

Ohio State Men's Basketball Records 1983-89

Season	Record	Coach
1983-84	15-14	Eldon Miller
1984-85	20-10	Eldon Miller
1985-86	19-14	Eldon Miller
1986-87	20-13	Gary Williams
1987-88	20-13	Gary Williams
1988-89	19-15	Gary Williams

Boston College Men's Basketball Records 1979-85

Season	Record	Coach
1979-80	19-10	Tom Davis
1980-81	23-7	Tom Davis
1981-82	22-10	Tom Davis
1982-83	25-7	Gary Williams
1983-84	18-12	Gary Williams
1984-85	20-11	Gary Williams

American University Men's Basketball Records 1975-81

Season	Record	Coach
1975-76	9-16	Jim Lynam
1976-77	13-13	Jim Lynam
1977-78	16-12	Jim Lynam
1978-79	14-13	Gary Williams
1979-80	13-14	Gary Williams
1980-81	24-6	Gary Williams

Coach Gary Williams By the Numbers

	Seasons	Wins-Losses	Winning Record
At Maryland	1989-2002	274-143	0.657
Elsewhere	1975-1989	207-128	0.618
Career Totals		481-271	0.640

Juan Dixon
2002 NCAA Final Four
Most Valuable Player

Date	Opponent	Points	FG-FGA	3-PT FG-FGA	FT-FTA
3-15	Siena	29	10-17	5-8	4-4
3-17	Wisconsin	29	10-19	4-7	5-6
3-22	Kentucky	19	6-15	3-8	4-4
3-24	Connecticut	27	10-18	3-5	4-4
3-30	Kansas	33	10-18	5-11	8-11
4-1	Indiana	18	6-9	2-4	4-4

Juan Dixon's 2002 NCAA Tournament Scoring Versus Regular Season Results

NCAA Tournament	25.8 points per game
Regular Season	19.3 points per game

Juan Dixon
All-Time Scoring Leader
University of Maryland Terrapins

YRF	G-FGA	3-PT FG-FGA	FT-FTA	PTS	PPG
1998-99	85-192	36-97	44-53	250	7.4
1999-00	234-506	49-135	113-143	630	18.0
2000-01	232-480	62-151	128-148	654	18.2
2001-02	251-535	92-232	141-177	735	20.4
TOTAL POINTS				**2,269**	

SOURCES

This book is based on more than 100 interviews with basketball players, coaches, writers, commentators and other experts. It is also based on interviews with Maryland officials, alumni, fans and friends, including people who have known Gary Williams from the time he was old enough to dribble a basketball until he cut down the net and won the 2002 NCAA Basketball Championship. The book reflects the insights of family members, especially Gary's daughter Kristin, as well as close friends who have shared victories and defeats with Williams both on and off the court. The book also is the product of reflections from Juan Dixon and numerous members of his family. Most of all, the book has been shaped by dozens of hours of interviews and discussions on a wide range of topics with the coach himself, who never ducked a question.

I want to thank everyone who spoke with me about Gary Williams and the University of Maryland. Without your help, this tale of triumph over adversity would have been incomplete. This is a book that had to be written, and this was the time. I am very grateful for your assistance and willingness to open up and talk about a man and his alma mater, making it possible for me to put this magnificent moment into perspective.

I was assisted in my research by the outstanding work of other journalists and authors. In learning about Gary Williams and the University of Maryland, as well as retelling the story of his earlier coaching assignments prior to returning to College Park in 1989, I relied heavily on contemporaneous newspaper and magazine articles as well as documentaries and articles from ESPN, game tapes and interviews provided by CBS Sports, and media guides, videotapes and other materials supplied by the University of Maryland and the NCAA. In understanding Juan Dixon, Tom Friend's excellent piece in *ESPN Magazine* and an ESPN SportsCentury special both contributed greatly.

I drew most extensively upon information from hundreds of excellent articles and columns in *The Washington Post* and *The Baltimore Sun,* the two major newspapers that closely chronicled day-to-day events with the greatest passion and precision.

Contemporaneous accounts of games and other events by beat reporters Josh Barr of *The Washington Post* and Gary Lambrecht of *The Baltimore Sun* were outstanding, thorough and provided real-time dialogue. The book also benefited from stories over the years, and a special commemorative issue, from *Sports Illustrated.* I relied on an accounting of the championship season from Maryland's student newspaper, *The Diamondback*, and The Associated Press. Other publications that I relied upon included *The Boston Globe*, the *Columbus Dispatch*, the *New York Times*, the *Los Angeles Times*, *USA Today*, the *Chicago Tribune*, *Baltimore Magazine*; *Washingtonian Magazine*, the *Richmond (Va.) Times-Dispatch*, *The (Cleveland, Ohio) Plain Dealer*, *The (Annapolis, Md.) Capital*, *The (Allentown, Pa.) Morning Call*, the *Washington Times*, the *San Diego Union-Tribune* and the *Quincy (Ma.) Patriot Ledger*.

Numerous books proved invaluable in the course of researching and writing *Sweet Redemption*. Noteworthy among them are: *A March to Madness, A Season on the Brink* and *The Last Amateurs*, by

John Feinstein; *They Call Me Coach* by John Wooden with Jack Tobin and Denny Crum; *A Coach's Life* by Dean Smith with John Kilgo and Sally Jenkins; *Lenny, Lefty, and the Chancellor* by C. Fraser Smith; *Never Too Young to Die* by Lewis Cole; *The Breaks of the Game* by David Halberstam; *Knight: My Story* by Bob Knight with Bob Hammel; *King of the World* by David Remnick; *When Pride Still Mattered* by David Maraniss; *Five Point Play* by Mike Krzyzewski with Donald T. Phillips and Shane Battier; *Cole Classics!* by John McNamara and David Elfin; *Sacred Hoops* by Phil Jackson with Hugh Delehanty and Bill Bradley; *More Than a Game* by Phil Jackson and Charlie Rosen; *True Blue* by David Dewitt; *Seabiscuit* by Laura Hillenbrand; *Secretariat: The Making of a Champion*, by William Nack; *Valvano* by Jim Valvano and Curry Kirkpatrick; *Friday Night Lights* by H.G. Bissinger; *CBS Sports Presents: Stories From The Final Four*, edited by Matt Fulks; *The Biographical History of Basketball* by Peter C. Bjarkman; *Blue Ribbon College Basketball Yearbook, 2001-2002 Edition*, edited by Chris Dortch; and the NCAA Official 2002 Men's Final Four Tournament Records and program.

If I have inadvertently failed to cite any published stories or broadcasts, I apologize. I am grateful to the many reporters, columnists, authors and broadcasters whose work influenced this book and made it more complete.

DAVID A. VISE

AUTHOR'S NOTE

Matthew Obernauer, my research assistant, is a talented journalist and a super guy. He brought energy, enthusiasm and expertise to every facet of reporting, writing and editing *Sweet Redemption*. He made the book process enjoyable while displaying a rare determination and passion from start to finish.

An astute student of the game and human nature, Matt contributed a valuable perspective. This is the second book we have teamed up on, and there is no one I would rather have in my corner. Matt is a pro. Any newspaper, magazine or broadcaster would be better off having him on their team, and I look forward to watching him thrive as a journalist in the years ahead.

—D.A.V.

ACKNOWLEDGMENTS

I am fortunate to be a reporter for *The Washington Post*, a great newspaper and a special place to be a journalist. My deep appreciation goes to Len Downie, executive editor, Steve Coll, managing editor, George Solomon, sports editor, Joe Elbert, photo editor, Bo Jones, Publisher, and Don Graham, chairman and chief executive officer, for their solid support of my efforts to write a book about the story behind the story of Coach Gary Williams and the University of Maryland Terrapins.

Any author would be lucky to be represented by my literary agent, Ron Goldfarb, who understood this tale and why it had to be told from the first moment he heard about it. He shared my passion for the subject, provided me with wise counsel and did an outstanding job finding the right publisher. I will forever be grateful to him for the role that he played in *Sweet Redemption.* He was also my link to the team at Sports Publishing, which has done a first-rate job in every way. My thanks to the entire organization, which is striving to become the ESPN of publishing, and especially to Senior Editor Joe Bannon Jr. and his editorial assistant, Erin Linden-Levy.

Max Pinson, the nation's top 12-year-old sports fan, contributed his insight and generous spirit to *Sweet Redemption.* Nobody besides the two of us will every fully appreciate and understand our collaboration on this book, but in addition to the desire to tell the story, there is the inspiration to find the words, and Max provided that for me. A fountain of ideas, Max was always ready to discuss the finer points of the game, sharing his observations about dedication, team work and what it takes to succeed. He is a winner, and I love him very much.

Barry Chasen, a diehard Terps fan and loyal friend, shared his affection for Maryland basketball with me. Without him, this book would not have been written, and I relish going to Terps games together. His wife Lyn, and their sons Brandon, Benjamin and Blake, witnessed Maryland's back-to-back journeys to the Final Four, attending countless games at Cole Field House and on the road. I know the Chasens will be in the Comcast Center rooting for the home team as Maryland basketball enters a new era.

A special thanks to Terry Arenson, a valued friend and adviser to Gary Williams. If we had not met on opening day when the Atlanta Braves won at Turner Field, and you had not introduced me to Coach Williams, *Sweet Redemption* would have been a nice title but there would have been no book.

My thanks to Cleo Long-Thomas, Gary Williams's executive assistant, Carole Bucco, administrative assistant, Maryland Sports Information Director Kevin Messenger and Video Coordinator Pat Shannon, for their assistance. And a special thanks to a pair of rabid young sports fans, Bobby and Michael Gottfried, for their help reviewing game films and compiling statistics. Under the tutelage of their father, my good friend P.G. Gottfried—whose moniker is "Mr. Ticket"—they have been to more games as toddlers and teenagers than most fans will attend in a lifetime. In all the best ways, it shows.

My appreciation also goes to Marty Franks, head of the Washington office of CBS and to Jennifer Sabatelle of CBS Sports, for their tremendous help. In addition, my thanks to ESPN and to Christian Whittaker for his assistance.

I attended Maryland's trips to the Final Four over the past two years with my good buddy Bruce Kershner, and I am glad he was a witness to the role of fate in *Sweet Redemption.* It was through his friendship, as well as his knowledge of cinema and sports, that the title for this book emerged. A former star catcher out of Bowie,

Maryland, Bruce has made the transition from player to fan as well as can be expected.

Our daughters, Lisa, Allison and Jennifer, enthusiastically play sports and have been attending basketball games since they could crawl. They are wonderful daughters and second-to-none as fans. They know how to win with dignity, lose with grace and move on to the next challenge. I love all three of them very, very much and enjoy sharing the joy of sports with them, whether we are playing, going to a game or watching together on TV.

When we moved to Washington in 1984, my wife Lori bought me a pair of basketball season tickets as a birthday present. While I know she would have preferred for us to attend a series of concerts or plays at the Kennedy Center, Lori shared and supported my life-long passion for sports. Some might say her willing indulgence of my hoops habit makes her an enabler; I say it is only one of many, many things that make her the greatest wife imaginable. She is also my best friend. Being married to Lori makes me the luckiest guy around, on or off the court, and inside or outside the arena. I love her very much and appreciate her extraordinary support and understanding of *Sweet Redemption.*

—David A. Vise